Aftershock

Aftershock

PROTECT YOURSELF AND PROFIT IN THE NEXT GLOBAL FINANCIAL MELTDOWN

SECOND EDITION

David Wiedemer, Ph.D.
Robert A. Wiedemer
Cindy Spitzer

WILEY

John Wiley & Sons, Inc.

Published by John Wiley & Sons, Inc., Hoboken, New Jersey.
Published simultaneously in Canada.

For general information on our other products and services or for technical support, please
contact our Customer Care Department within the United States at (800) 762-2974, outside
the United States at (317) 572-3993 or fax (317) 572-4002.

Wiley also publishes its books in a variety of electronic formats. Some content that appears in
print may not be available in electronic books. For more information about Wiley products,
visit our web site at www.wiley.com.

Library of Congress Cataloging-in-Publication Data:

Wiedemer, David (John David)
    Aftershock : protect yourself and profit in the next global financial meltdown /
David Wiedemer, Robert A. Wiedemer, Cindy Spitzer. — 2nd ed.
        p. cm.
    Includes bibliographical references and index.
    ISBN 978-0-470-91814-2 (cloth); 978-1-118-12750-6 (ebk); 978-1-118-12751-3 (ebk);
978-1-118-12752-0 (ebk)
        1. Finance, Personal. 2. Investments. 3. Financial crises. I. Wiedemer,
Robert A. II. Spitzer, Cindy S. III. Title.
    HG179.W5264   2011
    332.024—dc22
                                                            2011016577

Printed in the United States of America
10 9 8 7 6 5 4 3 2 1

Contents

Executive Summary

What Is a Bubble?

An asset value that temporarily booms and eventually busts, based on changing investor psychology, rather than on underlying fundamental economic drivers that are sustainable over time.

What Is a Bubble Economy?

An economy that grows in a virtuous upward spiral of multiple rising bubbles (real estate, stocks, private debt, dollar, and government debt) that interact to drive each other up, and that will inevitably fall in a vicious downward spiral as each falling bubble puts downward pressure on the rest, eventually pulling the whole economy down.

What Is the Bubblequake?

Phase I of the popping of the bubble economy, including the fall of the real estate bubble, private debt bubble, stock market bubble, and discretionary spending bubble.

What Is the Aftershock?

Phase II of the popping of the bubble economy. Just when many people think the worst is over, then comes the Aftershock, when the dollar bubble and the government debt bubble will burst.

Acknowledgments

The authors thank John Silbersack of Trident Media Group and John Wiley & Sons editors David Pugh and Laura Walsh for supporting this book. They also want to thank John R. Douglas for his very special role in making this book a reality.

David Wiedemer

I thank my co-authors Bob and Cindy for being indispensable in the writing of this book. Without them this book would not have been published and even if written, would have been inaccessible for most audiences. I also thank Dr. Rod Stevenson for his long-term support of the foundational work that is the basis for this book, which hopefully will be the second of many. I also thank Ruth Pritchard for her review of the manuscript. And I am especially grateful to my wife, Betsy, and son, Benson, for their ongoing support in what has been an often arduous and trying process.

Robert Wiedemer

I, along with my brother, want to dedicate this book to our father, the original author in the family, who died early this year. We also want to thank our brother Jim for his lifelong support of the ideas behind this book and our mother for inspiring us both with the joy of discovering the world and writing about it. I thank Ron Everett, my business associate, for his enthusiastic support of this project. I also want to thank Michael Lebowitz and Dan Cohen for their special contributions to the writing of this book. Chris Ruddy and Aaron De Hoog have been enormous supporters of *Aftershock*. It's been great to have such support. I also want to thank early supporters Stan Goldstein, Tim Selby, Sam Stovall, and Phil Gross. I am also grateful to Weldon Rackley, who helped my father to become an author and who did the same for me.

Of course, my gratitude goes to Dave Wiedemer and Cindy Spitzer for being, quite clearly, the best collaborators you could ever have. It was truly a great team effort. Most of all, I thank my wife, Serap, and children, Seline and John, without whose love and support, this book, and a really great life, would not be possible.

Cindy Spitzer

Thank you, David and Bob, for the true privilege of collaborating with two of the most intelligent, kind, and visionary people I know.

My deep appreciation and love go to my wonderful husband, Philip Terbush, my precious children Chelsea, Anya, and Zachary, and my dear friend Cindi Callanan.

I am also filled with a lifetime of gratitude for two fantastic teachers, the kind who, without realizing it at the time, change the course of your life: Christine Gronkowski, who at SUNY Purchase College in 1985 forced me to discover something in myself that I couldn't see on my own; and to my phenomenally gifted UMCP College of Journalism mentor, two-time Pulitzer Prize winner Jon Franklin, whom I haven't seen in more than two decades, yet whose lessons I still learn from daily.

Preface to the Second Edition
of *Aftershock*

Judging from the beginning-of-the-year media reports in 2011, as well as the forecasts of many investment professionals, it appears we have passed the financial crisis caused by the popping of the bubble economy, and there will be no Aftershock.

That would be welcome and comfortable news—if only it were true.

Instead, what happened in early 2011 is just as we predicted. As the four interacting bubbles (stocks, housing, private credit, and consumer spending) pop, they will put enormous pressure on the two remaining—and much more fundamental—bubbles in our bubble economy: the government debt and dollar bubbles.

That's because there has been an enormous incentive to further inflate the government debt and dollar bubbles in an effort to stall the popping of the other bubbles. And that is exactly what the government has done in two ways. First, it has increased its annual deficit by almost 550 percent from $250 billion in 2007 to $1.6 trillion today, pumping up the government debt bubble. And even more stunningly, it has increased the U.S. money supply by an unthinkable 200 percent (from $800 billion in 2008 to more than $2.4 trillion today), pumping up the dollar bubble.

By inflating these bubbles even more, we are temporarily preventing the other bubbles from deflating further and, in some cases, such as the stock market, we are actually reinflating the bubble to some extent. This was most clearly shown in late 2010 when Fed Chairman Ben Bernanke announced another round of money printing (via the second round of quantitative easing [QE2]), and the stock market not only avoided what would have likely been a 10–15 percent decline in the year but also enjoyed more than a 10 percent gain. By early 2011, the market was up more than 30 percent from when Ben made the announcement.

With great short-term benefits like this, further increases in the government debt bubble and the dollar bubble are likely to continue. Until we actually see inflation or have problems selling our government debt, there is no compelling, immediate reason to face, or even admit, any future problem with inflation or debt. Now that we have shown that we are willing to print money in order to buy our own government debt, we will always be able to sell it. So, the only real future problem with this scenario comes when inflation appears.

In fact, we could pump up the government debt and dollar bubbles even more and truly boost the economy into high gear. Double the deficit or triple the money supply again and, no doubt, stocks, housing, and the economy will improve dramatically along with the overall economy. Only if people fear the long term consequences of these actions, will they become a problem. The story of the economy and of financial markets has become less a story about various market forces and increasingly more a desperate fight between investor fantasy psychology and the deeper reality of what's actually happening in the economy.

As long as investors and politicians can ignore the future consequences, there is no short-term reason not to pump up the government debt and dollar bubbles. In fact, there is good short term rationale for continuing, because if we were to cut our federal deficit back down to where it was in 2007, before the financial crisis, we almost certainly would cause a major recession that would immediately pop the stock, housing, private credit, and consumer spending bubbles again. The same is true for the money supply. If we took out all the money we have printed in the last two years, we would certainly cause another bubble-popping recession.

But here's the catch. The only thing worse than the recession that would result from purposely deflating our government debt and dollar bubbles now will be the much, much bigger global depression that will eventually result from pumping them up even further. Deflating these bubbles now would pop our multibubble economy, but continuing to inflate them will eventually cause an even more massive and destructive pop in the future. We can either have pain now or a whole lot more pain later. As it stands, we have chosen a whole lot more pain later.

So, we have successfully postponed the Aftershock. How long we can postpone it for depends on the government's recklessness and the investment community's continued willingness to believe in the fantasy that nothing but good will come from massively expanding the government debt and dollar bubbles.

We don't think the Aftershock can be postponed much longer but, as we said in the book, that is largely a matter of governmental decisions and investor psychology. Could it be five years away? We think that is unlikely. Could it be just one year away? We think that is probably equally unlikely. Exactly when the Aftershock will hit is hard to say because there is no easy way to predict governmental actions or investor psychology. Best guess: two to four years.

Whatever happens, it will certainly be interesting to see how this story plays out, even if we already know how the story ends. It's too bad that it's not just a story.

Introduction

YOUR GUIDE TO THE SECOND EDITION
OF *AFTERSHOCK*

This second edition of *Aftershock* contains a number of important updates and clarifications to the previous book. We have been fortunate to have received lots of excellent feedback and suggestions from our readers, much of which we have incorporated into this new book. Some important changes include more information regarding personal finance in Chapter 6 and Chapter 7, applying the broad macroeconomic views of the book to specific real-world concerns, such as retirement, annuities, underwater mortgages, 401Ks, municipal bonds, and the many ways to buy and own gold.

In another important change, we replaced the chapter on STEP Evolution in the original book with a new Chapter 9, discussing where we believe the real trouble lies underlying our current economic dilemma—with the field of economics, itself. The underlying problem goes beyond the actions of the Federal Reserve, or specific government officials, investment bankers, or Wall Street, although all share some blame. Much more fundamentally, our current problems reflect an underlying lack of knowledge in the economics community about our economy, what brought us here, and how to get out of it. At its core, what we are experiencing is a fundamental failure of the economics profession. In the new Chapter 9, we look at why this has happened and where we believe the field of economics should be moving to finally get a full understanding of how our economy really works. In this discussion is the basis for answering questions about how to solve our current economic problems and moving forward to a much brighter, more productive and enjoyable economic world.

In this second edition of *Aftershock*, we also dropped the old Chapter 10 about life after all the bubbles pop. It really was a bit gloomy. Although we thought it was important to put into print our long-term predictions, there is no need to repeat them now. When one of our readers called it our "Dr. Zhivago chapter," we knew it was time to move on. However, both the STEP evolution chapter and the chapter on life in the postbubble world are important reading, so if you haven't already read the first edition of the book, you might want to pick it up or borrow it from a friend. Thanks to you, our readers, there are now a couple hundred thousand copies of the first *Aftershock* floating around out there, so you have a decent chance of finding one somewhere.

But the biggest difference between the first and second editions of *Aftershock* is our focus on the importance of the Federal Reserve's recent actions to massively increase the money supply, and the inflation this will eventually create. So important is this action by the Fed that we have devoted all of Chapter 3 to inflation—where it comes from, how it will hurt us and, most importantly the role it will play in helping to fully pop our multibubble economy. Although the Fed's actions do not change the final conclusions of the original *Aftershock*, they do significantly affect the short term path we will take to get there. Our updates regarding the Federal Reserve's latest actions and anticipated future actions have important implications for the short-term path of both the economy and how you can best protect assets and grow investments in this dangerous environment. The implications of the coming inflation have also been worked into almost every other chapter and are reflected throughout the book.

Finally, we want to take this opportunity to thank our readers for the incredible support they have shown us. We couldn't have asked for a better response. So many people have told us how much they enjoyed the book, sometimes reading it multiple times, and even giving extra copies to their friends and relatives. Wow—thank you, thank you, thank you!!! It is deeply satisfying to know we are being read, understood, and even appreciated. It's just fantastic!

It's also great that so many of you are helping us get the word out to help as many people as possible. That is so important to us. Hence, we give away free books, and we also make free presentations to worthy organizations. We want to get the word out as fast as we can, and as widely as possible. We hope that this second edition will be an important step in our mission to help people better understand what is going on with the economy, so that they can act now to protect themselves and to prosper in these most unusual times. We hope you find this second edition of *Aftershock* helpful in the months and years ahead.

PART

I

FIRST THE BUBBLEQUAKE,
NEXT THE AFTERSHOCK

CHAPTER 1

America's Bubble Economy

UNDERSTANDING HOW WE PREDICTED THE BUBBLEQUAKE FOUR YEARS AGO IS KEY TO UNDERSTANDING WHY OUR LATEST PREDICTIONS ARE CORRECT

When our first book, *America's Bubble Economy*, came out in 2006 (the book proposal was actually submitted 18 months earlier), we were right and almost everyone else was wrong. We don't say this to brag. We say it because it's important for understanding why you should bother to pay attention to us now.

America's Bubble Economy (John Wiley & Sons, 2006), accurately predicted the popping of the real estate bubble, the collapse of the private debt bubble, the fall of the stock market bubble, the decline of consumer spending, and the widespread pain all this was about to inflict on the rest of our vulnerable, multibubble economy. We also predicted the eventual bursting of the dollar bubble and the government debt bubble, which are still to come. Of course, back in 2006, our predictions were largely ignored. Two years later, they started coming true: The housing, private debt, and stock bubbles fell dramatically, causing a financial crisis here and around the world.

How did we see it coming? Certainly not by looking only at current conditions, which, at the time we wrote the first book, still looked pretty darn good. In fact, real estate prices in 2006 were close to their record highs. And with home values high and credit flowing, American consumers were still happily tapping into their home

3

equity and credit cards to buy all manner of consumer products, from designer diapers to flat screen TVs, importing goods from around the world, and boosting the economies of many nations. Businesses and banks appeared to be in good shape (very few banks were even close to failing), unemployment was relatively low, and Wall Street was still on an upward climb toward its record closing high (Dow 14,164) a year later on October 9, 2007.

With so much seemingly going so well back in 2006, how could we have been so sure that the housing bubble would pop, private credit would start drying up, the stock market would begin to fall, and the broader multibubble economy, here and around the globe, would begin a dramatic decline in 2008 and beyond? Our accurate predictions were not a matter of blind luck, nor were they merely a case of perpetual bearish thinking finally having its gloomy day. In 2006, we were able to correctly call the fall of the U.S. housing bubble and its many consequences because we were able to see a *fundamental underlying pattern* that others were—and still are—missing.

In this pattern, we saw bubbles. Lots of them. We saw six big economic bubbles linked together and holding up one another, all supporting a seemingly prosperous U.S. economy. And we also saw that each conjoined bubble was leaning heavily on the others, each poised to potentially pull the others down if any one of these economic bubbles were to someday pop.

Why would they ever pop? We knew they would eventually pop because we saw that the evolving economic facts on the ground did not justify the volume of the bubbles; therefore sooner or later, we knew they would have to burst. Later in this book, we will tell you more about these six big economic bubbles (the first four have already begun to burst and the other two will shortly) and how we knew they were bubbles. For now the point is that economic bubbles, by nature, do not stay afloat forever. Sooner or later, economic reality, like gravity, eventually kicks in, and bubbles do fall. After they burst, they never are able to reinflate fully and lift off again. In time, new bubbles may grow, but old popped bubbles generally do not take off again. When the party is over, it's over.

Most people, even most "experts," find it much easier to recognize a bubble (like the Internet bubble of the 1990s) *after* it pops. It is a lot harder to see a bubble *before* it bursts, and much harder still to see an *entire multiple-bubble economy* before it bursts. A single, not-yet-popped bubble can look a lot like real asset growth, and a collection of several not-yet-popped bubbles can look a whole lot like real economic prosperity.

We wrote our first book, *America's Bubble Economy*, in 2006 because, based on our unique analysis of the evolving economy, the facts on the ground did not support the bubbles in the sky. By that we mean high-flying asset growth that is not firmly pinned to real underlying economic drivers is not sustainable. For example, real estate prices are typically driven higher by a growing population (increasing demand) and the growing incomes of homebuyers (increasing ability to buy). When populations increase and incomes increase, home prices also increase. On the other hand, if you see home prices increasing, let's say, twice as fast as incomes, then that could mean something unsustainable is happening to the value of real estate. Why? Because home prices that high are not sustainable without a similar rise in the ability of buyers to keep paying those prices.

Asset bubbles are not always bad. On the way up, they can lift part or all of an economy and spur future economic growth. This certainly was the case with the housing bubble. On the way down, however, they can cause real problems. In fact, the bigger the bubble, the harder the fall.

America's Bubble Economy identified several economic bubbles that were once part of a seemingly *virtuous upward spiral* that first lifted and supported the U.S. economy over many decades, and are now part of a *vicious downward spiral* that will inevitably harm the U.S. and world economies as these sagging, co-linked bubbles weigh heavily on each other, and ultimately burst. These bubbles included: the real estate bubble, stock market bubble, discretionary spending bubble, dollar bubble, and government debt bubble. Despite how well the economy appeared to be doing in 2006, we predicted it would only be two or three years before America's multiple bubbles would begin to decline and eventually even burst.

And that is just what happened.

By the third quarter of 2008, home prices and sales had fallen significantly, mortgage defaults and home foreclosures were skyrocketing, commercial and investment banks were going under, unemployment was rising, and the stock market bubble had fallen from its peak of 14,164 in October 2007 to under 7,000 on the Dow Jones Industrial Average (DJIA) not much more than a year later.

Three years after publishing *America's Bubble Economy*, we released our second book, *Aftershock*, in November 2009, and now offer you this updated and revised second edition of *Aftershock* in 2011, as the rest of our conjoined economic bubbles are coming under increasing downward pressure.

Unlike any other moment in our history, there is something *fundamentally different* going on this time. Even people who pay no attention to the stock market or the latest economic news say they can just feel it in their gut. Experts keep saying we are on the verge of recovery, but something feels different this time. The difference that most of us feel but few can define is this: We are not in a typical "down market cycle" this time, awaiting an inevitable "up cycle." The difference this time is the *multibubble economy*. Falling bubbles cannot be reinflated by an "up cycle." With so many linked bubbles now on the descent, the impact of their combined future collapse will be far more dangerous than any downturn or recession we've experienced in the past. Unlike in a healthy economy, in this falling *multi-bubble* economy, the usual strategies for returning to our previous prosperity no longer apply. We have, in fact, entered new territory.

We call it a Bubblequake. As in an earthquake, our multibubble economy is starting to rumble and crack. Clearly, the real estate, credit, and stock market bubbles have already taken a serious fall, and the financial consequences for the broader U.S. and world economy have been significant.

Next comes the Aftershock. Just when most people think the worst is behind us, we are about to experience the cascading fall of several, co-linked, bursting bubbles that will rock our nation's economy to its core and send deep and destructive financial shock waves around the globe. The Bubblequake fall of the housing, credit, consumer spending, and stock bubbles significantly weakened the world economy. But the coming Aftershock will be far more dangerous. Despite massive efforts by the federal government and the Federal Reserve to hold up the falling bubbles with borrowing and massive money printing, the fall of a multibubble economy can be delayed, but it cannot be reinflated. Rather than home prices stabilizing and the U.S. economy recovering in the next year or two, as many "experts" want you to believe, we see serious, groundbreaking new troubles ahead. In fact, the worst is yet to come.

That's the bad news. The good news is the worst is yet to come (with emphasis on the word *yet*). There is still time for individuals and businesses to cover their assets and even find ways to profit in the Bubblequake and Aftershock. But first you have to see it coming.

Prescient Quotes from Our First Book, *America's Bubble Economy*

On the Stock Market

The idea that the stock market at any time is risk free is completely false. Every market has downside risk. Back in the 1950s, 1960s, and 1970s that was understood. It's been a very long time since the experts have tried to tell us there is no risk in the stock market. Guess when it happened before? The last time market cheerleaders tried to get Americans to think of the stock market as risk-free was just before the big 1929 stock market crash that led to the Great Depression. Coincidence? A bloated overvalued market (Dow up tenfold in 20 years), now "stable" from mid 2000 to 2005 (also known as stagnant), plus cheerleaders telling us that there is no downside risk, all add up to one thing: a Stock Market Bubble on the edge. (p. 110)

Bottom line: Most stocks are overvalued and on their way down. Will there be some ups and downs? Of course. Is it worth taking a chance on it? We think not. As with real estate, although there may be some potential growth left in the stock market, the timing is very tricky and it's not worth taking the risk. In the short run, you are about as likely to lose as gain. And in the long run, all you will do is lose significantly when stock values begin to seriously plummet. Again, we will show you much better places to put your money. (p. 139)

Fact: The Dow was at 12,100 when the first edition of this book was published in October 2006.

On Real Estate

In the near term, the slow collapse of the Real Estate Bubble (in some markets it won't be so slow) will weigh heavily on the stock market. The loss of housing construction jobs, plus the factory and service jobs that support housing construction, will further slow the economy, putting more downward pressure on the stock market. (p. 73)

Fact: The housing price index was at 205 according to Case-Shiller Top 20 Cities Index when our book was published, and fell to 142 by the end of 2010.

On Private Credit

All adjustable rate loans, credit cards and adjustable or variable mortgages will become an absolute disaster when the bubbles burst.

(continued)

Interest rates will rise dramatically and so will your mortgage and other payments if you don't get out of these soon. Now is a great time to lock in your low long-term interest rates. Don't take a chance; get rid of your evil variable rate mortgage and other big debts now! (p. 141)

Fact: Adjustable rate mortgages helped kick off the housing price collapse and are still one of the leading causes of mortgage default and foreclosure.

Because Our First Two Books Were Right, Now You Can Be Right, Too

Most people think the economy will get better soon. It won't. We can tell you what you want to hear, or we can help you enormously by showing you how to prepare and protect yourself while you still can, and find opportunities to profit during the dramatically changing times ahead. We may not give you news you like, but it will definitely be news you can do something about.

Now is not the time to look for someone to cheer you up. Now is the time to get it right because you won't care in five years if someone cheered you up today. What you will care about is that you made the right financial decisions. It matters more now than ever before that you get it right today. Please remember this important point as you go through the rest of the book: *It is only bad news for your personal economy if you don't do anything about it.*

And, you can do something about it. You can actively and correctly manage your investments and protect your assets now, before it's too late, and you can begin to position yourself to cash in on some really big profit opportunities in the longer term. This is a tricky time and it will only get trickier, which is why we want to help you come through each stage of the coming Aftershock (before, during, and after) in the best shape possible.

Before we go on, we should take a moment to assure you that we are neither bulls nor bears. We are not gold bugs, stock boosters or detractors, currency pushers, or doom-and-gloom crusaders. We have no particular political ideology to endorse, and no dogmatic future to promote. We are simply intensely interested in patterns, big evolving changes over broad sweeps of time. And because we look for patterns, we are willing to see them—often where others do not.

At the time we wrote *America's Bubble Economy*, we saw, and still continue to see, some patterns in the U.S. and world economies that others are missing. We see these patterns, in part because we are very good at analyzing the larger picture. In fact, co-author David Wiedemer has developed a fascinating new "Theory of Economic Evolution" (introduced briefly in Chapter 8 of the first edition of *Aftershock*, although not repeated in this updated second edition of the book) that helps explain and even predicts large economic patterns that most people simply don't see.

But there's more to it than that. We can see things happening in the economy right now that many others do not because, at this particular moment in history, it's very hard for most people—even most experts—to face what is actually going on. The U.S. economy has been such a strong and prosperous powerhouse for so long, it's difficult to imagine anything else. Our goal is not to convince you of anything you wouldn't conclude for yourself, if you had the right facts, based on objective science and logical analysis. Most people don't get the right facts because most financial analysis today is based on preconceived ideas about a hoped-for positive outcome. People want analysis that says the economy will improve in the future, not get worse. So they look for ways to create that analysis, drawing on outdated ideas like repeating "market cycles," to support their case. Such is human nature. We all naturally prefer a future that is better than the past, and luckily for many Americans, that is what we have enjoyed.

Not so this time.

Again, just to be clear, we are not intrinsically pessimistic, either by personality or by policy. We're just calling it as we see it. Wouldn't you really rather hear the truth?

At an April 2008 presentation about *America's Bubble Economy* to Hogan & Hartson, one of the nation's largest law firms, co-author Robert Wiedemer said he wished people would treat economists and financial analysts as doctors rather than people trying to cheer you up. What if you had pneumonia and all your doctor did was slap you on the back and say, "Don't worry about it. Take two aspirin, and you'll be fine in a couple days." Instead, wouldn't you prefer the most honest diagnosis and best treatment possible? But when it comes to the health of the economy, most people only want good news. Even in the face of some very damning economic facts, people still want convincing analysis of why the economy is about to turn around and get better soon. The vast majority of financial analysts and economists are simply responding to the market. That's what people want, and that's what they get.

Despite this universal desire for good news, and despite the fact that the housing and stock markets were both near their peaks in 2006, our first book did remarkably well. In fact, *America's Bubble Economy* has been discussed in articles in *Barron's, Reuters, Bottom Line*, and the *Associated Press*. The book was also selected as one of the 30 best business books of 2006 by Kiplinger's. Even before *Aftershock* was published, co-author Robert Wiedemer was invited to speak before the New York Hedge Fund Roundtable, The World Bank, and on CNBC's popular morning show *Squawk Box*. So clearly people are interested in unbiased financial analysis, even when that analysis says there are fundamental problems in the economy that won't be resolved easily or soon.

More recently, since the release of *Aftershock* in late 2009, support for our analysis and predictions has grown considerably. Dozens of newspapers, magazines, radio broadcasts, and television programs have featured and quoted from the book, and interviewed coauthor Bob Wiedemer, including the *New York Times, The Financial Times, Wall Street Journal, Associated Press*, CNBC, *Fox Business News*, and many more. While most of America still believes we are on the verge of economic recovery, there are cracks developing in that wall of good cheer, made evident to us by the fact that more than 230,000 copies of *Aftershock* are now in print, and our e-mails and voice mails are overflowing with people who want to find out more about how to protect themselves and profit in the months and years ahead.

Yet even within this supportive audience, and even among our most devoted fans, there is still a wish for optimism, a deep-down feeling that the future couldn't possibly be as bad as we say. We understand that. All we can offer is realism, based on facts and logical analysis. In the end, that is what's best for all of us.

Our original analysis for *America's Bubble Economy* showed us that the real estate bubble would be the first to burst, putting downward pressure on the stock market and discretionary spending bubbles, kicking off a major global recession. Now, in this book, we want to give you more details about the next round of bubbles to fall, while there's still time to protect your assets and position yourself to survive and thrive in this dangerous, yet potentially highly profitable new environment. Just as in the first book, our analysis is based on a reliable theory of economic evolution, backed up by cold, hard facts, and not random guesses.

Although much of what we predicted has come true, much that we forecasted in our first book hasn't happened yet, because most of the impact of the multibubble collapse is still to come. This is good news because it means you still have time to get prepared.

Didn't Other Bearish Analysts Get It Right, Too?

Not really. Back in 2006, there was a small group of more bearish financial analysts and economists who correctly predicted some slices of the problems we are seeing now. We say hats off to them for having the courage and insight to make what they felt were honest, if not popular, appraisals of the economy. It takes guts to yell "fire" when so few people believe you because they can't even smell the smoke.

However, there are times when smart people make the right predictions for the wrong reasons, or for incomplete reasons, and that makes them less likely to be right again in the future. In this case, there are important differences between our way of thinking and the typical "bear" analysis, which we think you ought to know about. For one thing, a lot of bear analysis tends to be apocalyptic in tone and predictions, sometimes going so far as to call for drastic survivalist measures, such as growing your own food. Unlike these true Doom-and-Gloomers, we see nothing of the kind occurring.

Another important difference is that so much bear analysis seems to carry moralistic overtones, implying that, individually and collectively, we have somehow sinned by borrowing too much money, and we will eventually have to pay a hefty price for our immoral ways. We certainly disagree that borrowing money is morally wrong. In fact, depending on the circumstances, borrowing money can be the best course of action for an individual, a business, or a government. Without the leveraging power of credit, it's very difficult to start a business, go to medical school, build a bridge, or lift an economy. Borrowing is not intrinsically "wrong." Clearly, some debts are a lot smarter than others. For example, borrowing money to go to college for four years en route to a lucrative career is smart. Borrowing the same amount to spend four years at Disney World is not. (More on "smart" versus "dumb" debt in the next chapter.) For now, the point is that borrowing money, in and of itself, is not the biggest problem—*stupidity* is. Other bearish analysts who complain about too much borrowing tend to miss this vital distinction entirely.

The biggest difference between our predictions and the rest is that the other bearish analyses tend to ignore the bigger picture of our *multibubble economy*. Even the most realistic bearish thinkers fail to see all the bubbles in today's economy, and they certainly miss the critically important *interactions* between them. Instead, if they mention any bubbles at all, they often focus on one singular bubble—like the credit crunch, or the housing bubble, or the growing federal debt. They are right to point out that all is not well, but they generally don't connect the dots from their single complaint to the larger multibubble economy. More importantly, they don't see the crucial interactions between all these bubbles that are currently pulling our economy down.

Honestly, if all we had was a credit crunch or a fallen housing bubble, our economy could get past it fairly unscathed. Unfortunately, our multibubble problem is much bigger than any one of its parts. As we discuss in more detail in the next chapter, these bubbles worked together in a seemingly *virtuous upward spiral* to lift the economy up in the longest economic expansion in U.S. history, and together these linked bubbles will work together in a *vicious downward spiral* to bring the economy down.

Partly because of their single-bubble focus and partly because people want to hear more optimism about the future, many bears were predicting a strong rebound in the economy as early as 2010. Grumpier bears said it could take several years, but most saw a fairly quick turnaround ahead.

Unfortunately, as we saw in 2010, a full economic rebound did not occur. Yes, in the last few months of 2010 the stock market recovered due to massive money printing and that has helped spur more consumer spending, but in terms of key areas such as job creation, new home sales, and auto sales, the economy remains well below the levels it hit prior to the financial crisis. The economy has not recovered because what we have this time is not a normal economic downturn on its way to an upturn. What we have this time is a multibubble economy on its way down. Multibubble economies certainly cannot stay afloat forever. There are real forces that push economies up and real forces that push economies down. These forces are not static, like repeating market cycles, but evolve over time. Based on our science-backed analysis of the evolving economy, which is neither bullish nor bearish, but simply realistic, the U.S. economy is in the middle of a long-term fundamental change. It is *evolving*, not merely cycling back and forth between expansion and contraction. Therefore, the multi-bubble economy will not automatically turn around and go back up again in the next few years. The idea that the economy is evolving, not merely expanding and contracting and expanding again, is a key difference between us and other bearish analysts; and it is certainly a huge difference between us and the bullish "experts."

Another reason that many "experts" did not (and still don't) see what is really occurring in the economy is that they don't fully understand the short term power of the federal government to make it look

We Said, They Said: Our Score Card

In Oct. 2006 we said	Experts said	What actually happened by December 2010
Stocks will fall	Stocks will rise	Dow fell from 12,100 to 11,000 and NASDAQ fell from 2350 to 2256
Housing will fall	Housing will rebound	Case-Shiller Top 20 Cities Composite Index fell from 205 to 142
Commercial real estate will fall	Commercial real estate will rise rapidly	Dow Jones U.S. Real Estate Index fell from 82 to 56
Dollar will fall	Dollar stable	The Dollar Index (DXY) fell from 86 to 81
Gold will rise	Gold already near its peak	Spot gold rose from $600/oz to $1,390/oz
Foreign stocks will go down	Foreign stocks will rise	FTSE 100 (London) fell from 5960 to 5530
Commodities will fall	Commodities will rise	Copper rose from $3.50/pound to $3.80/pound (China bubble at work). A broader commodities index, CRB, was flat at 304 in October 2006 and 305 in December 2010.

as if we are having a recovery when we are not. They see a financial crisis in late 2008, and then they see the short term positive impact of massive federal government borrowing and money printing on the stock market, helping to create the big stock rally of late 2010, and from there the experts conclude that the economy is getting back on track. It isn't.

How the "Experts" Got It Wrong

We enjoyed an article in the January 12, 2009 issue of *BusinessWeek* magazine so much that we thought we'd include some of it for you here. What follows are observations and predictions about the economy in 2008 by well-known and highly trained financial professionals, writers, investors, and economists. It is interesting to note that, in the course of our research for this book, we kept a file of predictions and observations that well-known analysts, investors, and economists make. In reviewing the file for this section of the book, we noticed that it is very hard to find *anyone* who will predict economic movements beyond a year. Hence, it limits just how wrong they can be. It also makes it very hard to compare our long-term predictions that were made in October 2006 with anyone else's predictions, since so few people in 2006 made predictions for 2008 or 2009. That we can show the accuracy of our long-term predictions against others' short-term predictions, which are much easier to make, shows the power of our financial and economic analyses in understanding the economy. For most investors, long-term predictions are really the most important because most investors are investing for the long term, whether it be for capital appreciation, capital preservation, or for retirement. Financial analysis has to be accurate long-term to really be valuable.

Here are the statements of interest from the January 12, 2009 issue of *BusinessWeek:*

Stock Market

"A very powerful and durable rally is in the works. But it may need another couple of days to lift off. Hold the fort and keep the faith!" A quote from Richard Band, editor, *Profitable Investing Letter*, Mar. 27, 2008.

What Actually Happened: At the time of Band's comment, the Dow Jones industrial average was at 12,300. By December, 2008 it was at 8,500.

AIG

AIG "could have huge gains in the second quarter." A quote from Bijan Moazami, distinguished analyst, Friedman, Billings, Ramsey, May 9, 2008.

What Actually Happened: AIG lost $5 billion in the second quarter 2008 and $25 billion in the next. It was taken over in September by the U.S. government, which will spend or lend $150 billion to keep it going.

Mortgages

"I think this is a case where Freddie Mac and Fannie Mae are fundamentally sound. They're not in danger of going under. . . . I think they are in good shape going forward." From Barney Frank (D-Mass.), House Financial Services Committee chairman, July 14, 2008.

What Actually Happened: Within two months of Rep. Frank's comments, the government forced the mortgage giants into conservatorships and pledged to invest up to $100 billion in each.

GDP Growth

"I'm not an economist but I do believe that we're growing." President George W. Bush, in a July 15, 2008 press conference.

What Actually Happened: Gross domestic product shrank at a 0.5 percent annual rate in the July–September quarter. On December 1, the National Bureau of Economic Research declared that a recession had begun in December 2007.

Banks

"I think Bob Steel's the one guy I trust to turn this bank around, which is why I've told you on weakness to buy Wachovia." Jim Cramer, CNBC commentator, March 11, 2008.

What Actually Happened: Within two weeks of Cramer's comment, Wachovia came within hours of failure as depositors fled. Steel eventually agreed to a takeover by Wells Fargo. Wachovia shares lost half their value from September 15 to December 29.

Homes

"Existing-Home Sales to Trend Up in 2008" from the headline of a National Association of Realtors press release, December 9, 2007.

What Actually Happened: NAR said November 2008 sales were running at an annual rate of 4.5 million—down 11 percent from a year earlier—in the worst housing slump since the Depression.

Oil

"I think you'll see [oil prices at] $150 a barrel by the end of the year"—a quote from T. Boone Pickens, one of the wealthiest and most respected oilmen today, on June 20, 2008.

What Actually Happened: Oil was then around $135 a barrel. By late December it was below $40.

Banks

"I expect there will be some failures. . . . I don't anticipate any serious problems of that sort among the large internationally active banks that make up a very substantial part of our banking system." Ben Bernanke, Federal Reserve chairman, Feb. 28, 2008.

What Actually Happened: In September 2008, Washington Mutual became the largest financial institution in U.S. history to fail. Citigroup needed an even bigger rescue in November.

Bernard Madoff

"In today's regulatory environment, it's virtually impossible to violate rules." Famous last words from Bernard Madoff, money manager, Oct. 20, 2007.

What Actually Happened: About a year later, Madoff—who once headed the NASDAQ Stock Market—told investigators he had cost his investors $50 billion in an alleged Ponzi scheme.

More Wrong Predictions

Following is another collection of predictions made about 2008 that was published in *New York* magazine. Again, these are all professional financial analysts who represent the opinions of many, many others, even if they are not quoted directly.

Stock Market

"Question: What do you call it when an $8 billion asset write-down translates into a $30 billion loss in market cap? Answer: an overreaction. . . . Smart investors should buy [Merrill Lynch] stock before everyone else comes to their senses." From Jon Birger in *Fortune's Investors Guide 2008*.

What Actually Happened: Merrill's shares plummeted 77 percent, and it had to be rescued by Bank of America through a deal brokered by the U.S. Treasury.

Housing

"There are [financial firms] that have been tainted by this huge credit problem. . . . Fannie Mae and Freddie Mac have been pummeled. Our stress-test analysis indicates those stocks are at bargain basement prices." Sarah Ketterer, a leading expert on housing, and CEO of Causeway Capital Management, quoted in *Fortune's Investors Guide 2008*.

What Actually Happened: Shares of Fannie and Freddie have lost 90 percent of their value, and the federal government placed these two lenders under "conservatorship" in September 2009.

Stock Market

"Garzarelli is advising investors to buy some of the most beaten-down stocks, including those of giant financial institutions such as Lehman Brothers, Bear Stearns, and Merrill Lynch. What would cause her to turn bearish? Not much. 'Our indicators are extremely bullish.'" Quote from Elaine Garzarelli, president of Garzarelli Capital and one of the most outstanding analysts on Wall Street, in *BusinessWeek's Investment Outlook 2008*.

What Actually Happened: None of these firms still exist. Lehman went bankrupt. JPMorgan Chase bought Bear Stearns in a fire sale. Merrill was sold to Bank of America.

General Electric

"CEO Jeffrey Immelt has been leading a successful makeover at General Electric, though you wouldn't know it from GE's flaccid stock price. Our bet is that in a stormy market investors will gravitate toward the ultimate blue chip." Jon Birger, senior writer, in *Fortune's Investors Guide 2008*.

What Actually Happened: GE's stock price fell 55 percent, and it lost its triple-A credit rating.

Banks

"A lot of people think Bank of America will cut its dividend, but I don't think there's a chance in the world. I think they'll raise it this year; they have raised it a little in each of the past 20 to 25 years. My target price for the stock is $55." A quote from Archie MacAllaster, chairman of MacAllaster Pitfield MacKay in *Barron's 2008 Roundtable.*

What Actually Happened: Bank of America saw its stock drop below $10 and cut its dividend by 50 percent.

Goldman Sachs

"Goldman Sachs makes more money than every other brokerage firm in New York combined and finishes the year at $300 a share. Not a prediction—an inevitability." A quote from James J. Cramer in his "Future of Business" column in *New York* magazine.

What Actually Happened: Goldman Sachs' share price fell to $78 in December 2008. The firm also announced a $2.2 billion quarterly loss, its first since going public.

Despite the hit to its stock, which has increased from $78 to nearly $150 (still about half the predicted price of $300), Goldman has by far the best management and skills on the Street and will have a consistently better performance than any other major firm.

Predictions from Ben Bernanke and Henry Paulson— We Trust These Officials with Our Economy

Federal Reserve Chairman Ben Bernanke and former Treasury Secretary Henry Paulson unfortunately make an incredible team for wrong forecasts. With the performance shown here, you have to wonder why they are given so much credibility.

March 28th, 2007—Ben Bernanke: "At this juncture . . . the impact on the broader economy and financial markets of the problems in the subprime markets seems likely to be contained."

March 30, 2007—Dow Jones @ 12,354.

April 20th, 2007—Paulson: "I don't see (subprime mortgage market troubles) imposing a serious problem. I think it's going to be largely contained." "All the signs I look at" show "the housing market is at or near the bottom."

July 12th, 2007—Paulson: "This is far and away the strongest global economy I've seen in my business lifetime."

August 1st, 2007—Paulson: "I see the underlying economy as being very healthy."

October 15th, 2007—Bernanke: "It is not the responsibility of the Federal Reserve—nor would it be appropriate—to protect lenders and investors from the consequences of their financial decisions."

February 28th, 2008—Paulson: "I'm seeing a series of ideas suggested involving major government intervention in the housing market, and these things are usually presented or sold as a way of helping homeowners stay in their homes. Then when you look at them more carefully what they really amount to is a bailout for financial institutions or Wall Street."

May 7, 2008—Paulson: "The worst is likely to be behind us."

June 9th, 2008—Bernanke: "Despite a recent spike in the nation's unemployment rate, the danger that the economy has fallen into a 'substantial downturn' appears to have waned."

July 16th, 2008—Bernanke: "[Freddie and Fannie] . . . will make it through the storm." "[are] . . . in no danger of failing.", ". . . adequately capitalized."

July 31, 2008—Dow Jones @ 11,378

August 10th, 2008—Paulson: "We have no plans to insert money into either of those two institutions" (Fannie Mae and Freddie Mac).

September 8th, 2008—Fannie and Freddie nationalized. The taxpayer is on the hook for an estimated $1–1.5 trillion. Over $5 trillion is added to the nation's balance sheet.

Where *We* Have Been Wrong

In the first edition of *Aftershock* we admitted that there is one area in which we have been wrong before, and we will likely be wrong again.

And now in this second edition of the book, we have to repeat that admission again. Timing exactly when each bubble will pop in the Bubblequake and Aftershock has been and remains nearly impossible to accurately predict. For example, in the last book we said the coming Aftershock could begin as early as 2011. But since we wrote the last book, the U.S. government has intervened in many ways to delay the coming economic collapse. For example, they enormously increased their borrowing, bailed out many of our largest financial institutions, bailed out our auto companies, gave significant tax credits to home buyers, put less pressure on banks to foreclose on defaulted mortgages, and began a program of massive money printing (see next chapter)—all of which helped temporarily support the sagging multibubble economy and delayed the inevitable fall ahead. (All this economic stimulus, by the way, is only going to make matters worse later, by putting more pressure on the debt and dollar bubbles, as you will see in Chapters 3, 4, and 5.)

In addition to huge government stimuli of various kinds, there is possibly some degree of manipulation of the markets for the purposes of keeping investor's psychology from turning too negative (for more on this, please see the Appendix).

So for a variety of reasons, our timing was a bit off in the first edition of *Aftershock* in 2009. In this updated second edition of the book in 2011, we believe the conditions necessary for the remaining bubbles to begin to fall (namely, rising inflation and rising interest rates) will likely be created in the next two to four years.

Timing is always tricky when making any forecast, but if you know what to look for, the *overall trends* of each phase are predictable, even if the exact moments when specific triggers that will activate them are not. That's why we try to give general time ranges for our ideas about future events, and we attempt to link these to other signs and events, rather than trying to predict specific dates.

While timing is tricky, knowing the overall trend is absolutely essential. If you know winter is coming, you can prepare yourself without knowing exactly when the first snowflake will fall. On the other hand, if you are expecting spring to begin, that first winter storm is really going to hit you hard.

An old stock market saying is "the trend is your friend." We say "the trend is your best way to defend" against the dangers of trying to time the Bubblequake and Aftershock. If you know the general trend, your asset protection and investment timing will, on average, be fine (see Chapters 6–8). Even if the trend seems to go against you for a while, if you follow a fundamental trend that you know may take years to play out, you will do fine. This type of fundamental, long-term trend thinking is key for success during each stage of the Bubblequake.

Within an overall trend, there will be moments, or trigger points, when dramatic shifts occur. For example, in the fall of 2008, the stock market dropped more than 20 percent within a few weeks of Lehman Brothers going bankrupt. Predicting the occurrence or the timing of that kind of specific event is essentially impossible. What we did predict with complete accuracy was the overall trend of an overvalued stock market bubble poised for a fall.

Specific trigger points are so hard to predict because their activation usually involves a high psychological component, and try as we might, the timing of human psychology is not especially predictable. For example, if you objectively analyzed the Internet stock bubble prior to its fall, you'd know that it was bound to pop at some point, but you'd be hard pressed to know precisely when and specifically what would kick it off. Even today, well *after* the fact, it is hard to figure out exactly what triggered the pop of the dot-com bubble in March 2000. Was it the collapse of Microstrategy's stock price due to the restatement of earnings forced on it by Price Waterhouse Coopers in March? That's a good guess, but not necessarily correct. Other people have their own guesses, but in talking to many investment bankers and venture capitalists, we have found no unified identification of the actual trigger point, even though they are experts in this area, and this was a major economic event that affected each of them quite personally. All we know with certainty is that we had a bubble in Internet-related stock prices, and in March 2000 investor psychology dramatically changed.

When thinking about how bubbles in general tend to burst, it's interesting to note that during the fall of the Internet bubble, NASDAQ didn't just collapse and go straight down. Over the course of nine months, it fell and recovered, at one point rising not too far from its peak, before its eventual final fall. Even right in the middle of the dot-com crash, most people didn't see it. In fact, the mantra among investors at the time was that we were simply moving away from a business-to-consumer model toward a business-to-business model, and then to an infrastructure play. The infrastructure play begat the rise of the fiber–optic companies in the summer of 2000, most notably JDS Uniphase, before it, too, collapsed. Ultimately, NASDAQ would rise and fall again many times, until it had fallen 75 percent from its all-time high of nearly 4700 in early 2000 finally hitting its low point of 1170 in September 2002.

The moral of the story is that it's hard to predict specific triggers before they happen. Even *after* the fact, it can be hard to understand the timing of specific events. Why did investors change their psychology in March 2000 instead of in August 1999? After March 2000, why did people think that infrastructure was the next big thing? Did they just want to keep the old Internet boom alive, or were they really sold on infrastructure? Most investor decision-making turned out to be based on psychology, not real analysis of the underlying trends. Eventually, all the stocks in the infrastructure play collapsed. Even wishful thinking can't grow a bubble forever.

So when people challenge us to tell them exactly when each phase of the Aftershock will begin, we don't take the bait. All we can say with certainty is that the transitions from each phase to the next will involve triggering events, the timing of which will be as hard to predict as the popping of the Internet bubble.

We do know that trends can take years to assert themselves fully, and along the way, long-term trends can be temporarily delayed, even briefly reversed, by a countering short-term trend. For example, the long-term trend of a falling stock market bubble was temporarily delayed by the short-term trend of the rise of the private equity company buyout bubble. With easy credit at very low interest rates, private equity and hedge funds raised enormous amounts of money and went on a company buying spree the likes of which we've never seen. Total merger and acquisition transaction values went from $441 billion in 2002 to $1.4 trillion in 2006 and $1.3 trillion in 2007, according to Mergerstat. This, plus generally good investor psychology, drove stock prices higher, helping to boom the Dow above 14,000 in 2007. Of course, it also made the stock market bubble much bigger, and therefore, much more vulnerable to the credit crunch, caused by the fall of the housing bubble and the private debt bubble (see Chapter 2).

In another example, the potential full negative impact of the collapse in home prices on the economy and stock market in 2008 was blunted, or at least delayed, by the short-term trend of lenders making much riskier loans in 2006. Historically, in July 2005 home prices stopped going up in many places or slowed their growth dramatically. They weren't falling, but they weren't rising rapidly anymore, thus setting the stage for the sub-prime and adjustable-rate mortgage collapse. Lenders' willingness to participate in riskier home loans in 2006 and early 2007 to some extent slowed the fall of the housing bubble and delayed its impact on the economy and the stock market for a while. In our first book, we couldn't give the exact timing of the housing bubble fall because it was hard for us to predict just how crazy lenders would get. We did know they could not keep it up forever, and in fact, they didn't. Lenders pulled back on their risky loans very dramatically in 2007, triggering an even bigger collapse in real estate prices.

Thus, our 2006 prediction of the long-term trend of falling housing and stock market prices began to emerge with a vengeance by the end of 2007 and early 2008, firmly establishing the start of the Bubblequake. And, if it were not for emergency measures by the Federal Reserve to print massive amounts of money combined with a massive increase in government borrowing, which were almost unprecedented, the stock market would have fallen much farther. But the dramatic government intervention only served to temporarily blunt (not stop) the effects of the underlying fundamental trend. In time, these trends will also include a major Aftershock that few others are anticipating: the bursting of the dollar and government debt bubbles. When will that happen? All we can say with any reasonable degree of confidence in 2011 is that the full force of the Aftershock will likely begin in the next two to four years.

While precise timing is very tricky because there are always so many intervening, complex factors, our predictions regarding the *overall trend* are well intact and still on track.

Love us or hate us—the fact is we got it right before, while others got it wrong. And unfortunately, we will be right again, for the very same reasons. As Paul Farrell, senior columnist for Dow Jones *MarketWatch*, said about our first book in February 2008, "*America's Bubble Economy*'s prediction, though ignored, was accurate."

Leave 'em Laughing

After reading some of the quotes from senior financial analysts and financial leaders you may be laughing or crying. But, to be sure you start the book with a little humor in an otherwise difficult situation; we thought we would close out the first chapter of the book with the following bit e-mailed to us by one of our supporters. It's not ours, but we honestly don't know who to give credit to. So, if someone knows who wrote this, e-mail or call us, and we'll post it on our web site.

You Know It's a Bad Economy When . . .

1. Your bank returns your check marked as "insufficient funds" and you have to call them and ask if they meant you or them.
2. The most highly paid job is now jury service.
3. People in Beverly Hills fire their nannies and are learning their children's names.
4. McDonalds is selling the quarter-ouncer.
5. Obama met with small businesses—GE, Chrysler, Citigroup, and GM—to discuss the stimulus package.
6. Hot Wheels and Matchbox cars are now trading at higher prices than GM's stock.
7. You got a pre-declined credit card in the mail.
8. Your "reality check" bounced.
9. The stock market indexes have been renamed: the Dow is now the "Down-Jones" and the S&P is the "Substandard & Very Poor."
10. Webster's is keeping its dictionary length constant by adding words that are commonly used, such as Twitter, tweet, and Facebook, and dropping those no longer needed, such as retirement, pensions, and Social Security.

He Said What?!

In an appearance on CNBC's *Squawk Box* in February 2008, co-author Bob Wiedemer offered what must have seemed like a wacky investment idea: *Start shorting housing stocks.* The analysts on the program cringed at what they considered yesterday's news—perhaps good advice the year before, but clearly no longer valid. Bob stood his ground. Based not on a lucky guess or some morbid wish for a crash, but based on the science-backed analysis of our first book, Bob knew the full collapse of the housing bubble (and therefore the construction industry) still lay ahead.

By now, we all know he was very right. Homebuilders' stocks fell by almost 50 percent over the next year, according to the Dow Jones U.S. Home Construction Index, which fell from 20 in February 2008 to 10 in December 2008. It would have been a tidy profit for any investor, especially if you were wise enough to use LEAPs (Long-Term Equity Anticipation Securities, which are publicly traded options contracts with expiration dates longer than one year)—one of our many investment suggestions. If you have an underlying theory that predicts overall trends, based on cold, hard facts, you don't have to run with the pack. Without trying to precisely "time the market," if you know the overall trend, you can stay out in front of the curve.

In fact, while the cameras were still rolling and the experts were still telling him he was dead wrong, Bob knew that eventually *all* the major publicly traded homebuilders would not just decline, they would eventually go bankrupt (and we still believe that). Naturally, he didn't dare say such a thing. (You don't get invited back on these shows if you are too pessimistic about stocks.) But, on that particular prediction, we know Bob will be quite right again. Without an underlying theory of economic evolution to base one's investment ideas on, even the "experts" don't realize just how fundamental the coming changes will be.

Phase I: The Bubblequake

POP GO THE HOUSING, STOCK, PRIVATE DEBT, AND SPENDING BUBBLES

W hat in the world happened? There we were, with the Dow over 14,000, U.S. home prices close to their all-time highs, and consumer and commercial credit flowing as freely as honey on a hot summer day. Then, seemingly overnight, things weren't so sweet. It may feel like the proverbial rug was randomly pulled out from under us, but in fact, we've been setting ourselves up for this multibubble fall over many years. Beginning with our decision in the early 1980s to run large government deficits, six co-linked bubbles have been growing bigger and bigger, each working to lift the others, all booming and supporting the U.S. economy:

1. The real estate bubble
2. The stock market bubble
3. The private debt bubble
4. The discretionary spending bubble
5. The dollar bubble
6. The government debt bubble

The first four of these bubbles began to burst in the Bubblequake that rocked the U.S. and world economies in late 2008 and 2009. Next, while most people think the worst is over, the coming Aftershock will bring down all six bubbles in the next two to five years.

We know this is hard to believe, and we wish it weren't true, but as you will see in this and the next chapter, all the evidence is right there, plain as day. You just need to know what to look for.

Bubbles "R" Us: A Quick Review of America's Bubble Economy

What is a bubble? This should be an easy question to answer but there is no academically accepted definition of a financial or economic bubble. For our purposes, we define a bubble as an asset value that temporarily booms and eventually busts, based on changing investor psychology rather than underlying, fundamental economic drivers that are sustainable over time.

For quite a few years, America's multibubble economy has been growing because of six co-linked bubbles, some of which you may find easier to believe in than others. These six bubbles are outlined next.

The Real Estate Bubble

Now that it's popped, the housing bubble is easy to see. As shown in Figure 2.1, from 2000 to 2006, home prices almost doubled.

Income Up 2%   Housing Price Up 80%

Figure 2.1   Income Growth versus Housing Price Growth 2001–2006
Contrary to what some experts say, the earlier rapid growth of housing prices was not driven by rising wage and salary income. In fact, from 2001 to 2006, housing price growth far exceeded income growth.
Source: Bureau of Labor Statistics and the S&P/Case-Shiller Home Price Index.

If nothing else, just looking at Figure 2.2 on inflation-adjusted housing prices since 1890, created by Yale economist Robert Shiller, should make anyone suspicious that there was a VERY big housing bubble in the making. Note that home prices barely rose on an inflation-adjusted basis until the 1990s and then just exploded in 2001.

However, while home prices exploded, the inflation-adjusted wages and salaries of the people buying the homes went up only 2 percent for the same period (according to the Bureau of Labor Statistics). The rise in home prices so profoundly outpaced the rise of incomes that even our most conservative analysis back in 2005 led us to correctly predict that the vulnerable housing bubble would be the first to fall. We have a lot more to say about what's ahead for the housing market later in this chapter. (Hint: It's not what they tell you to think.)

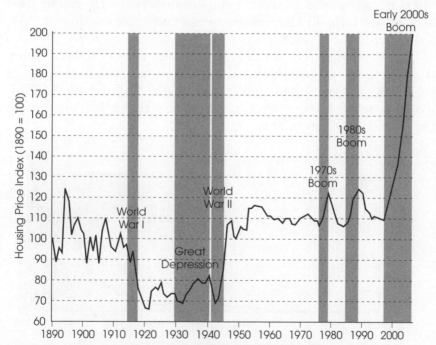

Figure 2.2   Price of Homes Adjusted for Inflation Since 1890
Contrary to popular belief, housing prices do not ordinarily rise rapidly. In fact, until recently, inflation-adjusted home prices haven't increased that significantly, but then they just exploded after 2001.

Source: Irrational Exuberance, Second Edition, 2006 by Robert J. Shiller.

The Stock Market Bubble

This one was almost as easy for us to spot as the housing bubble, yet many times harder to get other people to see. Stocks can be analyzed in so many different ways. We find the state of the stock market is easier to understand by looking at Figure 2.3. After decades of growth, the Dow had risen 300 percent from 1928 to 1982 (54 years). Yet in the next 20 years the Dow increased an astonishing 1200 percent, growing four times as much as before in 70% less time. But, that growth came without four times the growth in company earnings or our GDP. We call that a stock market bubble. It looks even more out of line when you consider that the population of the United States more than doubled in that previous period (1928 to 1982), and personal income more than doubled between 1950 and 1970 alone. In comparison, since 1980, our population has grown only 25 percent, and personal income barely has grown 10 percent. Population growth and personal income growth are the key drivers of GDP growth, and GDP growth is the fundamental driver of corporate earnings growth, and therefore stock prices.

Shown in a different way in Figure 2.4, the value of financial assets as a percentage of GDP held relatively steady at around 450 percent since 1960. But starting in 1981 it rose to over 1000 percent in 2007, according to the Federal Reserve. We call that prima facie evidence of a stock and real estate bubble.

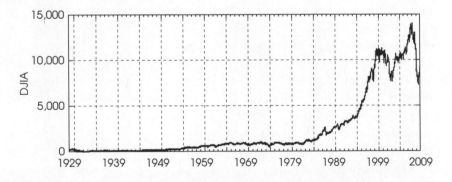

Figure 2.3   Dow Jones Industrial Average 1928–2009
Despite massive growth in the U.S. economy between 1928 and 1981, the Dow rose only about 300 percent. But after 1981 it rose an astonishing 1400 percent.

Source: Dow Jones.

Figure 2.4 Rise of the Financial Assets Bubble
Financial assets as a percentage of GDP: The exploding value of financial assets as a percentage of GDP is strong evidence of a financial bubble.
Sources: Thomson Datastream and the Federal Reserve.

The Private Debt Bubble

The private debt bubble, like all bubbles, is complex. But we will simplify it a bit by saying it is essentially a derivative bubble that was driven by two other bubbles: the rapidly rising home price bubble and the rapidly rising stock market bubble, which combined to make for a strong and growing economy. In both cases, lenders of all forms (not just banks) began to feel very comfortable with the false belief that the risk of a falling economy had been essentially eliminated, and the risk of any lending in that environment was minimal. This fantasy was supported for a time by the fact that very few loans went into default. Certainly, at the time we wrote our first book, commercial and consumer loan default rates were at historic lows.

The problem was not so much the amount of private debt that made it a bubble, but taking on so much debt under the false assumption that nothing would go wrong with the economy. Lenders felt very comfortable increasing the amount they lent for consumer credit card loans, home mortgages, home equity loans, commercial real estate loans, corporate loans, buyout loans, and, in fact, just about every kind of loan, due to increasing asset values and a healthy economy that no one thought would change.

For us, it was easy to see in 2006 that if the value of housing or stocks were to fall dramatically (as bubbles always eventually do), a tremendous number of loan defaults would occur. The private debt bubble was an obvious derivative bubble that was bound to pop when the housing and stock market bubbles popped.

The Discretionary Spending Bubble

Consumer spending accounts for about 70 percent of the U.S. economy (depending on exactly how you define *consumer spending*). A large portion of consumer spending is discretionary spending, meaning it's optional (how big a portion depends on exactly how you define *discretionary*). Easy bubble-generated money and easy consumer credit made lots of easy discretionary spending possible at every income level. Now, as the housing, stock market, and private debt bubbles pop and people lose their jobs, or are concerned they might, consumers are reducing their spending, especially unnecessary, discretionary spending.

This is typical in any recession, but this time the effect is much more profound for two key reasons. First, the private debt bubble allowed consumers to spend like crazy because of huge growth in housing prices and a growing stock market and economy, which gave them more access to credit than ever before, via credit cards and home equity loans. As the bubbles pop, that credit is drying up, and so is the huge consumer spending that was driven by it.

Secondly, much of our spending on necessities has a high discretionary component, which is relatively easy for us to cut back. We need food, but we don't need Whole Foods. We need to eat, but we don't need to eat at Bennigans or Steak & Ale (both now bankrupt). We need refrigerators and countertops, but we don't need stainless steel refrigerators and granite countertops. The list of necessities that can have a high discretionary component, complete with elevated prices, goes on and on. And all that discretionary spending is on top of completely discretionary spending, such as entertainment and vacation travel.

The combined fall of the first four bubbles (housing, stock market, private debt, and discretionary spending) make up what we call the Bubblequake of late 2008 and 2009. Unfortunately, our troubles don't end there. Two more giant bubbles are about to burst in the coming Aftershock.

The Dollar Bubble

Perhaps the hardest reality of all to face—the once mighty greenback—has become an unsustainable currency bubble. Due to a rising bubble economy, investors from all over the world were getting huge returns on their dollar-denominated assets. This made the dollar more valuable but also more vulnerable. Why? Because we didn't really have a true booming economy underlying the growth, we had a multibubble economy. The value of a currency in a multibubble economy is linked, not to real, underlying, fundamental drivers of sustainable economic growth (like true productivity gains), but to the rising and falling bubbles. For many years our dollars rose in value because of rising demand for dollars to make investments in our bubbles. Now the falling bubbles will eventually lead to falling-value dollars, despite all kinds of government efforts to stop it. (Don't believe us? You will by the end of the next chapter.)

The Government Debt Bubble

Weighing in at more than $8.5 trillion when our 2006 book came out, and expected to exceed $15 trillion by the end of 2011 as shown in Figure 2.5, the whopping U.S. government debt bubble is currently the biggest, baddest, scariest bubble of all, relative to the other bubbles in our economy. Much of this debt has been funded by foreign investors, primarily from Asia and Europe. But as our multibubble economy continues to fall and the dollar starts to sink, who in the world will be willing, or even able, to lend us more? (Much more on the fall of the impossibly huge government debt bubble in Chapter 4.)

From Boom to Bust: The Virtuous Upward Spiral Becomes a Vicious Downward Spiral

On the way up, these six linked economic bubbles helped co-create America's booming bubble economy. In a seemingly virtuous upward spiral, the inflating bubbles helped the United States maintain its status as the biggest economy the world has ever known, even in the last few decades, when declines in real productivity growth

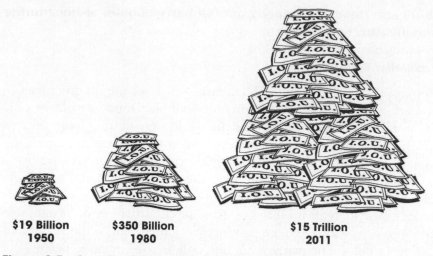

$19 Billion
1950

$350 Billion
1980

$15 Trillion
2011

Figure 2.5   Growth of the U.S. Government's Debt
The U.S. government's debt is massive and growing rapidly. With no plan and little ability to pay it off, the debt is quickly becoming the world's largest toxic asset.

Source: Federal Reserve.

could have slowed our expanding economic growth. Instead, these bubbles helped us ignore slowing productivity growth, boost our prosperity, disregard some fundamental problems, and keep the party going.

Not only did the U.S. economy continue to grow and remain strong, the rest of the world benefited as well. Money we paid for rapidly increasing imports poured like Miracle-Gro into developing countries like China and India, quickly expanding their burgeoning economies. The developed nations benefited as well. Because America's bubble economy was booming along with the developing nations, Japan and Europe were able to sell lots of their cars and other high-end exports, which helped their home economies prosper. The growing world economy created a rising demand for energy, pushing up oil prices, which made some Russian billionaires, among others, very happy. Growing demand for minerals, like iron, oil, and copper, pumped money into every resource-producing country. China and India's expanding appetite for steel boosted iron exports from the Australian economy. And on, and on. All combined, America's rising bubble economy helped boom the world's rising bubble economy.

Now, as our intermingled global party bubbles are beginning to deflate and fall, the virtuous upward spiral has become a vicious downward spiral. They are linked together and pushing hard against each other. Each time any one bubble sags and pops, it puts tremendous downward pressure on the rest. First, we had the fall of the U.S. housing bubble and its downward impact on the stock market bubble, the private debt bubble, and the discretionary spending bubble—what we call the Bubblequake. Next, in the Aftershock, the dollar bubble and the U.S. government debt bubbles will be pumped up even more to offset the other popping bubbles. But, when those final bubbles in America's bubble economy begin to burst, so will the world's bubble economy.

It is important to understand that the Bubblequake problems we are now facing are due to much more than merely a popped real estate bubble. If all we had was a burst housing bubble, it would not have created so much financial pain here and around the globe. In addition to the housing bubble, the private debt bubble and the stock market bubble also fell. And these problems are not going to be resolved anytime soon. Rather than the housing bubble, private debt bubble, and stock market bubble magically reinflating, they will instead continue to fall. This will continue to put downward pressure on the already vulnerable dollar bubble and bulging U.S. government debt bubble, eventually forcing both to burst, creating a worldwide mega-depression. Unless you know what to look for, the coming Aftershock will be hard to see until it's too late to protect yourself (see Chapters 6 through 8).

Once all six of our economy-supporting bubbles are fully popped, life in the post-dollar-bubble world will be quite different from the relatively quick recovery most analysts are now predicting. The vicious downward spiral of multiple popping bubbles will move the economy from the current Bubblequake to the coming Aftershock faster than the onset of the troubles we've already seen. And indeed the Aftershock will move quickly to the post-dollar-bubble world. So although there is much more economic change ahead, it will happen in increasingly shorter and shorter periods of time.

While it may seem chaotic and unpredictable, not all this change will be entirely random but will happen as part of a much bigger movement of ongoing economic evolution that will be the subject of a later book. That evolution will eventually involve some very effective solutions for the economy's problems that would be politically impossible to implement today.

If you've read the past few pages, you now know more than nearly everyone else about how we got ourselves into this mess. Now the big question is how bad will this Bubblequake get? How low will U.S. real estate, private credit, and stocks go? The rest of the chapter focuses on these three bursting bubbles.

Pop Goes the Housing Bubble

The most important thing to understand about the current housing crunch is that it's not a subprime mortgage problem whose contagion spread to other mortgages; it is a *housing price collapse*. If home prices had not declined there would never have been a subprime mortgage problem at all. If home prices had continued rising as they had been rising in the past, the low introductory, adjustable-rate subprime loans would have simply been refinanced into new low introductory, adjustable-rate subprime loans based on the higher equity in the home, and everything would have been just fine.

But, with a housing price collapse, the low introductory, adjustable-rate subprime loans were doomed. These subprime mortgages were not the cause of the problem; they were merely the first to get hit. If you have a housing price collapse and not just a subprime mortgage problem, then as housing prices continue to collapse, the Alternative A-paper (Alt-A, no documented income) "liar loans" start to fail. Loans made on investment properties also get hit. Fancy mortgages to people with good credit that allow the payer the option of paying less than the current interest owed and no principal at all (so called option adjustable-rate mortgages) take a hit, too. Home equity loans get pinched. Eventually, as the housing price collapse continues, perfectly good prime mortgages get hit as well. It's not a "spreading contagion" from the subprime problem, as the press so often tries to tell us. It's just the fallout from a continuously declining housing price bubble that is impacting more and more people.

The *falling equity value* (not subprime mortgages) is the single most important factor leading to mortgage default and foreclosure. Falling equity values make refinancing any adjustable loan very difficult. Home equity has been falling dramatically with the Bubblequake. As of the second quarter of 2007 it passed a milestone, with the percentage of equity Americans have in their homes falling below 50 percent for the first time since 1945 according to the Federal Reserve. It has fallen below 45 percent since then and continues to fall at a rapid rate today.

Because of the housing price collapse and the damage it caused to home equity, the number of mortgages that are *underwater*, meaning they have no equity or negative equity, is increasing extremely rapidly.

As the housing bubble pops, more homeowners will lose all of the equity in their homes. As of Q4 2010 more than 25 percent of homes with mortgages were underwater, up significantly from 14.3 percent in Q3 2008, according to Zillow.com. In Las Vegas, which was hit hard by the bubble pop, more than 80 percent of homes are now underwater. In Phoenix the number is 70 percent, and in Chicago it is almost 40 percent.

Co-author Bob Wiedemer likes to demonstrate the impact of falling home values on the economy by pushing a pencil into a balloon. The pencil represents declining home values. The balloon represents the economy. The more home prices fall, the deeper the pencil pushes into the balloon. As the pencil goes further and further into the balloon, more mortgages of higher grade are taken down at an increasing rate, taking the economy down with them. Ultimately, the balloon pops, because house prices can only go down so far before they trigger a major collapse in the mortgage market and the economy as a whole, a process we will describe in more detail later. Of course government intervention—such as massive purchases of mortgage bonds by the Federal Reserve—can slow things down temporarily but, in the long run, not only will this not save us from a big housing bubble pop, it will actually make the fall even worse, as we will show you in later chapters.

No One Thought Home Prices Would Decline

It was always assumed that subprime loans were risky loans, and so they carried a higher interest rate than non-subprime. What was not factored into anyone's calculations was the possibility (to us, the probability) that home prices would eventually fall. The models used by the bond-rating firms and investment banking firms that rated and sold the complex mortgage-backed securities (that included subprime loans) never anticipated home prices falling, at least not to any significant degree. As their analysts now readily admit, they anticipated various levels of home price increases—some low, some medium—but certainly not much of a home price decrease. Were these people crazy? Not a bit. After all, home prices have almost never declined in recent history. You would have to go back to the post-World War I recession to find any serious inflation-adjusted home price decline, and even then only for a short period of time. From 1916 to 1921 home values fell about 30 percent, according to data from the Case-Shiller Home Price Index.

Virtually no one in the investment world, or even outside the investment world, thought home prices in the United States would ever decline significantly, and certainly not for any extended length of time. There was no historical precedent for it to happen.

But, just as we predicted, happen it did. How come? Because home prices were in a *bubble*. As mentioned earlier, home prices were up 100 percent and income was up only 2 percent from 2000 to 2006. If that isn't a textbook example of an asset bubble, we don't know what is. That kind of price growth without comparable income growth to support it is just not sustainable for very long. It had to be a bubble; therefore, it had to pop.

People will give you a thousand reasons to justify the growing real estate bubble: "People love San Francisco," "There is limited land in Boston (or Manhattan, or LA)," "Washington, DC has a very stable job base," or "People enjoy living close to the city."

None of these reasons ever explained why prices were increasing so much in a fairly flat economy. And the economic growth that did occur in 2003 and 2004 was due in large part to rising home equity spending and rising home construction.

"Innovations" in the Mortgage Industry Made the Housing Bubble Possible

An important ingredient for growing such a large real estate bubble so quickly was the highly "innovative" mortgage industry. The industry developed new products and enhanced previous ones, such as the adjustable-rate mortgage, which had been around for a while but now was taken to a whole new level. Innovations included a low introductory interest rate—the same idea credit card companies used to hook consumers. Start with a low rate of 1 or 2 percent for the first two or three years and then jump to a normal adjustable-rate mortgage. Another "innovation" was the willingness to give these mortgages to people who could only afford them at the low introductory rate, not at the rate that was coming later. This made more expensive homes much easier for people to buy, often with the idea of selling them later for a big profit when home prices continued to climb.

The mortgage industry also innovated with no-documentation loans, called Alt-A loans or "liar loans." These loans had been around before but they were pushed much harder during the housing boom. Also, low credit scores were increasingly acceptable, and with the housing bubble on the rise more people lied about their incomes in order to get their hands on the keys to a piece of the housing boom.

Option ARMs were another incredible innovation. Every month you get the choice of making a full payment of interest and principal, or an interest-only payment, or—get this—a smaller payment that didn't even cover the interest due! The interest you didn't pay would be added to the principal of the loan until the loan value reached 110 percent or 125 percent of the original amount, at which point you would have to jump to full payment of interest and the payment on the new, much larger principal. No wonder they called them "suicide loans." More than 80 percent of folks who took these deadly loans paid the lowest payment option possible (who takes these loans if you want to pay more than the least possible?). Not surprisingly, the default rates on these loans will, by some estimates, soon reach 90 percent.

Mortgage brokers became much more prevalent during the housing boom, and they became much more aggressive in selling as many mortgages as possible. Bad loans were not their problem. The underwriter judged the quality of the loan. As long as the broker could place the loan with an underwriter, that's all that was necessary for the broker to get paid. What happened to the loan after that was not their worry.

Amazingly, in many cases, it was not the worry of the underwriter either. Many underwriters just wanted to repackage these loans into mortgage-backed securities and sell them in big multimillion-dollar bundles to large investors, often in other countries. The underwriter collected the underwriting fees and never had to worry if the poor suckers who took out the mortgages could ever make payments to the poor suckers who bought the mortgage-backed securities. The foreign and other investors who bought these mortgage-backed securities considered them as secure as government bonds, but with a higher interest rate. *The bond rating agencies, like Moody's and Standard & Poor's, encouraged these sentiments by giving most of the bond packages their highest AAA rating—which was the same as the U.S. government.* The high rating was often required for many investment funds to buy the bonds.

All of these and even more "innovations" by the mortgage industry were key to making the housing bubble possible. Now that these "innovations" are gone, lending has decreased substantially. In 2003, lending for single-family homes was $3.9 trillion. In 2008 it was half that amount, according to the Mortgage Bankers Association. And in 2011 the Mortgage Bankers Association predicts that lending for single-family homes will fall 50 percent from 2008 to less than $1 trillion. This huge decrease in lending has put enormous downward pressure on the housing bubble.

Had Home Prices Kept Going Up Rapidly, the Mortgage Industry Would Still Be Fine

In fairness to the mortgage industry, if home prices had kept going up and up, none of this would have been a problem. People could have easily refinanced their way out of all their fancy mortgages into other newer fancy mortgages based on the huge rise in home equity. Had home prices continued going up in value, there would have been little risk in making these higher risk innovative mortgages—that is, little risk that was not offset by higher fees and higher interest rates.

Had Home Prices Kept Going Up Rapidly, Home Buyers Would Still Be Fine

In all fairness to home buyers, if home prices had kept going up, it would have made tons of sense to buy the most expensive house you could possibly get away with. As long as you could make the monthly payments for at least a year (low introductory rate payments really helped with that) and as long as your home's price was going up 10 or 20 percent a year, you would be practically minting money.

For example, for a $500,000 house, a 10 to 20 percent rise in home prices annually created an increase of $50,000 to $100,000 in home equity every year. All you had to do was convert that growing equity into cash via a refinancing or a home equity loan, and you would have had plenty of money to make your house payments and buy lots of toys along the way. When the housing bubble was rising, you were actually getting paid to buy a home—paid a *lot* of money. What could be better? So please do not blame homebuyers; they were making excellent investment decisions—*as long as home prices kept rising rapidly.*

Had Home Prices Kept Going Up Rapidly, Wall Street Would Still Be Fine

No one thought housing prices would stop rising rapidly and actually go down. Even the best minds on Wall Street seemed blind to the bubble that they were helping to create. Remember, bubbles are a lot easier to see *after* they pop. And remember, too, that not noticing the housing bubble was making a lot of people very, very rich. So no one complained or criticized. Quite the opposite; they sang the praises of the brilliant new Wall Street mega-millionaires. Bear Stearns' profits were enormous, and many Wall Street insiders made out like bandits. And if the housing bubble had just kept rising, Wall Street would have been just fine.

But, as it turned out for Bear Stearns and the rest of Wall Street, making money by making bad investments and then selling those bad investments to others is a very bad long-term strategy. Even if the federal government comes along and partially bails you out, it's very painful when the boom busts.

And bust it did, because even the most "innovative" mortgages and creative new investment instruments could not get around one fundamental fact: Home prices cannot rise dramatically faster than incomes rise over any significant amount of time. It flies in the face of basic economic principles and has never happened before and never will again. Real estate bubbles don't last.

That is the kind of excellent and honest analysis that Wall Street could really have used before the housing bubble popped, but it would have been laughed at and ignored. Their lack of interest in such analysis has cost them very heavily indeed.

"Honey, we're homeless."

Where Do Home Prices Go from Here?

Even now, smart people continue to make the same mistakes as before. They feel that the fall in home prices has to stop and turn around fairly soon and they want to get a "bargain." And it's not just home buyers who are confused. In 2008, Alan Greenspan announced that home prices would stop falling by spring 2009. He was wrong, of course. He was just cheerleading. But even if he had been right for a short period of time and real estate values had begun to temporarily stabilize, they would only have started declining again. Why? Because it's a bubble! That means home prices are still higher than is justified by underlying, fundamental economic drivers.

There are only two ways to get home values to rise again: Either reinflate the bubble, which at this point is not possible, or have real economic reasons for a rise in home prices, which currently do not exist. While it is true that massive federal government support for the housing market has limited the fall for a while, it cannot reinflate the housing bubble. So, like it or not, the overall trend for home prices is to continue to go down, along with all the other bubbles in our multibubble economy.

Part of the reason the overall trend in housing is down is that the United States has lost a massive number of jobs. In fact, as can be seen in Figure 2.6 *the United States has lost almost every job that was created during the housing boom!* If people don't have jobs, they aren't very inclined to buy homes.

Bubbles don't rise and fall in a straight line because psychology is so involved and because the government will do many things to try to stimulate home buying and support prices. For these and other reasons, as we mentioned before, it is hard to predict the exact timing of the next drop down, but you can be sure that projections and proclamations by various economic experts that falling home prices are stabilizing and turning around are mostly conjecture.

You will notice that there is never much of a reason given for the predicted about-face. They don't say why home prices will stop falling

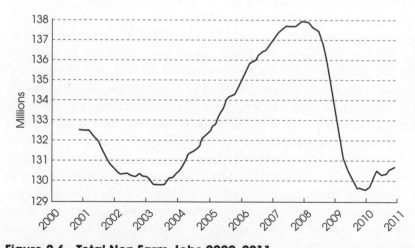

Figure 2.6   Total Non-Farm Jobs 2000–2011
The United States has lost almost every single job created during the housing bubble—no jobs, not much demand for homes.
Source: Bureau of Labor Statistics.

and start rising, or offer any analysis based on the fundamental forces driving real estate prices. Perhaps they just feel it "can't get any worse," so it has to get better soon. Home prices, after all, normally go up, and so the current decline has to be just a temporary aberration. This sounds a lot like what Wall Streeters might have said a few years ago. Instead of doing a careful analysis of the economics behind the asset values, they simply relied on the fact that, in the past, stock prices and home prices went up, so in the future, they would have to go up too. Apparently, they don't listen to their own disclaimer: "Past performance is no guarantee of future results."

All these projections by Greenspan and others are optimistic conjecturing at best, and pure cheerleading at worst. Either way, they are telling people what they want to hear because that's what gets the biggest audience. By the way, we like to hear it, too. We also own houses.

Pop Goes the Stock Market Bubble

The fall of the housing bubble caused many mortgages to default, particularly the riskier subprime mortgages given to people who often could not afford them in the longer term. Some of these subprime mortgages probably would have gone into default even if the housing price bubble was still afloat, because they were risky loans. But once the housing bubble started to fall, and lots of people had mortgages greater than the value of their homes, mortgage defaults began to rise dramatically. This caused unexpectedly large losses in the massive mortgage-backed securities market, felt both by the investors who bought mortgage-backed securities and the investment banks that held mortgage-backed securities. Because the mortgage-backed securities market was so big, these losses roiled the entire credit market.

The credit markets began to freeze up partly driven by fear of not knowing which financial institutions were holding what losses (the financial institutions themselves didn't even know, so it was hard for anyone else to know). More importantly, credit froze because investors who thought they were buying highly secure AAA bonds lost confidence. If AAA bonds could go bad, what was next?

The collapse in credit market confidence and in the value of banks helped start the popping of the stock market bubble. Had the stock market not been in a bubble, it would not have fallen so far so quickly. Not only were stock prices in a bubble, but about two-thirds of the increase in the value of the stock market from 2005 to 2007 was due to increases in financial and energy stocks. With these financial institutions losing the value of many of their assets, their stock prices began to fall. This spread to the rest of the stock market as investors began worrying about a major market correction. Rising financial stocks had been the key driver of the rising stock market, so now that financial stocks were collapsing, the fears of investors were quite valid.

The Collapse of the Mortgage-Backed Securities Market Popped the Private Equity Buyout Bubble, Creating the Credit Crunch

In addition to harming the value of financial stocks and overall investor confidence in the stock market, toxic mortgage-backed securities helped punch a hole in the private equity buyout bubble. On its way up, private equity buyouts helped boost the stock market in 2006 and 2007. Back then, private equity firms were able to take on massive amounts of debt on incredibly favorable terms to buy increasingly larger companies. New records for the sheer size of these transactions were being made monthly. At its peak in 2006, 11,750 deals valued at $1.48 trillion were completed, according to Mergerstat. It seemed as if every few days another large public company was bought, and always at a big premium to the market price. The name of the game wasn't to pay a low price; instead the private equity Masters of the Universe competed to pay the highest price possible for a company.

It was all very exciting, and the stock market loved it. The market didn't need many reasons to go up. The economy was good and the market players were in a good mood. The private equity buyout bubble was just the tonic needed to push the Dow from the 11,000 range in 2006 to a peak of 14,164 in late 2007. Even after the private equity buyout bubble began to slow, the momentum it had created in the market continued.

Like all bubbles, it eventually popped. Ultimately bondholders, frightened by the credit crunch, began to worry about the incredibly favorable terms being offered to sellers by buyout firms. Many of the loans for the deals required little equity and were called "covenant lite," meaning the borrowers had few benchmarks to meet in order to maintain their loans in good standing. Even riskier, many loans did not even require that interest be paid in cash. Instead, the interest could be paid in more debt, or payment-in-kind (PIK).

But, as the mortgage-backed securities debacle continued, investors became increasingly afraid. All of a sudden, there was a greater perception and awareness of risk, which amazingly, investors did not have during the peak of the private equity buyout bubble. Lenders started asking for better terms. They quit agreeing to covenant lite loans and, most importantly, they wanted more equity. They wanted the buyout firms to share more of what they now saw as a growing perceived risk. This, of course, put the kibosh on the private equity buyout bubble. Many deals in negotiation fell apart. Even some already agreed-to deals were called off.

An even bigger problem was that many investment and commercial banks were on the hook for transactions that had recently taken place. They had lent out the money to complete the transactions, fully expecting to be able to sell that debt to other investors. When the money musical chairs came to a halt, a lot of that debt became unsellable, except at a loss, and sometimes at a very big loss.

For the stock market, the party had been ruined. The private equity buyout boom had ended and so had the glorious tonic that had driven up the market to record highs. The decline of the mortgage-backed securities market and the popping of the private equity bubble caused the Bear Stearns implosion in spring 2008, and then the fall of Lehman Brothers in fall 2008.

It Isn't a Liquidity Problem, It's a Bad Loan Problem!

The mantra during the credit crunch following the collapse of Bear Stearns, and the even worse global credit crunch after the collapse of Lehman Brothers, was that we had a "liquidity" problem, and all the U.S. Federal Reserve and other central banks had to do was inject liquidity into the markets. However, it wasn't a liquidity problem at all—it was a bad loan problem.

A liquidity problem occurs when a bank has sound financial assets (meaning their loans are good loans that will eventually be paid back), but for some reason people want to pull money out of the bank. This used to be called a "run on the bank" and happened frequently before the Fed was created to help prevent such a problem. By loaning the bank money (a.k.a., "injecting liquidity"), the Fed made it possible for the bank to pay off the people who wanted their money. But, that assumed that the bank's underlying assets were sound and the loans were good loans and would eventually get paid back. The banks were sound; however, the people who wanted their money back were unsound in their fears.

In the case of the latest credit crunch, quite the opposite is true. The bank's assets are unsound (because the loans are not good loans and many or most would not get paid back), while the people who want their money back are very sound, indeed. Therefore, the problem is not fundamentally a liquidity crisis, but a *bad loan crisis*. Investment and commercial banks made a lot of bad loans and hence, they had a lot of bad assets. It is not a crisis of confidence; but a crisis of bad investments that is scaring people. Interestingly, bankers are *still* making a lot of bad loans on the false assumption that the economy will turn around and asset values will not fall much more. The loans the Fed and other central banks, primarily the European Central Bank (ECB), made to these banks were essentially to cover losses. How much of a loss is still unknown, but one thing we do know: These losses will continue to increase as the value of the assets declines further. As the bubbles pop and asset values decline, these loans and other loans the central banks will make in the future, will also decline in value, and the Fed and the ECB will face horrendous, mounting losses. Rather than being repaid, central banks will take write-offs—which means they will let the money they have created to make these loans to the banks simply remain in the money supply, eventually causing significant future inflation (as you will see in the next chapter).

So, when you hear the experts talking about the "credit crunch" in relation to the stock market or the banks, simply insert these words, instead: "Bad loans going south." These bad investments ultimately impacted the stock market—most directly and initially on the most vulnerable part of the stock market—the private equity buyout bubble.

The Key Forces Driving the Stock Market Bubble

The private equity buyout bubble was the first part of the stock market bubble to get hit, because it was the *most vulnerable* part of the market. However, there are other stock market drivers creating downward pressure, such as the dramatic decline in large, high-priced merger and acquisition activity by corporations and the massive decline in corporate stock buy-backs.

As with the real estate market, most stock market analysts don't like to look at these fundamental drivers of price but, instead, assume the stock market will rebound, because it has gone up before and it "inevitably" will continue to go up again. The implication is that the gains will be significant even if not at the level of the last few years before the recent market collapse.

However, as like with housing, these projections of a rebounding stock market are mostly conjecture. There is never much of a reason given for the coming positive change. It's not an analysis based on the fundamental forces driving the stock market. As in real estate, it is more of a feeling that stock prices have gone up a lot in the past 30 years and sooner or later they will begin that inevitable rise again. However, as we know, past performance is no guarantee of future performance!

When Will the Stock Market Turn Around and Go Back Up Again?

Because we had a bubble in stock prices, there are only two ways to go back to high prices again:

1. Reinflate the bubble, which is not possible at this point because the previous drivers of the stock bubble are gone.
2. Temporarily stimulate the stock market with massive money printing by the Federal Reserve, which has been occurring for the last two years and is behind the bull markets of 2009 and late 2010. Unfortunately, this temporary stimulus is, well, temporary. And even worse, it will cause us much bigger problems later, with rising inflation and rising interest rates (as explained in the next chapter).

We know the stock market is a bubble in part because the Dow rose fourteen-fold from 1982 to 2007, while company earnings rose only three-fold for the same period. That means we had a stock bubble. And the rise in company earnings has been a bubble. Over the long term, as Nobel Prize–winning economist Milton Friedman and others have shown, earnings rise about as fast as GDP. Certainly the GDP didn't rise 300 percent as earnings did or 1400 percent as the stock market did during that period. So that means stock prices have been too high compared to earnings, and earnings have been too high compared to real economic growth.

For visual proof, it's worth looking again at Figure 2.3 on the growth of the Dow, which shows relatively normal growth from the 1920s until 1982, when it skyrockets upwards. Also, look at the Figure 2.4 that shows financial assets as a percentage of GDP skyrocketing upward at the same time. It is the classic picture of a bubble.

Of course, the market has been rebounding since March 2009 when the Federal Reserve began its massive money printing operations, but it has not regained its earlier peak. However, if the Federal Reserve keeps printing money, it may. Of course, the reinflated stock market bubble will pop again when the Fed's "medicine" (printed money) becomes poison (high inflation)—more on this in Chapter 3. What this emphasizes is that you have to be able to differentiate short-term volatility from long-term trends and the long-term economic fundamentals that ultimately drive those trends. But, the long-term trend for the market based on economic fundamentals is definitely negative.

Pop Goes the Private Debt Bubble

The full credit crisis hasn't kicked in yet. That will only happen in the Aftershock, when the dollar bubble and the government debt bubble pop. When consumers can still get low interest rate financing on a new car, you don't have a credit crisis. When you can get a 5 percent, 30-year fixed-rate mortgage, you don't have a credit crisis. In spring 2009, Toll Brothers was even offering a 3.99 percent 30-year fixed-rate mortgage on the homes they built. Of course, these loans were only to qualified buyers. From 2002 to 2006 mortgage and auto loans often went to unqualified buyers, so that is a bit of a change. We got so used to credit flowing to anyone willing to take it that now we actually think if an *unqualified buyer* cannot get a loan or cannot get the best interest rate possible, then we have a credit crisis.

We also do not have a credit crisis for business loans. Companies like Walmart do not have to pay 20 percent interest on their inventory loans, and they aren't being turned down for loans entirely. It's true that construction loans for buildings that won't make money are being turned down, as are loans for buying commercial real estate at prices that are way too high. But we can't exactly call that a credit crisis. It's more of a return to credit rationality, which apparently is very foreign to many of us.

However, when the dollar bubble pops, we will most definitely have a massive credit crunch. Very few businesses or individuals will be able to get loans at that point. More importantly, not long after the dollar bubble pops, the massive government debt bubble will burst and the U.S. government will no longer be able to get credit either.

The Private Debt Bubble Will Pop Twice: In Phase I, Bad Loans Go Bad. In Phase II, Good Loans Go Bad

In Phase I (the Bubblequake of 2008 and 2009), the private debt bubble started to pop, with some bad loans going into default. This will continue in 2011 and 2012 when more bad loans go bad with the help of a continuing downturn in the housing market and high unemployment.

However, in Phase II (the Aftershock—when the dollar bubble pops and *good* loans go bad), the private debt bubble will more fully collapse. This is because even good loans (those with reasonable leverage ratios that normally could withstand a modest economic downturn) will not be able to survive the kind of high interest rates, inflation, and economic collapse that will follow the popping of the dollar bubble (explained in Chapter 4). In this chapter, we are focusing only on the first stage of the private debt bubble pop in Phase I.

The Basis for Many Bad Loans Was the Good Times—And Thinking They Would Go on Forever

Optimism was the basis for the colossal bad loan collapse in mortgages. As we have mentioned many times before, *everyone, including bankers,* thought home prices would just keep rising no matter how much they had already risen beyond people's incomes. This same mentality affected commercial real estate loans as well. Plus, many of those loans were short-term, because it was a "sure bet" they could always be refinanced, thus keeping rates very, very low.

Huge corporate buyout loans with very high leverage ratios were fine, too, because who thought the value of these companies would ever go down? Why not loan 90 percent or more of the value of the company—it never goes down, right? And history was on their side. Bob recalls talking to a friend at one of the largest banks in the United States in 2006. He was in the workout group that handles bad commercial loans. When Bob spoke with him, he joked that he wasn't in the workout business anymore. He said there was no more need for workouts. If they had the rare bad loan, they could just repackage it and sell it off to another lender. Same for the FDIC—no banks were going under. Workout departments and the FDIC were like the Maytag repairman. Loans and banks almost never went bad. All they had in 2006 were good loans on their books.

Of course, the good times did end, which should not have been a surprise to anyone. Yet it was a 10,000 volt electric shock to the people in the financial community who made the loans. Now the FDIC couldn't be busier, and yes, Bob's friend at the large bank is hiring like crazy to expand his workout group.

A Nation on the Edge of Default

Consumer credit card balances and other loans were looked at the same way. Americans never thought they would have trouble finding a job or getting more credit. Why would the good times ever go bad? So, no one saved much for a rainy day. A study in early 2009 by Metropolitan Life Insurance showed that more than 50 percent of U.S. households do not have enough savings to cover their monthly expenses for more than two months if a breadwinner loses a job. And, it's not just your average Joe or Jane having problems. Over 27 percent of those making over $100,000 a year in household income don't have enough savings to make their monthly expenses for more than two months.

It doesn't take a Certified Financial Planner to tell you that a lot of people are in for the shock of their lives, when they find that rainy days can, in fact, happen. And that's one reason that the economy can turn down so quickly. Not only are a lot of our expenses discretionary, which means they are very vulnerable to deep cutbacks in a recession, but we are terribly vulnerable to job loss because we have no rainy-day savings (let's not even discuss retirement savings!). If job loss hits someone, expenses, even non-discretionary expenses, will get cut fast. This will also create a huge increase in riches-to-rags stories of people going from six-figure incomes to low-wage jobs in just a few months.

Figure 2.7 tells the story of a nation on the edge in terms of rapidly rising household debt.

Figure 2.7 Household Debt as a Percentage of Disposable Income
Consumers are having to service an increasing amount of debt relative to their income, making defaults much more likely as the economy goes down.

Sources: Federal Reserve and U.S. Bureau of Economic Analysis.

One Laid Off, Three More Worried

In a high-spending consumer society like ours, layoffs of small numbers of people can have a big impact on the economy, because the large number of people still employed get frightened that they, too, might get laid off. They then cut back on their discretionary and capital goods spending. In reality, it may be too late to start saving for a rainy day but people cut back on their spending anyway. And it makes sense even if it is too late. But that very fast, very deep drop in discretionary spending also means a very fast, very deep drop in economic activity, and more job losses are a result.

The Feedback Can Really Be Annoying

This feedback loop of job loss creating more job loss is ultimately what really puts the economy in a tailspin. It's not the credit crunch so much as the big downturn in people's spending. Credit is available, but there is a lack of interest in taking on more debt, combined with a lack of interest by the banks in making more bad loans to unqualified borrowers.

If banks were more willing to make the kind of reckless loans they made in 2004 and 2005, the economy would be better off—for a while. But with so many banks being burned by bad loans, they are losing their appetite for and ability to make bad loans. And, of course, making more bad loans would only be a short-term cure that would ultimately harm the banks even more. And, in any case, people who fear losing their jobs are simply less willing to take on new debt for discretionary items even if their credit is good.

A good example of the unwillingness to buy because of layoff and financial fear is the auto industry. Interest rates for auto loans are very low now. When combined with the incentives being offered by some automakers, there has probably never been a better time in the last 20 years to buy a car. But, sales are still down quite a lot, despite a recent uptick during the latest stock market rally. It's not a lack of credit, it's primarily a lack of buyer interest and also a lack of qualified borrowers. With more layoffs and little hiring, the lack of interest in buying and the lack of qualifications to borrow are growing daily. So the lack of interest in buying due to fear of job loss continues to pound the economy, further adding to that annoying feedback.

Key Drivers of the Private Debt Bubble Collapse

The current thinking in financial and government circles is that we need to clear the *toxic assets* (their term for bad loans going south) out of the banking system. They are wrongly assuming that this group of toxic assets isn't growing much and can simply be flushed away. Of course, nothing could be further from the truth. As we have discussed, the number of toxic assets is growing, not staying the same. But wait, it gets worse. Not only is the number of bad loans growing, these bad loans are becoming increasingly toxic because they are *losing value every day*. As commercial real estate prices continue to go down, and housing prices continue to go down, the value of the assets behind these loans is decreasing constantly. Government intervention that allows banks not to write down assets or allows them to keep bad assets on their books without foreclosing on them can make the situation look better on the surface. But, underneath, the value is declining and, more importantly, will decline much more significantly, even devastatingly, when the dollar and government debt bubbles pop.

Government regulators and financial analysts desperately want the situation for bank assets to look better than it really is. Otherwise, if toxic assets are instead growing rapidly, how can they be flushed away, and if they can't be flushed away, what will happen to the banking system? That sort of fear is impeding rational analysis and hence, supporting the mistaken view that the toxic assets are limited mostly to subprime mortgages and the real estate bubble in states like Florida and California.

All of These Problems Happen in a Relatively Good Economy, but Phase II (the Aftershock) Will Be Far Less Gentle on the Banking System

Let's not forget that Bear Stearns went bankrupt when the economy had low unemployment, low interest rates, and low inflation. None of those were much higher when Fannie Mae and Freddie Mac had to be bailed out. Again, they weren't much higher when Citibank, Bank of America, and other big banks had to be bailed out. The same was true when Lehman Brothers, Merrill Lynch, and AIG were bailed out. The economy really wasn't all that bad in October 2008.

But, as we said before, the good times won't last forever. The economy grew worse in 2009 but has recovered somewhat in 2010. However, unemployment remains high and will continue to be high, especially if discouraged unemployed and underemployed are counted. Hence, bad loans will continue to default. And all that will still be far better than when the dollar bubble pops in Phase II. At that point, sky-high inflation and interest rates will put the banks under tremendous pressure. They are simply not designed to handle interest rates and inflation of 50 to 70 percent. After the dollar bubble pops, even very good loans will go bad.

When Will the Private Debt Bubble Turn Around and Go Back Up Again?

Because we had a bubble in private debt, there are only two ways to go back to where we were before: Either reinflate the bubble, which is not possible at this point (the previous drivers of the private debt bubble are now gone), or have real, underlying economic reasons for a rise in private debt, which currently do not exist. So, the private debt bubble—just like the housing bubble and the stock market bubble—will continue to fall, along with all the other bubbles in our multibubble economy. Why? Because, just like real estate and stocks, private debt has been a bubble, too. Of course, massive government intervention can keep the bubbles from popping faster and maybe even keep them from popping further—for a while. But that intervention is occurring with borrowed and printed money, which will only make the popping of the government debt and dollar bubbles that much more destructive when they eventually pop.

Pop Goes the Discretionary Spending Bubble

A disproportionately large share of the U.S. economy is "discretionary spending," meaning a good deal of what people have been buying in this country has been optional. Easy money from a rising multibubble economy made big-time discretionary spending possible and fun. Abundant high-limit credit cards and plenty of home equity loans fed the buying party at every income level, from luxury jet-set buyers to everyday Walmart consumers.

Now, with a popping housing bubble and high unemployment, credit is getting harder and harder to come by. In fact, home equity withdrawals declined rapidly from their peak of $144 billion in the second quarter of 2006 to $7.2 billion in the fourth quarter of 2008 according to the latest information from the Federal Reserve. Undoubtedly, no net home equity withdrawals have occurred since the fourth quarter of 2008. That's a big pop!

As an incredible example of just how much money home equity withdrawal gave consumers, a study by Alan Greenspan and James Kennedy found that between 2001 and 2005 homeowners gained an average of $1 trillion per year in extra spending money! Now that's a little extra in your pocket.

However, now Americans at every level are no longer rushing out to buy things they don't really need at the same level they did before. Who's going to run out and buy new granite countertops for their kitchen, for example, when they've lost their job or house? And even if you still have income and a home, the old kitchen will probably do just fine for a while longer. Food, basic utilities, and other essentials, yes. New granite countertops, not so much.

Plus, consumers' credit cards are under increasing pressure. The Bloomberg Index of delinquent credit cards (more than 90 days late) remains elevated at 2.0 up from 1.4 in 2006. Hence, banks are being more careful about who they give credit cards to and how much credit they give. Consumers are losing the ability to borrow money from home equity and credit cards at a rapid rate. Even if they wanted to spend, it's getting harder and harder to do so.

And it will likely get much worse since much of the credit card debt held by credit card companies is subprime. In 2009, almost 31 percent of Bank of America's credit card loans were subprime, 30 percent of Capital One's credit card loans were subprime, and 27 percent of Citibank's credit card loans were subprime according to Keefe, Bruyette & Woods, Inc., a financial firm that specializes in the financial services industry. While it is true that credit card losses have begun to stabilize in 2010, and credit card purchases have increased from their rapid drop after the financial crisis of 2008 and 2009, it is also true that credit card spending is no longer fueling as much of the economy, and that will continue to be the case for quite some time.

More importantly, there will be no easy home equity loan bailouts for credit card holders. In the past a lot of home equity loans were used to retire high-interest credit card debt. So, home equity loans were a shadow support to the credit card boom that is no longer there, which puts more downward pressure on discretionary spending.

If the other bubbles were not popping, or if discretionary spending was a much smaller slice of the U.S. economy, a decline in discretionary spending would not pose so much of a problem. But our economy is so deeply dependent on discretionary spending that there is simply no way we can return to business as usual, when more and more businesses just don't have the buyers they had in the past. How can we easily go back to the level of spending we once enjoyed when we no longer have the other big bubbles (housing, stock, credit) to push us back up? And how can the other falling bubbles possibly turn around and go back up, unless we have lots of discretionary spending? They can't.

The stock market increases of 2009 and 2010 have helped encourage consumer spending by the top 20 percent of income earners in our country, who make almost 40 percent of the consumer purchases. This has been a key part of the stabilization we have seen in consumer spending but, with high unemployment, lower home values, and minimal increases in credit card debt, discretionary spending remains challenged, especially among the middle and lower income groups.

In a multibubble economy, co-linked bubbles rise and fall together. With the huge pink cloud of good-times discretionary spending being replaced by pink slips, our other falling bubbles have no viable way to reinflate themselves. And without the other bubbles, especially the private debt bubble and the real estate bubble, discretionary spending has no "bubble fuel" to keep it going at previous levels. The American consumer—that Energizer Bunny of bubble maintenance here and around the globe—is finally running out of bubble steam.

What can turn all these falling bubbles around and force them back up again? The economic cheerleaders, who are pinning their hopes on "market cycles," just say, "wait a while and everything will get better soon." But they never tell us *how* that is supposed to happen. With the housing bubble, the stock market bubble, the private debt bubble, and the discretionary spending bubble all popping and falling together, what will reinflate our economy? Certainly not a rebound in big discretionary spending by the American consumer.

The only thing that is temporarily delaying the coming multibubble crash is massive money printing by the Federal Reserve (see next chapter), and even that cannot save us because massive money printing will eventually cause massive inflation and rising interest rates (in two to five years) that will only make our multibubble crash all the worse. In the meantime, massive money printing by the Fed will continue to hold up the previously falling stock market bubble until significant inflation hits. Hardly a real recovery.

This Is No Ordinary Recession

Back when we were doing presentations about *America's Bubble Economy* in spring 2008, we said the watchwords for 2009 would be "Job Loss." Long before the housing and stock bubbles popped, we knew significant unemployment would be hard to prevent in 2009 and 2010, as home construction, consumer spending (related to rapidly declining home prices), and commercial construction began to rapidly decline. All that came true.

Next, for 2011 and 2012, we predict the mantra will be "This Is No Ordinary Recession." By then, more people will realize that we are not in a down economic cycle that we can move out of soon. Instead, as

(continued)

the economy continues to decline, it will become increasingly obvious that we are not in a typical recession. In fact, this is a multibubble pop. There will be no automatic recovery—the curve of change is not U-shaped, not V-shaped, not L-shaped, not any shape!

The feeling that this is no ordinary recession will have a chilling effect on consumers who will continue to be cautious just when everyone will be hoping for more spending, especially on large purchases, such as autos and houses. As one person put it, the realization that this is no ordinary recession will slowly dawn on people the same way that you might slowly realize you have married the wrong person. It's not a problem that's simply going to disappear.

Massive federal government borrowing and printing certainly made 2010 better than it might have been. It has certainly helped the stock market significantly and has helped keep the housing market from declining even more. The same will likely be true in 2011. But no amount of government intervention is going to keep these bubbles up forever. It may slow the onset of the full fall but it certainly will not reinflate the bubbles, and therein lies the rub: Falling bubbles—even when temporarily supported—are destined to fall.

The Biggest, Baddest, Bad Loan of Them All

As bad as the financial judgment of private sector bankers and investment bankers is, even worse is the incredible irresponsibility and bad judgment of the public sector—the U.S. government. The government has been involved in the biggest bad loan of them all: the monstrous government debt bubble. We can't possibly pay it off. Our tax base in a good year is only $2.5 trillion. In a bad year, it's more like $2 trillion. The total government debt bubble will soon be over $15 trillion and rising rapidly. If you look at the loan from the perspective of any rational loan officer at a bank, you would see a debt-to-income ratio of over 7 to 1. That's pretty steep. Most loan officers would not approve such a loan. And that's assuming interest rates stay at their current incredibly low level. What if interest rates rose to 10 percent? We would have a hard time just paying the interest!

Our track record of repayment is not too good, either. Except for some token payments in the best years of the last couple of decades, we have *never* made any payments to reduce the debt. It's clearly a bad loan, the biggest bad loan in world history. A technical default on our huge government debt will have history-making consequences. Just when most people think things will improve and the Bubblequake is ending in Phase I, the next shoe will drop in Phase II, the Aftershock, as described in the next chapter. What then?

The economic cheerleaders say recovery is on the way. All we have to do is sit back and be patient. Sooner or later, a reliable "up-market cycle" is going to come along and turn this frown upside down. It's just a matter of time.

Of course, they never explain exactly *what* is supposed to bring about this magical up cycle. And even more telling, they never, *ever* said anything about a future *down cycle* back when the economy was doing well. Oh, no. As long as the economy was booming, no one said a word about a possible down cycle ahead. They only pull out the "market cycles" theory when they want people to think everything is going to be okay.

We say it is a bubble pop, not a cycle or a normal recession. However, big gains in real productivity could pull us out. But, we haven't made big improvements in real productivity in more than three decades, and there isn't much hope of pulling a quick, economy-saving productivity rabbit out of the hat now. Very large real productivity improvements, such as moving from a nation of 90 percent farmers to less than 3 percent is, by its very nature, a slow process. Equally unlikely is a big jump in demand right now. The recovery of strong demand and the possibility of creating real productivity gains in the future are going to take some time, considerable resources, and of course, the political will to make tough decisions. So, we can't count on productivity improvements or strong demand to help us right now.

How about more rising bubbles? Would that help us? Sure they would, at least for a while. The trouble is, four of our six bubbles have already begun to burst. So, it is hard for a new bubble to be created.

How about big government spending on stimulus packages and bailouts? Won't that save us? At another time, they might have, but not now that we have a multibubble economy on the way down. No amount of stimulus spending can possibly reinflate all these big falling bubbles. And even if it could, how long would that last? Bubbles, by nature, do eventually fall. Big stimulus spending will not be able to bring us back to a strong nonbubble economy. Stimulus spending isn't how a strong nonbubble economy is created in the first place.

Even if you believe in the "market cycles" idea, you still need *something* to get a new up-cycle going. We may throw all kinds of spending and bailouts at the economy, and we may even have periods in which people swear a recovery is just around the corner but, in truth, without rising bubbles, or real productivity gains, or a rebound in strong demand, or a previously strong nonbubble economy to revive, we are out of ammo.

Without something to turn this falling multibubble economy around, what do you suppose will happen next? Follow us now to the next chapter where the current Bubblequake will become the Aftershock few people recognize we are about to face.

The Medicine Becomes Poison: Dangerous Inflation Ahead

Inflation is always and everywhere a monetary phenomenon.
—Milton Friedman, Nobel Prize–winning
expert on monetary theory

In the last chapter we told you how and why the real estate, stock, private debt, and discretionary spending bubbles began to pop before and during the financial crisis of late 2008. In the next chapter, you will see how these first four bursting bubbles will help bring down the last two: our vulnerable dollar and massive government debt bubbles.

But first, wedged in between these bursting bubbles, we offer you an in-depth look into something that we feel you absolutely must know about right now. Something so pressing and dangerous that if you believe nothing else in our books, you must give serious consideration to what we are about to tell you. Why? Because unlike some of our other predictions, this future threat has actually already become inevitable. Like a submarine missile that has already been launched, it is silently hurtling towards us. We are just waiting for impact.

This already launched missile heading our way is *inflation*. Not too many people are currently worried about inflation because right now inflation is low and poses no immediate threat. But inflation is the most significant future danger to the dollar, and understanding where it comes from and what it will do is essential for understanding why and when the dollar and government debt bubbles will fully collapse, bringing down what remains of the stock, real estate, private debt, and discretionary spending bubbles. This new chapter on inflation is one of the key additions to this updated second edition of *Aftershock* and is the basis for many of the other important updates we've made throughout the book—incorporating a greater focus on both the current causes and future impacts of inflation.

A note to the easily bored: If the seemingly dry subject matter is tempting you to skip this chapter, please don't. Please give us a few minutes to explain what inflation is, how it hurts, and what has already happened that will cause it in the future.

By the end of this chapter, you will be among the few people who know that this dangerous missile has already been launched and why it is so critical to the future of the economy. More importantly, you can begin to take steps now to brace yourself for impact, while most people have no clue that significant and dangerous inflation is ahead. In fact, our investment advice later in this book regarding asset protection and potential profits will make much more sense to you in light of this chapter. If nothing else, knowing that inflation is coming will save you from being entirely surprised when this already launched missile finally hits.

What Is Inflation?

Inflation is an increase in the price of goods and services *not* due to growing demand or shrinking supply for those goods and services (which also affects price) but due instead to the dollar losing its buying power. For example, if the annual inflation rate is 10 percent, then a box of cereal that cost $4.00 last year would sell for $4.40 this year, up 10 percent from the year before. In this example, the demand for cereal has not gone up, nor has the supply of cereal gone down; this cereal just costs more because the dollar is worth less. As someone once said, "In inflation, everything gets more valuable—except money." Actually, nothing gets more valuable, everything just costs more. Prices go up because the buying power of the dollar goes down.

What Causes the Dollar to Lose Buying Power?

For those of us who are relatively new to the sometimes unfathomable world of economics, it may come as a bit of a surprise to learn that the dollar's buying power or value comes from the very same economic forces that set the value (or price) of everything: *supply and demand.* For example, if a lot of people want to buy diamonds (big demand) relative to how many diamonds are available (small supply), then the price of diamonds is high. On the other hand, if diamonds were to become as plentiful as, say, sand grains on a beach (big supply) or if people become less interested in owning diamonds (small demand), then diamonds would become far less valuable. It's hard to think of money this way, but the truth is that the value of money is also affected by supply and demand: If there are too many dollars available, like sand instead of diamonds, their value falls. Therefore, *inflation is caused by an increase in the nation's money supply.*

But increasing the money supply does not always cause inflation. That's because, for an economy to run smoothly, the amount of money in circulation has to more or less match the need for that money, based on the size and growth rate of the economy. As the economy expands, more money must be created in order to facilitate and keep pace with the amount of trading that is taking place. When additional dollars are created in a *growing* economy (in the correct amounts to keep up with and encourage that growth), the value of those dollars does not fall, despite the fact that more money has been created. In fact, rather than the value falling, the value of those dollars may rise because more and more people want to own that currency, so they can take part in that booming economy.

However, when the money supply is dramatically expanded in an economy with no or slow growth—as is happening today—the value of the dollar will eventually decline. In short, too many dollars (too much supply), relative to the slow growth of the economy (too little demand), leads to the falling value of the dollar—a.k.a. inflation. *The real cause of inflation is increasing the money supply beyond what is needed to keep up with economic growth.*

Who is increasing our money supply beyond what is needed to keep up with our current rate of economic growth? As we will see shortly, the size of the U.S. money supply is controlled by the Federal Reserve, and the Fed can add to or subtract from our money supply any time it wishes, by either buying or selling government bonds, as a way of trying to control the money supply. By properly controlling the growth of the money supply, it will help the economy grow without creating inflation. However, in the last two years, the Fed has massively increased the U.S. money supply beyond what is needed to keep up with economic growth in an attempt to stimulate the economy. This massive increase will stimulate the economy, and especially asset prices, such as the stock market, in the short term, but longer term it will create much higher inflation. More on this shortly. But first, we have to answer another pressing question.

Why Is Inflation Bad?

At first look, inflation might not seem so bad. After all, if the cost of everything goes up and if your income goes up, too (because it is part of the cost of everything going up), then there really is no change to your bottom line. You just get paid more dollars, and you spend more dollars. As long as these increases are more or less consistent across the board, nothing has really changed, right?

The first problem is that your income may not rise as fast as inflation. As one of our publishing friends said, "I know that there is inflation, it's just not in my salary!" To be sure, that will be an increasing problem going forward, but right now, we are going to focus on the other big problem with inflation, especially in a bubble economy.

And that problem is that, as inflation rises, so do interest rates, and as interest rates rise, *asset values fall.* And again, it is important to emphasize, this is a particularly bad problem when assets are in a bubble because this makes them very vulnerable to a fall when inflation hits. In a bubble, the asset prices will go up with inflation, but like our friend's income, they won't go up nearly as fast as inflation.

Let's break that down into its parts. Rising inflation eventually causes rising interest rates, because when the dollar is losing buying power each year (rising inflation), the only way you can get someone to lend you dollars is if you offer to pay them an interest rate that at the very least compensates them for the inflation rate, plus a bit more so they can make a profit on the loan. Therefore, in time, interest rates tend to be a bit higher than the inflation rate.

Okay, so increasing the money supply causes inflation, and inflation causes interest rates to rise. So what?

Here is where the impact of that already launched inflation missile starts to do its terrible damage. Rising inflation causes interest rates to rise, which makes money more expensive to borrow. When money is more expensive to borrow, less lending occurs. When less lending occurs, less buying occurs, and when less buying occurs, the demand for assets—like our homes, stocks, savings accounts, artwork, jewelry, cars, and all dollar-denominated assets—falls. Demand falls, supplies go up (because fewer buyers), and asset values go south.

How far south will asset values fall? Well, in a normal, healthy, non-bubble economy, not too far south. Certainly, we have had rising inflation before, and we've had rising interest rates before, and although it wasn't great for the economy, nothing too terrible happened.

But in an already falling, vulnerable multibubble economy, high inflation and high interest rates will make asset values across the board drop like a rock. Rising interest rates will cause bond values to fall, businesses to do poorly, stock prices to drop, and home prices to decline even further. In a multibubble economy on the way down, rising inflation and rising interest rates lead to *falling asset values.* What economists call "nominal prices" go up due to inflation, but in inflation-adjusted dollars "real prices" do not go up. In a falling bubble economy, real prices go down, which means wealth (mostly "bubble money") is disappearing. Can you see why rising inflation and rising interest rates are bad, especially in a falling multibubble economy?

Inflation is not just bad for the general economy, it is bad for *your* investments. During inflation, the real value of your assets will fall significantly, and those asset value losses could be tremendous. But, in addition, any income from those investments (interest, dividends, rent, etc.) will have to outpace inflation for you to receive any real income. It's as if your investments are on a boat trying to go upstream: the only way to make any headway is to travel faster than the current pushes you backwards. The same goes for your job. With inflation, you will have to get a pay raise every year equal to the annual inflation rate just to stay even. Otherwise you are getting paid less and less, even if the dollar amount on your paycheck is unchanged.

Inflation does have some limited silver linings. If the value of the dollar declines with inflation, we get to pay back our previously borrowed loans, mortgages, and other debts with cheaper dollars than we originally borrowed, assuming these debts are at fixed interest rates that do not increase. Inflation makes it possible for the government to pay back some of its debts with cheaper dollars than the dollars they originally borrowed.

But, what's good for borrowers is bad for lenders.

For the federal government, which has to keep refinancing its debt over and over again because a lot of its debt is short term, each time it refinances its debt, the new refinanced debt is subject to higher and higher interest rates, which can get very expensive very quickly. Having to keep refinancing massive debt and also running massive budget deficits means the federal government—and the massive government debt bubble—is acutely vulnerable to massive inflation-generated increases in interest rates.

Higher interest rates also spell trouble for the already falling real estate bubble. Higher interest rates will mean more expensive mortgages, which will discourage home buyers and keep home values from rising as everyone would like. When higher interest rates stop many people from buying homes, home inventories will rise and home prices will fall further (falling demand plus rising supply equals falling prices). Even a 3 percent rise in interest rates can have dire consequences for real estate and other asset values. Figure 3.1 shows just how much home prices have to go down to maintain the same mortgage payment, if mortgage rates increase even fairly modestly from 4 percent. Remember when mortgage rates were 15 percent in the early 1980s? A mortgage rate of 7.5 percent is pretty reasonable, but it would mean that home prices would have to decrease by 32 percent.

Even worse, as interest rates rise, the value of mortgage bonds falls drastically, which means there won't be much mortgage money to lend, even if home buyers wanted to borrow it at the high rate. So rising inflation and rising interest rates will help further pop the real estate bubble. Increasingly, lenders won't grant mortgages at fixed rates. They will only lend if the interest rate adjusts with inflation. That will make it very difficult for most home buyers to borrow money to buy a house. As mentioned in the last chapter, the falling real estate bubble negatively impacts the wider economy in many, many ways.

And our troubles won't end there. Higher interest rates will also mean that businesses won't borrow as much as they would at lower interest rates. With less borrowed money, businesses don't make as many purchases from other businesses, so there is no good reason for businesses to expand their outputs or hire more employees. That adds to rising unemployment, hurting the economy further. And of course, rising interest rates have a negative impact on the value of stocks and bonds, and the higher interest rates go, the deeper stocks

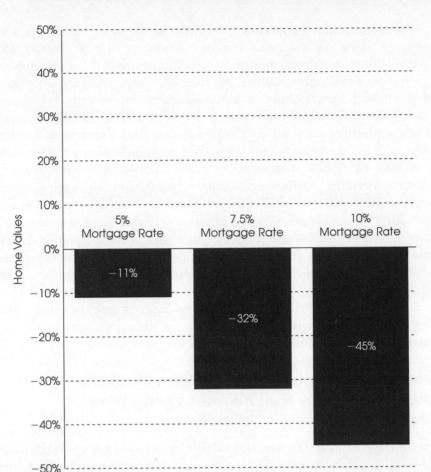

4% baseline Mortgage Rate

Figure 3.1   Decrease in Home Values When Mortgage Rates Increase
The chart assumes the current mortgage rate is 4 percent. An increase to
5 percent would force home prices down 11 percent to maintain
the same monthly payment.

Source: The Foresight Group.

and bonds fall. Moderate inflation and interest rates don't cause
immediate, significant damage, but as inflation and interest rates
continue to rise, the negative consequences accelerate until no one
wants to lend money anymore, or they offer impossible terms.

So the limited benefits of inflation are far overshadowed by
the huge negatives to investors, businesses, real estate, the federal

government, and the overall economy. While rising inflation and interest rates are not great for any economy, they are really bad for a falling multibubble economy. It is true that with tremendous government stimulus, falling bubbles can be temporarily blocked from falling further and sometimes even temporarily reinflated to a moderate extent. But even tremendous stimulus cannot push falling bubbles back up to their previous highs or support them for very long, because in time that tremendous stimulus itself (massive increases in the money supply and massive government deficit spending) ends up causing high inflation and high interest rates, which will eventually help deflate the bubbles. In a normal, healthy, nonbubble economy, a bit of stimulus can do the trick without very bad consequences later. But any temporary boost to a falling bubble economy is doomed to fail, when the negative consequences of high inflation and high interest rates eventually kick in.

Fortunately, right now inflation and interest rates are quite low, so why do we say that future inflation is racing toward us like an already launched missile?

Printing Money Is Easy Short-Term Medicine for the Economy That Becomes Long-Term Poison in the Form of Inflation

With current inflation low, the value of our money is in no immediate danger. The trouble is, we have a multibubble economy on the way down, including a slow economy caused by a global financial crisis that hit in late 2008, from which we have not recovered. Faced with so many falling bubbles (stock, real estate, private debt, discretionary spending), the Federal Reserve had to do something to try to rescue the economy and its bubbles. In a bold move that helped spare us immediate, but not long-term, pain, the Fed began in early 2009 to purchase almost $2 trillion in U.S. mortgage and treasury bonds with printed money in an effort to help stimulate the economy. The technical term for these big bond purchases is "quantitative easing" or QE, but in plain English it simply amounts to *printing a whole lot of money.*

The Fed's first round of bond purchases (QE1) massively increased the U.S. money supply from $800 billion to $2.4 trillion—an unprecedented 200 percent increase. More recently, in November 2010 the Fed began more bond purchases (QE2), adding an additional $600 billion to the nation's money supply over the following eight months. And, there is a very high likelihood of even more QE to come.

The goal of the money printing is to stimulate the economy back to health, like trying to jump-start the stalled heart of an otherwise healthy person. The trouble is, the falling bubble economy is *not* a healthy economy having a heart attack; it is a falling bubble economy that is falling because that is what all bubbles eventually do. The financial crisis in late 2008 was not a random economic heart attack; it was the logical and inevitable consequence of the popping real estate and private debt bubbles, coupled with a vulnerable stock market bubble. Together they helped bring down the discretionary spending bubble, resulting in worldwide recession. That is not a random economic heart attack; that is a lot of conjoined bubbles starting in earnest to fall and the full fall is not over.

Money Printing (Quantitative Easing) Is Doing Great Things for the Economy (in the Short Term)

The short-term stimulative benefits of printing money are many. First, the federal government and other bond sellers get to raise money at lower interest rates than if the Federal Reserve was not a buyer. In addition, the stock market is well supported by printing money, because a lot of money that would have gone to buying or holding bonds is now available to buy stocks, so that makes stock investors happy. The rising stock market indirectly makes American consumers, especially those who own stocks, feel more confident, boosting consumer spending a bit. The top 20 percent of income earners account for than 40 percent of consumer spending, and it is those consumers who are most likely to own stock and are most affected by higher stock prices. So higher stock prices help encourage the most important consumers in the country to buy more goods and services.

As we said, printing money keeps interest rates low in the short term, which is good for businesses that want to borrow money to expand and hire employees, good for home buyers who want low-interest-rate mortgages, and good for anyone making payments on adjustable-rate debt, like many consumers and the federal government. All these short-term benefits and stimulants to the economy are what the Fed is hoping to buy with QE1, QE2, and possibly more QE in the future.

Fed chairman Ben Bernanke and others are fully aware that massively increasing the money supply carries the potential risk of eventually causing inflation and rising interest rates, which would be bad for the economy, but that is a risk they are willing to take, rather than letting the stock market go down again, housing go down further, and the economy not recover quickly.

The Fed is thinking that when the economy picks up again, they can eventually reduce the money supply by selling the bonds that they bought with QE1 and QE2 to willing investors, taking the money "off the books" so to speak, thus reducing the money supply before dangerous inflation and high interest rates can kick in. The Fed is banking on a future booming economy, in which they will find lots of willing investors to buy these bonds from them, thus avoiding future inflation and rising interest rates.

Money Printing Is a Great Short-Term Plan with a Fatal Long-Term Flaw: We Have a Falling Bubble Economy

This is the part that these otherwise smart individuals (at the Federal Reserve and elsewhere) seem to be missing, or at least ignoring. The long-term success of money printing depends not only on an immediate boost to the economy, but also on that economy being able to sustain enough economic growth so that the increase in the money supply can either be absorbed by the rapidly expanding economy, or it can be reversed without negative consequences by selling the bonds back into the market place, thus reducing the money supply without causing a sharp economic downturn.

If, instead of a sustainable recovery and economic growth, the falling bubble economy does not fully recover, or has only a partial or short-lived recovery, the U.S. money supply will have been increased by an astounding 300 percent or more, with no hope of pulling that additional printed money out of the supply (because the economy is not yet strong enough), leading to the one thing that we can absolutely count on to happen when the money supply is massively increased in an economy that is not growing equally quickly: *Future Inflation*.

It's the Size of the Increase in Our Money Supply That Makes Inflation So Likely and So Large

Future inflation is headed our way, and it's going to be big. Amazingly, many financial analysts and economists today believe (for reasons we will explain later) that massively increasing the money supply will *not* lead to significant inflation. We believe it will. In fact, given the enormous size of these increases, we feel we are now on the road to 10 percent inflation and, in time, much higher inflation, and of course, the even higher interest rates that will eventually follow.

Size matters! If the Fed had increased the money supply by, say, 10, 20, or even 30 percent, there would be little reason for concern. But as you can see in Figure 3.2, the money supply has been increased almost three-fold since late 2008 and as of this writing in spring 2011, it is still growing.

This is a stunningly large increase, and its eventual consequences will be equally enormous. Nothing like this has ever occurred before in the United States, and certainly not in our recent history. Although many people recognize we are printing more money, few people talk about the sheer magnitude of this increase. Again, *size*

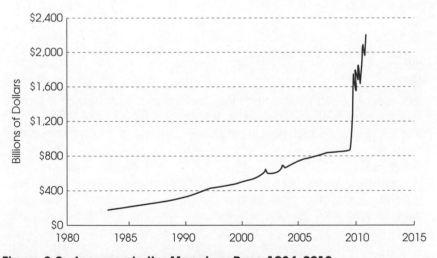

Figure 3.2   Increase in the Monetary Base 1984–2010
Our money supply has increased massively with the Fed's recent money printing operations—the fuel for the fires of inflation.

Source: St. Louis Federal Reserve.

matters. A small increase in the money supply that roughly tracks the increase in the GDP would not increase inflation that much, as can be seen in recent U.S. history. But massive increases in the money supply that dramatically outstrip the growth of GDP most definitely will.

Because we have so massively increased the money supply, big future inflation—like an already launched missile—is on its way. In fact, unless the Fed can reverse this massive money printing fairly soon, which the currently slow economy will not allow them to do, increasing the money supply by a whopping 300 percent will translate into double digit inflation and higher. And, of course, interest rates will eventually be even higher than inflation.

The Important Difference between Inflation and Real Price Increases

Too often people refer to a price increase as inflation. Just because the price of something, such as oil, increases, does not mean this price increase is due to inflation. As Nobel Prize–winning economist Milton Friedman said, "Inflation is always and everywhere a *monetary* phenomenon," meaning it can only be created by a central bank, such as the Federal Reserve, creating more money. Instead of inflation, the price of oil could be going up because we are running out of easy-to-find oil, or demand has gone up because China's rapidly growing economy is demanding more oil. That's not inflation; that's a real price increase due to the forces of *supply and demand*. True inflation occurs when the Fed increases the money supply at a faster rate than the economy needs it. Think of the Fed as simply a money factory. Increase the money supply very fast, and you get inflation. Slow or stop the increase in the money supply, and you get almost no inflation.

Often, inflation is created by governments to avoid raising taxes or cutting spending—they simply "print" money instead. This is also why deflation will not be a significant problem in the future. Any real decrease in the prices of goods or services (deflation) due to a depressed economy will be more than offset by the Fed printing money to try to stimulate the economy and deal with declining tax revenues (eventually causing inflation).

Why Don't More People See the Threat of Inflation? Because Inflation Is as Hard to See as the Housing Bubble Before It Popped

We believe the reason more people don't see the threat of future inflation (which will bring down the dollar bubble) is because the threat of inflation *before* it begins is as invisible to most people as the threat of the rising housing bubble was *before* it popped. When home prices were going up, almost nobody saw the bubble and few people paid attention to us when we warned about it in our first book. Even most financial analysts and economists denied there was a housing bubble, or at least much of one. Rapidly rising home prices were considered no more than just "a little froth on the coasts," as Alan Greenspan put it so mildly.

It is the same for the threat of future inflation. Few people see it. In fact there is still some debate over whether we might be heading for deflation, not inflation (see the sidebar titled "Inflation or Deflation?" later in this chapter). So, the authors see the massive money printing and the inflation it will cause as the hidden "housing bubble" of today. In fact, eerily, the timing of the coming inflation won't be all that different from the popping of the housing bubble. Although the housing bubble started to pop in the summer of 2005, it really didn't melt down until fall of 2008—about 3½ years later. That's within the general timeframe that we see future inflation kicking in (see "Exactly When Will Inflation Begin?" later in this chapter).

Interestingly, the patterns of how the housing bubble popped and how inflation will develop are also somewhat similar. In the case of housing, the prices stopped rising substantially in many hot real estate markets in the country (although they kept rising in others) in late 2005. When buyers pulled back somewhat in early 2006, the response from lenders was to make even more outrageous and aggressive loans than ever before—subprime loans, no-doc "liar" loans, option ARM "suicide" loans, etc. Lenders did this to combat declining buyer enthusiasm in the real estate market that had suddenly cooled. With names like "liar" and "suicide," you might think some of these loans would have people sounding the alarms, but instead this easy money worked to keep the housing bubble from popping, and everything rolled on fairly smoothly through 2006.

But by 2007 it was becoming increasingly obvious that many of these easy money loans were really bad and were defaulting quickly. Most importantly, there was not enough easy money to bring the real estate bubble back. Buyers became less excited about paying very high prices for real estate that was no longer increasing in value very fast, or not increasing at all in many cases, and even declining in some cases. But, we still made it through 2007 on the feeling that the housing market had bottomed out and there were lots of bargains to be had. Plus, lending requirements of borrowers were still fairly lax, allowing many people to qualify for high-priced homes. However, a few people were starting to see some big fundamental problems in the housing market and were increasingly fearful of a big collapse.

More importantly, by 2008, buyers were getting increasingly tired of buying high priced homes when home prices were no longer going up and were even falling. Plus, many of the earlier irresponsible loans were starting to fall apart. At this point, things were starting to get bad for the housing industry. By spring 2008 Bear Stearns had failed. But, even then, the housing bubble was still hard to see. Instead, most people thought it was a subprime mortgage crisis, and they thought that crisis was more or less over. It was just a subprime crisis where lots of bad loans were made to subprime borrowers.

That summer went okay with no major problems, bolstering what many, including our Fed Chairman Ben Bernanke, said about the housing problem: It was all over with Bear Stearns. But then in the fall of 2008, formerly AAA mortgages had suddenly become XXX. Fannie and Freddies' $5 trillion in mortgages had to be taken over by the federal government. And with the collapse of Lehman Brothers, the government was forced to bail out nearly every major commercial and investment bank in the country to prevent the whole financial system from collapsing.

Wow, what an overnight disaster! But, it wasn't actually overnight at all. It started 3½ years earlier when the real estate bubble (and housing prices) stopped going up.

What does this bit of real estate bubble history have to do with the coming inflation? We think it is eerily similar to the scenario that is dead ahead—a combination of real financial and economic changes coupled with slowly (and then suddenly) changing investor psychology, leading to a big bubble pop, pop, pop.

Inflation Will Hit Us Much Like the Housing Bubble

The scenario for future inflation will be similar to the real estate bubble scenario we just outlined. The inflation scenario has already begun. In spring 2009, the Fed decided to buy huge numbers of bonds thus massively increasing the money supply in response to a number of factors: the meltdown in the stock market; growing unease with the financial system; the potential inability of the Treasury to sell all of the massively increased debt the government needed to sell in order to cover its greatly increased deficit; and the inability to sell more mortgage debt in a bad market.

Seeming like just the right stimulus at just the right time, buying bonds with printed money in 2009 was powerfully effective in reviving the stock market and guaranteeing that the Treasury, Fannie and Freddie bond markets had no problems. More importantly, just as with the invisible housing bubble before it burst, almost no one saw this as causing future inflation.

However, by 2010, it became obvious that even that big first round of bond buying was not enough to put the economy and the stock market in high gear. Economic growth clearly slowed in spring 2010, and the so-called recovery's "green shoots" were turning brown. The flash crash of May 2010 and the sluggish summer stock market were all that was needed to prove to the Fed that more needed to be done. This scenario is similar to when the mortgage lenders started to lower lending requirements in an attempt to boost housing sales, and, in effect housing prices.

By late 2010, the Fed once again increased the money supply with QE2 (our monetary version of "liar loans" or perhaps more fittingly, "suicide" loans) to help boost the economy, the stock market, and the housing market (stocks and housing being our most important economy-supporting bubbles). However, this second round of bond buying (QE2) has started to make a few investors more anxious over inflation. So now the dollar has more problems, gold rises, and people are a bit more concerned about buying long term debt. Not many people are worried about inflation, but a few more are beginning to get worried—very much like the few people who began to see a more fundamental problem in housing in 2007.

How much longer will this general group inflation blindness go on? One thing that helps the blindness is the way the government calculates and reports inflation is misleading (more on this later in the chapter). But even using the unrealistically low CPI, the official inflation rate will creep up over time and it will become increasingly apparent to some investors that we may have a problem. Many more will say not to worry, that some inflation is good or at least is not significant.

However in the next few years, inflation will become more apparent, possibly moving into the 4 to 10 percent range. More investors will become more noticeably skittish about the dollar, and gold will go higher. At this point, real problems start to happen, just as they did with Bear Stearns and Lehman in 2008. That's because the reality will finally begin to dawn on people that all this money that the Fed printed will truly cause significant inflation, and there is no easy way of pulling that money back out of the economy when financial markets are so fragile. Like the inflated housing bubble, the inflated money supply is like a big bubble, too, and there will be no easy way out.

In fact, rather than reversing this money printing, it is very likely that the Fed will have to do *far more* money printing just to maintain some degree of financial stability, as discussed in the next section, especially with many foreign investors starting to leave their dollar investments. Of course, increasing the money supply yet again just makes the situation even worse, creating even more fear of future inflation. The panic that will come once inflation passes 10 percent will grow rapidly. Like the housing bubble in 2008, inflation will have reached its turning point, where it is painfully clear that significant inflation really can happen—just as it became painfully clear in 2008 that housing values could fall dramatically, it really was a bubble after all, and much of the debt backing up those mortgages had essentially gone bad.

Of course, when the government has problems, it is a much bigger threat than when the housing market has problems, because the government can bail out the housing market and financial system, but the government cannot bail out itself. This escalation in bubble danger is similar to how the Internet bubble was not as much of a problem as the housing bubble. Now the housing bubble will pale in comparison to the inflation bubble (part of the dollar bubble, which fully pops in the next chapter).

Why the Federal Reserve Will Be Forced to Greatly Expand
the Money Supply Later Even If It Doesn't Want To

1. The federal government will continue to have a very large deficit. That deficit will be expanding as interest costs rise, in large part due to inflation-driven interest rate increases. With inflation scaring off foreign investors, the Fed will be forced to be the buyer of last resort and will buy what will be a continuing flood of bonds needed to finance the enormous borrowing needs of the federal government.
2. As discussed later in this chapter, the Federal Reserve will likely pay increasing amounts of interest to banks to hold excess reserves. The Fed will do this to prevent the onset of inflation but will have to do it with printed money.
3. Inflation will be putting downward pressure on the economy as we just discussed. This pressure on the economy and financial system will require support from the Federal Reserve in the form of big increases in the money supply.

The Fed won't want to print so much money, but it will do so because it feels the alternative is worse. It's very much the same attitude they have towards printing money today.

It's Not Hyperinflation—No Wheelbarrows Needed

Although many people who are concerned about inflation think we might have hyperinflation, that won't happen. We will be able to control our inflation long before it becomes hyperinflation of over 1,000 percent annually. Basically, we will decide to reverse the inflation pressures previously discussed. We will balance the federal budget, inflate away the debt, stop paying banks interest on excess reserves, and we won't print massive amounts of money to boost the economy or resurrect a financial system that will have pretty well failed. At a certain point, the inflation will be much worse than the alternative of changing the necessary policies to get rid of inflation.

But, Even Relatively Small Inflation Can Do a Lot of Damage

However, just because there won't be hyperinflation doesn't mean there won't be big problems. Even inflation that takes one dollar and turns it into five in five years will completely destroy the bond markets as well as stocks and real estate. Actually, even taking one dollar and turning it into two via inflation in five years will pretty well devastate the bond, stock, and real estate markets.

Many Experts Don't See That We Are in a Bubble Economy So They Aren't Worried About Inflation

If you think more than tripling the U.S. money supply with QE is too much money printing, wait until you hear what economist and Nobel laureate Paul Krugman wants to do. Krugman says a mere $2–3 trillion of additional money is nowhere near enough to save our economy. In fact, Krugman thinks the Fed might need to do $8–10 trillion of money printing to save our weak economy. In fairness, this is not Krugman's first choice. He would much prefer to use fiscal, rather than monetary stimulus. In other words, he would prefer that Congress agree to a lot more stimulus spending. But if there is no stimulus spending, then the next best stimulus is printing money.

Why do so many experts, like Krugman and others, seem to like printing money or at least don't rail against it? The answer is frustrating but painfully simple: They don't realize (and don't want to realize) that this is not a healthy economy having a random heart attack; this is a falling bubble economy on the way down, and even shockingly high stimulus cannot stop the inevitable fall.

Instead of facing the facts of a falling bubble economy, Krugman and most analysts are deeply committed to the false idea that we are merely in a down market cycle. The beauty of the market-cycles thinking is that every down cycle is eventually followed by an up cycle. It's just a matter of time, and maybe some big stimulus—like shock therapy, to get things going again. During the rise of the multibubble economy, we've had several up and down cycles, all within an overall up trend, and now most people desperately want to count on more of the same.

Unfortunately, these experts don't understand, or more accurately, they don't want to face, the current bubble economy. We do not have a temporary down cycle that we can just wait out until the next up cycle comes. This is not winter, which will inevitably be followed by spring. This is a multibubble economy on its way down! Massive expansion of the money supply can certainly delay the fall, but it ultimately cannot save us. In fact, it will only make things worse when inflation rises, pushing the bubbles down even faster. The enormous collapse of asset values (including the value of the dollar) that we will soon face is not typical of a healthy economy going through normal up and down cycles. Only a falling bubble economy behaves this way. So unless the "experts" are able to face the fact that we have a falling bubble economy, their ideas about what is happening and what to do about it are not helpful.

The problem is not that these people aren't smart enough; they are very well educated and very well versed in the history of economics. But like military generals out of touch with some basic realities on the ground, many economics experts today are trying to fight the last war, the Great Depression, while ignoring the current situation. Even modest money printing would have prevented the Great Depression before it happened or solved it very quickly once it was underway. Simply not decreasing the money supply as they did during the Great Depression would have been a huge help. But today's circumstances are not like the Great Depression. Unlike 1929, today we have a falling multibubble economy, and adding massive money printing to a falling multibubble economy is like throwing timed-release gasoline on a fire. It may seem as if it will do us some good in the short term, but it will only make matters much worse in a few years.

Inflation or Deflation?

In the ongoing debate over whether we will have inflation or deflation in the coming months and years, we see no contest at all. In all our research, we have yet to come across an article or academic paper that shows that massively increasing the money supply by 200 percent or more has ever, or will ever, cause the value of money to increase and deflation to set in. Increasing the money supply causes inflation, not deflation.

It is true that asset prices, like home prices, will fall due to falling demand and rising supply, but that is not deflation; that is real falling asset prices. True deflation is caused by the money supply shrinking or not growing enough to keep pace with economic growth. The money supply is not shrinking now—it is growing. Therefore, future deflation is not the problem—inflation is.

The Arguments against Future Inflation Don't Hold Up

Although at this point, it may seem obvious to many readers that we will eventually have dangerously high inflation that will drive up interest rates, which will help burst the remaining bubbles, many more people do not believe that future inflation is a real threat. A few of their most important arguments and our rebuttals are presented in the sections that follow.

Why No Inflation Now? Understanding Lag Factors

Inflation doesn't immediately occur after an increase in the money supply, even after very large increases in the money supply, because of what economists call "lag factors." These lag factors normally delay inflation for 18 to 24 months. In fact, our own Ben Bernanke, along with several other authors (Laubach, Mishkin, and Posen), wrote a paper in 1999 that examined past periods of inflation and determined that about a two-year lag was the most common estimate among the research they examined.

The delay between the time of increasing the money supply and the onset of inflation can exceed two years in certain situations, such as in a bad economy. It can also be delayed if the Fed takes measures to reduce inflationary pressures, such as paying interest on excess bank reserves to keep banks from lending money, which it is currently doing. All those actions create more lag time. This is discussed in more detail later in this chapter.

Interestingly, the positive impacts of increasing the money supply occur much more quickly than the negative impact of inflation. For example, during and after World War I, when Germany wanted to raise money for the war without raising taxes and then was forced to pay billions of dollars in war reparations that it simply did not have, the government decided to print more money. Lots of it. Some people may remember the German Weimar Republic for its pictures of wheelbarrows of paper money. What few people remember is that when Germany began to rapidly expand its money supply, it experienced very rapid economic growth and unemployment of less than 1 percent. Of course, the positive impacts of printing lots of money also came at a heavy future price: the worst hyperinflation the industrial world had ever seen. By late 1923, it took 42 billion German marks to buy just one U.S. cent. And it took

726 billion marks to buy something that once cost just one mark four years before.

So the joys of printing money come quickly, while the pain comes later. Or, we could say lots of short-term gain, and lots and lots and lots of long-term pain. And, needless to say, it is very hard to control inflation once it gets going because getting rid of inflation causes even more economic pain.

Won't a Bad Economy Save Us from Inflation? Lessons from Zimbabwe

Every time coauthor Bob Wiedemer hears this question, he likes to pull out a 100-trillion-dollar bill from Zimbabwe that he keeps in his wallet. Clearly, a bad economy did not protect Zimbabwe from inflation. It's a short and sweet answer that's really quite accurate. A bad economy will not save us—or any other nation—from inflation.

It's also a complete myth that bad economies have low inflation, and good economies have high inflation. In fact, it is just the opposite. Bad economies have high inflation. Think of Brazil 10 or 20 years ago. Its inflation was over 1,000 percent. Its economy was not in good health. Now its economy has inflation of less than 10 percent. Its economy is in much better shape. The reason bad economies have high inflation is that in a bad economy the government has difficulty raising money from taxes. Hence, it has to resort to inflation to get the money it wants.

It's not just other countries that show this pattern. The United States is the same way. When did we have high inflation most recently? We had high inflation in the early 1980s when we also had very high unemployment and an economy in a major recession.

There are several more specific arguments related to the idea that a slow economy protects us from inflation that we'd like to address in the sections that follow.

Lack of Wage Pressure Will Save Us   One popular version of this "bad economy gives us protection" argument is that the current lack of wage pressure and underutilized factories will keep inflation under control. This is an argument currently championed by Janet Yellen, Vice Chairman of the Federal Reserve. A good way to counter this argument is to assume that we increased the money supply by 1,000 percent and assume that the nation's GDP only increased by 1 percent. In such an environment, prices would go up because all that money isn't being used as part of a growing economy. Instead it would have to go toward increasing prices. Even if the economy is declining by 1 percent and has downward wage pressure and lots of factory space operating under capacity, the same logic holds true.

Low Monetary Velocity Will Save Us   Another version of the bad economy protecting us from inflation idea comes from people who say that the slow blow of the money winds (low velocity) will protect us from inflation. Velocity is the speed at which money flows through an economy, and hence, when it slows, the theory is that inflation will be lessened. We heard this argument a lot in late 2010, but it seems to be used less now.

That's not uncommon in these arguments. They are faddish with a short shelf life. We're not sure if people really believe them, or even understand them. It seems more likely that people are just trying to come up with arguments for why we won't have inflation. But, it's still worth discussing.

In the case of monetary velocity, yes, a slower economy will reduce the velocity of the money supply. However, velocity can only change so much since people can only slow down payments so much. Also, in a low interest rate environment, they have relatively little incentive to slow payments that much, since the cost of money is low. Right now, lower velocity does help to reduce inflation, but in the face of a 300 percent increase in the money supply, lower velocity is like a sand castle trying to hold back a rising tide.

Lack of Bank Lending Will Save Us   In another version of the argument that the bad economy will protect us from inflation, some people say inflation will be held off because banks aren't lending. The idea here is that if banks don't lend money because we are in a slow economy, we won't have inflation. There is some truth to this.

When banks don't lend, there won't be a "multiplier effect" on the money supply, which will greatly reduce the amount of inflation. But, that doesn't stop inflation when the money supply is increased; it just doesn't magnify it.

Won't the Smart People at the Fed Save Us?   There is no question that there are many smart people at the Fed who could know all this. However, they may be ignoring much more of this than they should. That's only human nature, since the implications otherwise are pretty severe. But, what can they do to prevent inflation? From our research, we have found the following solutions to be most commonly suggested.

Maybe the Fed Will Sell Back Those Mortgage and Treasury Bonds It Just Bought   This is the simplest and best way to combat inflation: Reduce the money supply by selling those mortgage and treasury bonds. The trouble is, the Fed will not do it even if it talks about it. Why? Because if it tried to sell such a large number of bonds, it would significantly raise interest rates and cause great economic pain by further deflating the real estate bubble. Also, doing so could spook the bond markets, making it even more difficult to sell so many bonds.

This is exactly what the Fed was trying to prevent by buying all those mortgage and treasury bonds in the first place. In addition, if the Fed was able to sell the bonds, it would soak up a lot of the money that has gone into fueling the stock market rally of 2010—one of the greatest in history. That wouldn't be good for the stock market. There are real costs to decreasing the money supply, especially in a bubble economy, so selling bonds, although effective at controlling inflation if enough are sold, would also greatly hurt the economy. It's a nonstarter. Again, this is part of the reason inflation is so hard to control.

Maybe an Economic Rebound Will Save Us   We think this is the key to the Fed's thinking. Like many other people, they are assuming that we are in a simple cyclical downturn, and all we need to do is provide massive monetary and fiscal stimulus, which will take us to the other side of the cycle. At that point, we can then sell bonds or otherwise reduce the money supply without hurting the economy too much.

Of course, this assumes that we are in a simple economic cycle and not a multibubble economy that is popping. As we have said before, all we are really doing with this fiscal and monetary stimulus is maintaining the bubbles. The economy is not restarting. Almost all of the stabilization and growth in the economy has come from massive government intervention. We are not in a down cycle that will be self-correcting. This is really a bubble economy that is popping.

Maybe Congress Will Get Religion and Make Great Strides toward Balancing the Budget and Take the Pressure off the Fed to Print Money Although the Fed discusses this solution publicly, they have been careful not to push it too hard, since there is tremendous support in Congress for keeping the budget highly unbalanced. However, people we know inside the Fed indicate that there is some hope there that this may happen. Honestly, we don't see it. There may be some possibility that Congress will reduce the deficit a little, (although we have had a huge increase in 2011 even though the economy is getting better), but with tax revenues still down significantly and so many politically powerful groups requesting financial support, this suggested solution seems unlikely to occur in time to prevent inflation. We want to emphasize that we think it will occur, just not soon enough to prevent double digit inflation.

How the Fed May Delay the Onset of Inflation

Once the Fed massively increases the money supply, inflation is inevitable unless they can reduce the money supply before the inflation occurs. Without a significant economic recovery, however, removing money will cause a major crash, so instead of reversing the money printing, the Fed will likely take steps to try to *slow the onset* of high inflation. Here are four ways we think they will try to slow the onset of inflation:

1. **Paying Interest on Excess Reserves**
   The Fed's most powerful tool for delaying inflation is to pay interest on banks' excess reserves. By law, all banks are required to keep a certain amount of funds in reserve so they can meet their customers' needs for withdrawals. These reserve requirements prevent banks from lending out all of their money. *Excess* reserves are any reserves that banks keep *beyond* what is required. Normally, banks don't keep any excess reserves for obvious reasons. Why would a bank want to keep excess reserves when it could lend out that money and make a profit on it?
   The Fed, however, can encourage banks to keep excess reserves by paying banks interest on those excess reserves thus stopping banks from lending out this money.

Why would the Fed want to do that? They would do it in order to limit "the multiplier effect" that we mentioned earlier. The multiplier effect greatly increases the amount of inflation that comes from money printing because a relatively small amount of new money can create a greater number of loans. By limiting that multiplier effect, inflation can't be prevented, but the speed with which it occurs can be limited, thus helping to postpone its onset.

As can be seen from Figure 3.3, excess reserves are currently at historically unprecedented levels of more than $1 trillion. As you can see, for the last 60 years banks have held *no* excess reserves, which makes sense since they don't make any money on them and it isn't required by the Fed. However, banks are now holding massive excess reserves not only because the Fed is paying banks interest on this money but also because the banks want to help support the Fed. After all, the banks were recently bailed out and they certainly would like that kind of support again if needed. So it is a bit of pay back for the Fed's support, as well as a bit of future insurance in case they need the support of the Fed again.

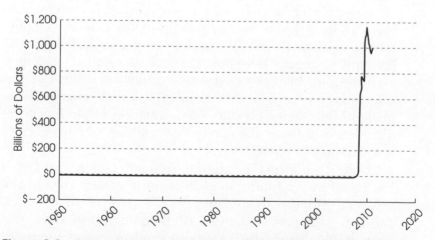

Figure 3.3   Amount of Excess Reserves Held by Banks 1950-2010
For the past 60 years banks have held no excess reserves, but in the last two years excess reserves have soared to over $1 trillion.
Source: Federal Reserve.

Of course, the Federal Reserve funds those interest payments by, you guessed it, printing more money, so that also contributes to future inflation. But, not immediately. The immediate effect is to reduce the multiplier effect and postpone the onset of inflation.

We expect the Fed to increasingly use this tool to limit the inflationary pressure of its massive increases in the money supply. We also expect that the amount of interest paid to banks on excess reserves will rise dramatically as the Fed sees a significant onset of inflation and sees banks holding less excess reserves. Already, the amount of excess reserves is declining, and the Fed will have to decide when it wants to react.

In the short term, paying interest on excess reserves will likely be one of main reasons that inflation will be slow to begin. Of course, it is also one of the reasons that inflation will take off with a vengeance, once we reach the end of the Road to 10 Percent.

2. Manipulating the Measurement of Inflation

"Figures never lie, but liars always figure." The Fed can manipulate the measurements of inflation. The CPI, the primary measure of inflation the Fed uses, could be manipulated to reflect a lower rate of inflation. Earlier, Alan Greenspan actually changed the way the CPI is calculated to lower its growth rate and help support his easy money policies, as well as to reduce cost of living increases in Social Security payments. To show the power of those changes, according to Shadow Government Statistics, if the CPI was calculated the same way it was in 1990, before changes were made in how the CPI is calculated, inflation would now be at 6 percent instead of the current calculation, which indicates it is around 2 percent.

Even if no formal changes were made to how the CPI is calculated in the future, the CPI is not a perfect measure of inflation. Housing costs comprise 30 percent of the CPI, and that large part of the CPI will be going down as the real estate bubble pops, which will mask the true rate of monetary inflation caused by increasing the money supply. This will be especially true in the next couple of years as house prices are falling and the effects of inflation on other parts of the CPI are still relatively weak. Long term, these won't matter because inflation will be climbing so high that relatively small biases in calculation will be of little importance. However, in the early stages of inflation, these biases will make a difference, and the inflation rate will appear lower, effectively postponing the onset of observed inflation.

3. Cheering the Advent of Early Inflation

This delaying technique may seem silly, but it works. The Fed, and many cheerleading economists and financial analysts, will actually praise the onset of early inflation. Because inflation will be small, they will say it's a good thing and a sign of a more robust and growing economy. Thus, by praising a small amount of inflation, they will limit the early negative reactions to it.

As with the other strategies, this will not stop inflation, but it will effectively postpone the onset of observed inflation by reducing the fear that inflation is bad or will increase due to the massive increases in the money supply. The cheerleader mantra will be that early inflation is not due to massively increasing the money supply, but instead it is due to a healthy growing economy. Hence, no need to worry, right?

4. Creating a Lag between Inflation and Interest Rates

As we have said, the worst effect of inflation in a bubble economy is increased interest rates. Increasing the money supply rapidly by purchasing massive amounts of bonds will keep interest rates from rising as fast as inflation. This works only in the early stages of inflation. Eventually interest rates will actually rise faster than inflation.

Wait! Didn't We Survive High Inflation in the 1970s? What's So Different This Time?

It's true that we did have significant inflation in the 1970s and early 1980s, and we did get out of it. But circumstances were considerably different. We didn't have a bubble economy. The Fed could reduce the money supply and raise interest rates substantially to reduce inflation. With much lower housing and stock prices, high interest rates were painful, but not devastating. Also, we were at the beginning of the tidal wave of foreign capital that moved into the United States, which greatly reduced inflationary pressures. That tidal wave is just about to go the other way, greatly increasing inflationary pressures by increasing the need to rapidly expand the money supply. This all means that the "Volcker Medicine" for the inflation of the 1980s won't work today.

Exactly When Will Inflation Begin?

It's hard to predict exactly when any given event will occur. As with the housing bubble, the onset of inflation depends a lot on changing psychology. For housing prices, it was faith that housing prices could never fall too significantly that kept us going for so long, until that faith finally died. For inflation, it will be faith that massive increases in the money supply never cause significant inflation or that it can be easily controlled before inflation gets too high. Once that faith dissolves, the domino fall of our remaining bubbles (described in more detail in the next chapter) will begin.

Of course, the same people who are now saying that increases in the money supply will not cause inflation or will cause only mild inflation that can be easily be controlled, are the very same people who said housing prices could not fall significantly enough to cause major financial problems for the United States and the world. You wonder how these people maintain such high credibility on such important economic issues even after being horribly wrong on such other incredibly important economic issues, like the fall of the real estate bubble or the stock market crash of 2008. Of course, we know why they maintain such high credibility. They say what the cheerleaders want to hear.

So what is our best guess about when inflation will start? Due to the "lag factors" we described earlier, it typically takes about 2 years from the time the money supply is increased for significant inflation to begin. We will also likely have some additional lag factors due to some of the ways we just described that the Fed will use to hold off inflation or the appearance of inflation. Hence, given the usual lag factors, plus the extra lag factors, our best guess (as of the spring of 2011) is that significant inflation will begin in the 2013–2015 range.

But regardless of the precise timing, this much we know for sure: Very significant inflation, like an already launched missile, is hurtling our way. Why? Because we have a falling multibubble economy that will not be fully revived by massively increasing the money supply, and massively increasing the money supply will eventually cause massive inflation.

The Deeper Causes of Inflation

Before we leave this inflation chapter and move onto the final fall of the dollar and government debt bubbles, we'd like to give you a broader perspective on what we believe are the underlying causes of this inflation. We've already given you the technical and proximal cause of inflation, which is massive increases in the money supply well beyond the growth rate of the economy.

But there are deeper causes of this inflation, as well. What economic forces have driven ours and other governments in the last 50 years to increase their money supplies so massively and so fast? To put it in three simple words, it's a "failed tax system." By failed tax system, we mean a tax system that does not collect enough taxes to cover government expenditures. Of course, you could also say the problem is not due to taxes being too low, but due to spending being too high. That's probably more the case in many countries. But, in many countries, which have the highest inflation, their tax systems are so corrupt or so arbitrary as to be completely ineffective. Either way, whether it's too much spending or too corrupt a tax system, the government isn't collecting enough money to cover its expenses and hence resorts to inflation instead of reforming its spending and taxation systems.

This has happened many times in European countries, like Italy and Turkey, or in many South American countries. These countries have tax systems in which many people avoid taxes by using the black market, corruption, or other tax avoidance schemes. Part of the reason so many people don't pay taxes is because they feel other people aren't paying taxes. Or, they feel the money is being wasted on corruption and patronage jobs. In addition, the economy may be low growth or very sluggish, providing a very poor tax base for the government.

Turkey provides an excellent example of how to change this. Only five years ago, if you went to Turkey and wanted to buy a bottle of Coke, you had to be a millionaire. It took at least 1 million Turkish lire to buy a bottle of Coke. Turkey had been plagued for decades by ineffective tax systems. Many people avoided taxes, there were lots of patronage jobs—the government had over 50,000 tea servers on its payroll—and the government didn't have the money to fund its spending. So, it printed the money.

Needless to say, the long-term effects of printing more money did not help the Turkish economy at all. It was hard to do financing in Turkey and hard to keep capital in the country (they even tried capital export controls to combat this). But, finally, they put their economic house in order by implementing many reforms including controlling government spending, improving their tax system, and borrowing money (that will cause big problems down the road, but it helps with inflation). In 2006, they changed every 1-million-lire note to the new Turkish lire, literally stripping six zeroes off their currency. Since those reforms, Turkey's economy has boomed with some of the highest growth rates in the world, in part because they have gotten rid of inflation.

Now simply having an out of balance budget doesn't guarantee inflation. Even countries that don't have failed tax systems, like Japan, or that have sterling credit ratings, like the United States, can instead borrow a lot of money and avoid printing it, thus avoiding inflation. From an economic standpoint borrowing money is more expensive than spending cuts or raising taxes, but it is much more politically saleable. Borrowing money is also less damaging (less expensive) to the economy than raising money by printing it.

However, once the United States had problems borrowing money—as we did during the spring of 2009 after the financial crisis—we had the equivalent of a failed tax system that is driving the desire to print massive amounts of money. If we don't want to reduce spending (in fact we are increasing it enormously) even if our tax revenues fall, and we don't want to raise taxes, and we cannot borrow all that we need and want, then we have the equivalent of a failed tax system. It's not that different from Turkey. There is a lot of pressure to print more money because the short-term costs of printing more money are very low.

Printing money is the easy way out of governmental financial problems. But, as we are about to find out in the coming years, it is also the most expensive, especially if you are in a bubble economy.

Inflation and Real Estate: Will Home Prices Go Up or Go Down?

We are often asked about the future of real estate values and whether our predictions for future inflation will cause home prices to go up or down. Our seemingly contradictory answer is *both*.

On the one hand, when inflation kicks in, real estate prices, like the prices of most things, will go up with inflation because the buying power of the dollar will go down, pushing all prices up. But here is the catch: In "real" dollars (inflation-adjusted), real estate values will actually decline because of rising supply and falling demand. Too many homes for sale (due to increasing foreclosures and increasing numbers of people who can no longer afford their homes) coupled with too few buyers (due to rising mortgage interest rates and climbing unemployment) will force what is left of the real estate bubble to fully pop and for home values to significantly decline. Commercial real estate values won't be any better off for the same reasons: rising supply and falling demand.

So the inflation-adjusted value of real estate will fall, while inflation will push nominal prices higher. Regardless of what the resulting sticker price will be, most real estate will be worth much less than before—and that is all that really matters if you are a home owner or a real estate investor. (For more about primary residences, vacation homes, rental properties, commercial real estate, and farmland, please see Chapter 6.)

For more information on inflation timing and its effects, please visit our website at www.aftershockeconomy.com/inflation.

Phase II: The Aftershock

POP GO THE DOLLAR AND GOVERNMENT DEBT BUBBLES

In our presentations, we often tell people that the biggest impact of the bursting housing, stock, private debt, and discretionary spending bubbles is not the immediate problems caused by the popping itself, although that has been very upsetting and very costly to the economy. The biggest impact of these four bursting bubbles is the terrible *downward pressure* they are now exerting on our two remaining bubbles: the dollar bubble and the government debt bubble.

It won't be hard to convince you that we have an enormous government debt bubble, so we'll get back to that in a few pages. Right now, we'd like you to keep an open mind and consider the possibility that we have a vulnerable dollar bubble. We know this is hard to believe. All we ask is that you read on a bit more before coming to your own reasonable conclusions. If we are right (and based on our first book in 2006, we have an excellent track record), you cannot afford to ignore this. We know it feels fundamentally wrong, but please let icy cold logic be your guide.

The Dollar Bubble: Hard to See without Bubble-Vision Glasses

Remember how hard it was to see the Internet stock bubble *before* it popped in early 2000? Remember when buying real estate was considered a great quick-flip investment before the housing bubble began to burst in 2007? Unpopped bubbles really can be very deceiving. Of course, *after* they pop, that's another story. Hindsight is 20/20. But *before* they pop, you need special bubble-vision glasses in order to see an unburst bubble.

Here are your bubble-vision glasses for the dollar. Once you look at the dollar this way, you'll see for yourself that this bubble has no choice but to pop.

To use your bubble-vision glasses, you must look at the dollar through the two lenses of *supply and demand*—the same two forces that determine the value of any asset.

In the simplest terms, growing supply (due in part to recent massive money printing by the Fed) is driving the dollar bubble up. And in the future, falling demand (due to factors we will explain shortly) will drive the dollar bubble down. Unless there is significant demand, no asset—bubble or no bubble—can retain its value.

While these concepts are logical and straightforward, accepting that the mighty U.S. dollar is actually an asset bubble getting ready to pop is pretty hard to swallow. It means that we have to accept that the future value of the U.S. dollar has nothing to do with what a great country we are, or how we have been the greatest economic power the world has ever seen. The future value of the U.S. dollar depends heavily on *supply and demand*.

We have already devoted most of the last chapter to the growing *supply* of the dollar, via massive money printing by the Fed, so let's focus now on *demand*.

Clearly, past demand has been spectacular. Prior to the bubble economy, demand for dollars was strong and growing stronger due to our growing economy and rising productivity. But once we started to inflate our bubbles, beginning in the 1980s, the rising demand for dollars was no longer entirely driven by rising productivity but also by our growing asset bubbles. Rising stocks, bonds, real estate, and other dollar-denominated assets were very, very profitable, which naturally attracted many investors from around the world. In fact, foreign-owned U.S. assets grew from $661 billion in 1981 to $22.3 trillion in 2010 according to the Bureau of Economic Analysis.

Foreign investors bought up many U.S. assets over the years, not because they wanted to help us out, but because their investment returns were stellar. The tremendous and growing demand for U.S. assets made the dollar increasingly more valuable. Foreign investors wanted more and more U.S. assets and needed more and more U.S. dollars to buy them—creating lots of demand for dollars.

Sounds great. So what's the problem?

There was no problem with this at all, as long as we were growing our economy with big improvements in productivity, such as laying railroad tracks from coast to coast, which greatly boosted trade, or when we developed mass-produced automobiles, or innovated to create other big jumps in output and productivity. All that helped grow a stronger U.S. economy and helped increase demand for U.S. dollars.

The trouble started when demand for U.S. dollars by foreign investors was driven less by increasing productivity and more and more by something else: rising asset bubbles. In a multibubble economy, the value of a currency can do nothing else but to rise and fall as the bubbles rise and fall.

Why? Because the value of any currency is set by *supply and demand*. When a multibubble economy is on the way up, investment returns go up, and therefore demand from foreign investors for dollars to buy those investments also goes up. And when a multibubble economy is on the way down, investment returns go down, and therefore demand for dollars to buy those investments also goes down.

For many years, our rising bubbles created rising demand from foreign investors for dollars, and therefore the value of the dollar rose. More recently, the falling bubbles are beginning to create falling demand for dollars, and therefore the value of the dollar is declining, despite all kinds of government efforts to keep this from happening. While not a sharp, quick rise, the value of the euro, compared to the dollar, has risen pretty steadily from a low of around 87 cents in 2000 to around $1.40 in 2009. Although the euro fell in 2010, it has recovered back to the $1.35–$1.45 range, as of spring 2011. We expect the euro to continue to be volatile due to the ongoing and growing European debt crisis, as well as due to some government manipulation.

But, in the long term, we see the euro doing well *relative to the dollar* because the demand for dollars is driven by demand from foreign investors to purchase U.S. assets, and the demand to purchase U.S. assets will fall. When our bubbles fully burst, demand for U.S. assets—including the dollar—will crash, driving up the value of the euro and other foreign currencies *relative to the dollar* over the next five to ten years.

It may be hard to imagine the dollar taking such a future beating, but in fact the start of the beating has already occurred. The dollar

The Hardest Bubble to See Is the One You're In

Back in 2007, everyone we spoke to at presentations about our 2006 book, *America's Bubble Economy*, could see the housing bubble. Housing prices had stopped growing and were heading down substantially in some parts of the country. However, they had a hard time seeing the stock market bubble because the market was still moving steadily upward. And they had a really hard time seeing the dollar bubble because, at that point, the dollar looked fine.

Then, starting in spring 2008 and especially in spring 2009, few people had any trouble seeing the stock market bubble after the Dow had fallen 40 percent from its peak. The housing bubble was also easy to see because home prices had fallen substantially in every part of the country and in some parts by 50 percent from their peak. But they had a hard time seeing the dollar bubble, because the dollar still looked fine, like a safe haven in stormy times. If anything, the dollar seemed like an even safer bet due to the European debt crisis. This makes the dollar bubble even harder to see.

But in a few years—after it starts to fall more—the dollar bubble will no longer be so hard to see. Initially, that fall will be driven largely by growing inflation (due to massive money printing by the Fed, increasing supply), which will hurt U.S. stocks, real estate, and especially U.S. bonds. In time, as inflation creeps up to and past 10 percent, there will be a more rapid decline in stocks, real estate, and bonds. As a result, foreign demand for dollars, which have been heavily in demand to buy U.S. bonds and other assets, will significantly decline as well. At that point, everyone will be able to see the popped dollar bubble, just as the real estate bubble and the Internet bubble both became painfully obvious *after* they popped.

What we have seen with a vengeance in the past few years is the fact that *the hardest bubble to see is the bubble you are in*. No matter what the price is, as long as your bubble is moving upward, that is the right price. A stock market that slowly moves from 10,000 to 11,000 is thought to be priced properly, and so is a market that very rapidly goes from 11,000 to 14,000. As long as it is moving up, it's priced right.

The dollar is the same. As long as it is relatively stable (or better yet, growing), people assume it is priced just right. And the forces that might push it down in the future, like massively increasing the money supply or huge government borrowing with no hope of paying it back, don't really affect people's thinking about the value of the dollar, because the government must be printing and borrowing just the right amount—certainly not enough to negatively affect the dollar in any significant way! Whether we are borrowing $100 billion a year or $1.5 trillion a year it's always fine, because the dollar isn't falling *too* much, so it *must* not be in a bubble, just as real estate was not a bubble—until it popped. As long as a bubble is heading in the right direction (up), it can't be a bubble. That's why, as Alan Greenspan said, it's hard to see a bubble until it bursts.

has already lost significant value over the last decade. And it is quite vulnerable to further decline.

What could make the dollar decline further? The answer, as always, is *falling demand.*

Since the 1980s, the rising bubble economy has become increasingly dependent on foreign investment for its capital, and that foreign investment can easily pull out when the excellent returns investors used to receive become not so excellent anymore, or worse, they turn into losses. As we said in *America's Bubble Economy,* foreign investors did not invest in our dollar-denominated assets because they love us; they did it for the fabulous profits. And foreign investors will not slow their purchases of dollar-denominated assets because they hate us; they'll also do it because our investments aren't very good anymore. They'll also do it to protect their assets from losses, especially foreign exchange losses.

But, what could possibly give foreign investors the idea that they may not be able to make as much profit on their U.S. assets in the future as they did in the past?

How about more declines in our four big already-falling bubbles?

Falling Stocks, Real Estate, Credit, and Spending in the United States Create "No Gain, Lots of Pain" for Foreign Investors

When U.S. real estate was going up, stocks were going up, easy credit was flowing like joy juice, and everything about investing in the United States was oh-so-good that there was no reason not to invest here. It was safe, it was easy, and it produced high returns. What more could any investor ask?

In the reverse, however, falling real estate and stock values, along with declining consumer spending and evaporating credit, make the United States a far less attractive place to invest. Separately, each popping bubble makes investors—including foreign investors—lose a lot of money. On top of that, the combined effect of these falling bubbles is negatively impacting the broader U.S. economy, including driving up unemployment and threatening our banking system. That isn't too attractive, either.

But all that will not be enough to drive foreign investors away. After such a wonderful party, it's hard for foreign investors to imagine that the good times could really end, and most will stick around for a while and hope for the best. In the short term, many foreign investors will simply move from riskier U.S. investments, such as stocks, to less-risky U.S. investments, such as government bonds. Also, for a while, U.S. Treasuries will be viewed as a safe haven in a world of turmoil. The huge inflows into U.S. bonds in 2010 were strong evidence of that.

Many foreign investors, just like domestic investors and economists, believe (or want to believe) that the U.S. economy will start growing rapidly soon, and they naturally want to be ready when their U.S. investments start to pick up. However, because there is nothing that will magically reinflate these bubbles or quickly bring us huge productivity gains or skyrocketing demand in the next few years, we know that the slow economy will have no option other than to continue. But even so, foreign investors will not run away.

However, as inflation and interest rates rise (see Chapter 3) and as the expected rebound of the economy doesn't happen, investor psychology (both foreign and domestic) will begin to change. Perhaps at first this change will only cause foreign investors to buy slightly fewer U.S. stocks, bonds, and other dollar-denominated assets. Buying a little less is perfectly reasonable. Remember, it only takes a small increase in interest rates to cause a big drop in bond values. With interest rates currently so low, small movements up will have big consequences.

At some point—and we believe that will likely be when inflation is around 10 percent—investor psychology will take a more decided turn toward the negative and demand for U.S. assets, and therefore dollars, will drop. Instead of risking their money on our dollars, foreign investors will put more of their investment resources into their own countries, thinking they can always reinvest in the United States when things improve.

But, as we've said, falling bubbles have no viable way to reinflate themselves, and therefore, falling bubble economies cannot possibly recover very fast. Instead, they keep falling until there are some real economic reasons for solid economic stability and sustainable growth. Until then, foreign investors will continue to adopt a very reasonable "wait-and-see" approach.

Unfortunately, there's nothing like a very reasonable wait-and-see investment approach to really kill a falling bubble economy that is so deeply dependent on foreign investors. How can things possibly turn around when not enough of the people responsible for our past growth are willing to stay in the market or buy more?

Although it's too early to see much of a change in foreign investment sentiment right now, we are starting to detect the beginnings of a change. According to the U.S. Treasury, net inflows of long-term capital into the United States fell by more than 50 percent from 2007 to 2008—from $1 trillion to $414 billion. In 2009, with the recovery in the U.S. stock market, the inflow increased to $639 billion, but still much less than the $1 trillion in 2007. This large drop in late 2008 and early 2009 was one of the key reasons that the Federal Reserve had to step in and buy over a trillion dollars worth of bonds—foreign buyers were disappearing at a rapid rate. In November 2008, gross foreign purchases of U.S. Treasury bonds fell almost 40 percent before recovering to more normal levels in June 2009.

Foreign inflows of long-term capital increased in 2010 to $824 billion largely due to safe-haven purchases of bonds, but it is still significantly below the level of 2007, which was less than 2006. The overall trend, despite a recent upturn, is down.

When the bubbles pop again and we know they will because there is nothing to stop them, despite government intervention through massive borrowing and money printing, more and more foreign investors will lose interest in buying U.S. assets. Dropping demand for these assets will put increasing downward pressure on the value of the dollar, creating a negative feedback loop of falling demand leading to falling prices, leading to falling demand. And, that massive government intervention of printing and borrowing that helped support the dollar so much in the short term will begin to have terribly negative consequences on the dollar due to inflation (see Chapter 3) and increased fear of more inflation due to the size of the U.S. debt.

At first, just a few foreign investors will decide to end their wait-and-see approach and will want to sell some of their U.S. holdings. Some of that early selling may be by sophisticated investors, as well as by foreign pension funds and life insurance companies that have to be somewhat risk-averse in their investments because of the nature of their fiduciary responsibility to protect the assets of their retirees and beneficiaries. This early selling will lower demand even further, and prices will drop even more, motivating more foreign investors to flee. Fairly quickly, the number of foreign investors selling their U.S. assets will hit a critical mass, and a perfectly rational panic will kick in, further bringing down the already bursting asset bubbles, including the dollar. It's all about falling demand.

One way to look at this is to think of the United States as a big mutual fund. When our performance is good, foreign investors throw their money at us, but when performance is not so good, they throw less money at us. And when performance becomes bad enough, they are going to want to take their money and go home. And the future inflation that will result from the Fed's massive money printing to stimulate the economy will only reinforce this desire to go home.

Based on our analysis, we foresee foreign investors beginning to significantly lose confidence in their U.S. holdings sometime in or after 2013, and increasing over time, with the likelihood of a mass exit by or before 2016 becoming very high. Again, we must keep in mind that massive amounts of borrowing and money printing can delay the timing of this for a while, but it will also heighten the loss of foreign investor confidence when that finally starts to occur.

Needless to say, not too many U.S. investors will want to stick around at that point, either. And some of them will move their money out of the United States early along with the foreign investors, making enormous profits in the process. Fear *and* greed will drive the process of pushing the dollar down: foreign investors' fear of losing money, and U.S. investors' greed to make money by moving money into rapidly rising foreign currencies.

Before we move on to the next big bubble pop, we need to answer a question that is probably on your mind right now: If the United States is no longer a good investment, where will foreign investors go? Won't the United States still be the best place to invest, relative to other countries whose economies will be in even worse shape than ours?

The U.S. Will Remain a Reserve Currency after the Aftershock

This might surprise people because if the dollar collapses, many people think that means it won't be a reserve currency. Currently about

61 percent of foreign exchange reserves around the world are held in dollars and about 26 percent in euros, according to the International Monetary Fund. The euro's percentage has grown about 10 percent in the last 10 years and the dollar's percentage has fallen about 10 percent. Clearly, the dollar and the euro completely dominate the reserve currency market. What makes a currency good as a reserve currency is scale and liquidity. These characteristics make a currency excellent for world trade. Hence, it will be easy for a nation, such as South Africa, to trade with Brazil using the dollar.

Also, huge reserves of dollars are being held by China and to a lesser degree Japan, not for trade, but to manipulate the price of the dollar in favor of their exports to the United States. After the Aftershock, those manipulations will fail and their reserves of dollars will decline precipitously, making the euro an increasingly important reserve currency by default. But, simply due to the size and scale for our economy and its worldwide trade, the dollar will remain a reserve currency for future trading, even if it falls to being the second most important reserve currency after the Aftershock.

The Biggest Myth about the Dollar Is That Foreign Investors Have No Place Else to Go

Lots of people we talk to find it difficult to believe that foreign investors will ever significantly pull out of their U.S. investments because many Americans believe that most foreign investors have no other profitable place to go. Bob has found in his presentations to financial analysts and asset managers that there is rather strong agreement that U.S. investments are not performing as well as they did in the past. There is also pretty strong agreement that the trade deficit is putting downward pressure on the dollar. And people don't argue with the fact that the value of the dollar has already declined. In fact, the U.S. Dollar Index (DXY), a basket of foreign currencies whose value is tracked against the dollar, is down more than 30 percent from its value in 2001. Against the euro, the dollar's value is down almost 60 percent from its peak in 2000.

What people do not agree with is the idea that foreign investors have profitable non-U.S. choices for investment. The most common question we get about a potential fall in the value of the dollar is "Where else would foreign investors put their money except in the United States?" We've heard this from individual investors, highly respected economists, senior Wall Street asset managers, and even senior Federal Reserve officials.

Apparently, many otherwise intelligent Americans simply don't realize that foreign investors *already* put most of their money in other places! It's a bit arrogant on our part to think that foreign investors have to invest *all* of their money in the United States. In fact, they often keep most of their investment capital in their own local or regional investments. Think about it. If foreign investors actually did put all of their money in the United States, how would other countries get any capital at all? This idea is really very silly.

As the U.S. bubbles continue to fall, foreign investors will simply decide to reduce their dollar-based investment exposure and keep a little more money at home. Wouldn't you? There is always some foreign exchange risk in any investment outside your own country. Certainly U.S. investors think about this when considering investments in another country, and foreign investors do the same when they weigh the costs and benefits of investing in the United States. This is perfectly reasonable. Fluctuating foreign exchange rates can make foreign investments less attractive.

This is especially true over the long term with low yield investments, such as government bonds. For example, a euro bond may yield 3 percent, and a U.S. bond may give a more attractive 3.5 percent, but if the exchange rates move even 1 percent, the advantage of owning the more profitable U.S. bond instead of the euro bond is entirely wiped out, and there is a loss. When exchange rates become volatile, this risk only increases and is an important consideration for foreign investors when deciding whether to buy U.S. bonds and other U.S. assets or to buy their own countries' bonds and other assets.

It is important to recognize that this is part of an overall flight to safety by foreign investors. Not only will foreign investors reduce their foreign exchange exposure, they will also reduce their exposure to riskier assets in their own countries, especially stocks. So, when they bring their money back home, they won't be putting it into stocks, but instead will be putting much of it in short-term debt instruments and precious metals.

Money Does Not Have to Flow Out of the United States for the Dollar to Decline; It Just Has to Flow In Less Rapidly

Foreign investors don't have to take their money out of the United States for the dollar bubble to fall; they just have to reduce the enormous amounts they are now putting in. People forget how much money we take in from foreign investors. We currently receive about $2 billion of foreign capital *every day*. Even if not a penny is taken out of the United States and the only thing that happens is that this big inflow of foreign capital drops to, say, $1 billion or $500 million a day, the value of the dollar would drop significantly.

So pushing down the dollar will not require a major withdrawal. All it will take is a slowdown of foreign capital flowing in. No money has to actually flow out in order to pop the dollar bubble.

Maybe the United States Is Too Big to Fail?

Some people think that since the dollar and U.S. government bonds are so important to the world economy, the rest of the world won't let the dollar fall or the government debt bubble burst. This is often used as a reason why China will want to maintain the dollar's value—because it is so heavily invested in dollars. The reality is that China does not control the market. In fact, no one group comes anywhere close to controlling the market. Because of that, it is in everyone's individual best interest to get out of dollars, even if it is not in the group's best interest. As we have said many times before, last one out is a rotten egg, and no one will want to be the rotten egg.

Most Foreign-Held Investments in Dollars Won't Flow Out of the United States—They Will Go to "Money Heaven"

Remember Bear Stearns? In early 2008, the value of its stock went from about $28 billion to just $2 billion, practically overnight, but not because $26 billion was actually moved out of Bear Stearns stock. In fact, only a small portion of stock was sold before the stock price collapsed. Where did that $26 billion in wealth go? We like to say it went to "Money Heaven," meaning it simply disappeared.

When the dollar bubble falls, most foreign-held investments in dollar-denominated assets will not have a chance to run out of the United States. Instead, that capital will go to the same place your home equity went when the housing bubble popped. It will go to the same place your 401(k) and other retirement account funds went when the stock bubble dropped to half its peak value. It will go to the same place that all bubble money goes when a bubble pops: It's all going to Money Heaven.

A Small Change in Demand Can Create a Big Change in Value

You only need a relatively small change in demand to significantly impact value. For example, if the last person at the end of the day buys GE stock for $100 per share, then all GE stock is worth $100 a share even though almost none of the people holding that stock paid $100 a share. Conversely, if the last share of GE stock sells for $50 at the end of the day, all GE stock is worth $50 a share, regardless of what price you paid before. Asset values can go up and down very quickly because they are priced at the margin.

The same thing will happen to the dollar. It won't take the sale of a lot of dollars to make the value of the dollar drop significantly. Like stocks, dollars are priced at the margin. Once it starts to seriously decline, the value of the dollar can and will fall very rapidly—so rapidly that most foreign investors won't have time to sell (just as you may not have had time to sell a given stock before the price went way down). Only those who sell early will escape Money Heaven, which is a big motivating factor in the sell-off as the dollar starts to fall—no one will want to be stuck holding dollars or dollar-denominated assets after

All Dogs Go to Heaven, and So Will a Whole Lot of Money!

People often ask where the massive amount of investment capital in stocks, bonds, and real estate will go in the future. The answer is Money Heaven. Most investment money will go to Money Heaven in the future because most people won't pull their money out of falling stocks, real estate, and bonds soon enough. Anyone who doesn't move money out early won't be able to move it out at all. That's because other people will have moved their money out of those investments earlier. Most importantly, there will be little demand for those investments afterwards. Hence, the value of most people's investments will decline dramatically.

At that point most people will realize they should have moved their money out, but it will be too late. Their portfolios will have been automatically rebalanced for them, heavily weighted toward Money Heaven. For the money managers and financial advisors who will preside over this reweighting of investors' portfolios into Money Heaven, it's going to feel a lot less like Money Heaven and a lot more like Money Hell.

the dollar collapses. Again, last one out is a rotten egg. So this early selling will only accelerate the fall.

We believe that during this period there will be a fierce fight to save the dollar by central banks around the world and by the U.S. government, including a variety of federal interventions to attempt to stop or slow the sell-off. Such interventions will delay but not prevent the dollar's full fall.

Once the dollar bubble falls significantly, foreign and U.S. investors together will start moving their money out of the United States in hot pursuit of the enormous profits to be made by selling falling dollars and buying rising assets elsewhere, such as foreign currencies and gold (see Chapter 7).

The Second Biggest Dollar Myth: In a Worldwide Recession, the Relatively Good U.S. Economy Will Always Make the Dollar More Valuable Than the Euro and the Yen

First of all, the dollar is already worth 30 percent less than it was in 2001, according to the U.S. Dollar Index. More importantly, the value of the dollar is *not* a function of the relative strength of the U.S. economy compared to economies of other countries. Even if the United States has a stronger economy than Europe and Japan in the coming years (and it will), the value of the dollar will still be determined entirely by *supply and demand*. Demand for dollars always depends on how attractive our investments are. So, if U.S. investments do poorly, the dollar will still go down because the foreign investors will go back to lower-risk investments in their own countries where there is no foreign exchange risk.

Why would foreign investors consider investments in economies doing worse than ours as safer than U.S. investments? Because, as we mentioned before, investments in their own countries will carry no foreign exchange risk.

But, as mentioned before, when the Aftershock begins to hit, foreign investors will make a general flight to safety. They won't sell U.S. stocks and invest in European or Japanese stocks. They will invest in short term, highly liquid cash securities. Foreign investors will prefer their own countries' cash securities over U.S. bonds because there is no foreign exchange risk involved in buying cash securities in their home countries. This has nothing to do with the relative strength of economies; it's all about investor safety.

Also, some foreign investors, and U.S. investors, will be piling into gold to greatly improve their returns over short term debt securities.

The Real Reason Most People Don't Believe the Dollar Can Collapse Is That the Consequences Are Too Terrible to Think About

The debate over the future of the dollar is not academic. If the dollar falls, it will deeply and negatively affect everyone in the United States and most people around the world. That is pretty scary. Unfortunately, this fear colors the debate about what is ahead, with most people carrying a strong bias against the possibility that the dollar could actually ever fall. This makes open and honest discussion about the future value of the dollar much more difficult, especially for financial journalists, financial analysts, and economists, most of whom would be deeply and negatively affected personally and professionally by a collapse.

Some people avoid the debate entirely because they assume the collapse of the dollar will mean the end of the world. It won't! It may be the end of the world as we know it, but it won't be the end of the world. All we ask is that you not let fear stop you from absorbing the facts. Based entirely on logic and the evidence at hand, there simply is no other plausible scenario. The dollar can and will fall. Again, if we didn't have a falling *bubble* economy, things would be very different. And if we weren't so heavily dependent on a constant inflow of foreign capital, things would be very different. Unfortunately, falling bubbles are exactly what we have, and a decline in the massive inflow of foreign capital to the United States is all it will take to start bringing the dollar (and all the other bubbles) down.

Hasn't the Dollar Been a Safe Haven Currency Recently?

Yes it has, and it will continue to be so to some degree until inflation begins to hit the U.S. dollar. Also, international investor psychology has to change to catch up with the new reality of the dollar. In the past, the U.S. dollar has always been the strongest and most reliable currency in the world. Many international investors still view it as such.

But that view was created before the new conditions of the dollar were created with a massive government debt of $14 trillion and rising due to a massive deficit of nearly $1.6 trillion. The view of the safe haven dollar was also created long before we had the massive inflow of foreign capital into our country chasing and aiding our economic bubbles. It was also created long before we decided to triple our money supply and before our likely increases in the future.

Although the economic conditions surrounding the dollar have been changing for many years, international investor perceptions have not been as quick to change. They are similar to U.S. investors. They don't really see the fundamental economic bubble until it begins to pop, and then they see it all too quickly.

Also, the speed with which those fundamental economic conditions are changing for the worse has increased rapidly. In fact, the stress can be seen in the need for the Federal Reserve to buy nearly $2.4 trillion worth of government bonds, Freddie Mac bonds, and Fannie Mae bonds since spring 2009. Clearly, the world's appetite for our dollar-denominated debt is limited, or the Fed wouldn't have to buy the bonds.

The Federal Reserve is acting as an enormous buyer of last resort. This has helped boost international investors' confidence in the dollar in 2009 and 2010 and will likely continue to do so in 2011, since it guarantees there will be no confidence-shaking failed Treasury auctions. Right now a failed auction would be highly damaging to investors' confidence in the dollar. But in the long run, the purchase of these bonds damages investors' confidence since it runs the high risk of creating dollar-damaging inflation. It's a short-term move that boosts the dollar with very bad long-term consequences. Sound familiar?

In the Bursting of Japan's Bubble Economy, the Yen Didn't Collapse

You wouldn't expect it to collapse. Japan's bubble economy only had two major bubbles—stock and real estate. It didn't have a yen bubble, a private debt bubble, or a public debt bubble that were anything like those of the United States. It didn't have to increase its money supply to handle a massive collapse in the private credit markets. It didn't further massively increase its money supply to buy its own government bonds to help save its stock market, stimulate the economy, and finance a massive public debt bubble. Hence, there was little threat of inflation. Also, Japan had high internal savings rates, relative to the United States, until recently and it did not have a huge inflow of foreign capital over decades chasing its economic bubbles.

Japan had a very different and much milder bubble economy. In fact, it was less of a bubble economy and more like an economy that had experienced very high real growth rates due to rapidly increasing productivity that simply saw its high productivity growth, and hence, economic growth, come to an end.

The Fierce Fight to Save the Dollar

As you might expect, the United States and other countries will make all sorts of heroic efforts to save the dollar. Keeping the dollar bubble pumped up is now and will continue to be a major focus of central banks around the globe, especially the Chinese central bank, which now has bought over $1.3 trillion to prop up the dollar's price. Japan has over $800 billion but it is no longer accumulating a significant number of dollars.

China's primary motivation in buying dollars is to keep the price of their currency, the yuan, lower relative to the dollar, and thus keep the price of their goods low for their number-one customer, the United States. The more goods they sell to us, the more jobs they create at home, and with more jobs comes more political stability. If China stops producing jobs, political instability will rise and Chinese political leaders fear that another Tiananmen Square, or worse, would not be far off.

Of course, China exports to other countries, as well, but no other customer base has been as large as the United States over the past five years. In large part because of our voracious rising-bubble appetite for their low-labor-cost goods (clothing, furniture, kitchen gadgets, tools, lamps, towels, pens, shoes, and so much more), China's economy has been growing at an astounding rate of around 10 percent annually. Even now, during the global Bubblequake recession, China is still growing at a fast, but more modest 9 percent rate although much of that growth is due to the government's enormous construction stimulus program. That stimulus program is funded with printed money, which will eventually create high inflation, some of which is already showing up in the Chinese economy. Most importantly for the dollar, at some point, the Chinese central bank will no longer be willing—or for that matter, able—to keep buying our dollars in order to support its price.

Government Manipulations to Hold Up the Dollar Will Ultimately Fail

The U.S. Federal Reserve and the central banks of other governments, such as China, will work hard to hold up the value of the dollar.

There is not much the Fed can do to directly manipulate the value of the dollar because it normally does not buy dollars, but it can encourage other central banks to buy dollars. And it can take other indirect actions, like raising interest rates to attract more foreign investors, but that would also damage the U.S. economy. However, there is one thing the Fed could do to directly support the dollar that it has never done before. If necessary, the Fed could borrow currencies from other countries and use them to buy dollars. But such actions can have big negative consequences. So, short of that, we are really quite dependent on the kindness of strangers— in this case, foreign central banks—to support the dollar.

Manipulations of the value of the dollar by foreign central banks make it difficult to predict movements in the dollar's value in the short term. But we must emphasize *short term*. In the long term, market forces, meaning the *supply and demand* for dollars by foreign investors, will ultimately determine the value of the dollar. In the meantime, expect governments to manipulate the value of the dollar as best they can, for as long as they can, by buying dollars (lowering supply) and supporting its price.

Why are they helping us? They do it because the value of the U.S. dollar is not only our concern; the whole world is impacted by it. No one wants to see the dollar fall and all major governments will work hard to keep it up because the international losses and global financial instability caused by its fall will hurt everyone.

However, wanting a strong and stable dollar is not the same thing as being able to buy dollars indefinitely to hold up their value. So expect a lot more talk than action, and some of the talk will not be entirely positive because many people and governments will get increasingly angry that the dollar and the U.S. economy are falling and hurting them.

Ultimately, good investor psychology and active government manipulation will not be able to overcome fundamentally bad investment performance. As the financial bubbles that were so attractive and profitable for foreign investors fall and pop, no one is going to be very interested in supporting (buying) the dollar, supply will rise, demand will drop, and the dollar bubble will pop.

"It's just a flesh wound. I got it defending the dollar."

The Huge Government Debt Bubble Is Also Putting Downward Pressure on the Dollar Bubble

Expected to be nearing *$15 trillion* by the end of 2011 (up from $12 trillion just two years earlier), the U.S. government debt bubble is certainly the biggest, scariest bubble of all. As we mentioned earlier, debt, even big debt, is not intrinsically bad. But debt only makes sense when it is in reasonable proportion to the debtor's ability to pay it back within a reasonable amount of time. As Figure 4.1 indicates, our current $14 trillion debt is nearly *seven times* our government's current annual income (taxes) of around $2 trillion. That makes it impossible to pay back. How many banks would lend money to a company or an individual with a debt-to-income ratio of 7 to 1, with no plan to pay it off, and projections of further huge increases in their future debt?

But that's comparing our debt to income. It is much more common to compare the government's debt to GDP. Looking at it that

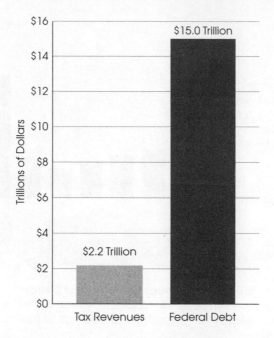

Figure 4.1   Ratio of U.S. Government Debt to Tax Revenues 2011
Our debt-to-income ratio is 7 to 1 and heading towards an incredible
8 to1. Is that a good debt?

Source: Office of Management and Budget.

way, our debt is about one times our GDP. But we don't pay our government debt with GDP, we pay it with taxes and, again, our debt
is *seven times* our tax income. People use the comparison to GDP
partly as a way of making the debt look smaller and more manage-
able than it really is.

As Figure 4.2 indicates, our annual federal deficit has been on a
high growth track since 2001, but it has gone into overdrive since the
financial crisis of 2008, when it has consistently run in the $1.5 tril-
lion range (expected to hit $1.65 trillion this year), and even the gov-
ernment expects it to stay above $1 trillion for years to come. Since
we spend almost $3.5 trillion each year, that means that more than
40 percent of everything our government spends comes from borrowed money. When the federal government's income goes down, it
doesn't even consider spending cuts as states have to—it just borrows
more money to make up the difference! In fact, the federal government spends far more money when its income declines. What a life!

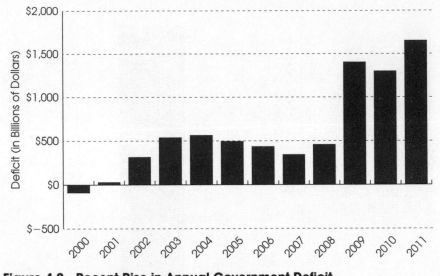

Figure 4.2   Recent Rise in Annual Government Deficit
Our annual government deficit is exploding, which is shining a very bright spotlight on our already enormous government debt (our accumulated annual deficits).

Source: Federal Reserve.

Who is lending us all this money? Much of this debt has been funded by foreign investors, primarily from Europe and Asia. In fact, the percentage of U.S. debt held by foreign investors has almost doubled since 1980, climbing from 15 percent to almost 30 percent. Yep, those same foreign investors who we know for a fact are going to slow their buying of U.S. assets, such as U.S. stocks, are also going to lose their appetite for buying U.S. Treasuries.

The Fed's massive money printing, which the Federal Reserve calls quantitative easing, is contributing mightily to the growth of the money supply and hence, future inflation. That doesn't make foreign investors too happy, either. In fact, the money supply has skyrocketed since late 2008, as Figure 4.3 shows.

All those bonds purchased by the Fed, which have increased the money supply, make it much easier for the government to borrow money and expand its debt. And, there is no guarantee we won't have to borrow even more than $1.6 trillion a year in the future. The government is not predicting we will, but when inflation hits and the economy slows down even more, the deficit will rise again.

Why Not a 100 Percent Tax Cut to Stimulate the Economy?

Even better than our "triple-zero" plan for reviving the housing market (in that plan the government guarantees mortgages at 0 percent interest, $0 down payment, and zero credit check) is our 100 percent tax cut stimulus package! Now this will really get the old economy going. No more arguing about who pays what taxes; let everybody get a complete tax cut! It surely will get very broad bipartisan support. Instead of collecting taxes, we can just borrow all the money from foreign investors! If we can borrow $1 trillion a year to stimulate the economy and never worry about paying it off, why don't we borrow more and really stimulate the economy?

Of course, no one would ever do this because it uncovers a big unmentionable problem: Eventually we'll have to pay the money back, or inflate our currency, or default on our government debt. Whether it's $14 trillion going up at a rate of $1.6 trillion a year, or $14 trillion going up at a rate of $3.5 trillion a year, it really doesn't matter, but it certainly looks a lot worse if we fund 100 percent of our expenses with borrowed money rather than 40 percent. It also makes it more obvious how irresponsible we really are—whether we borrow $1.3 trillion a year or $3.5 trillion—in an attempt to maintain our bubble economy.

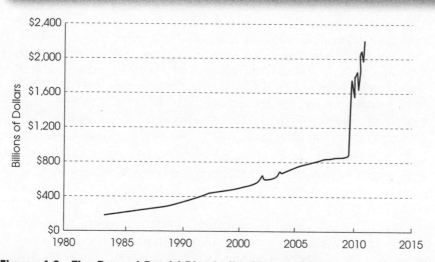

Figure 4.3 The Recent Rapid Rise in the Money Supply
The Fed has massively increased the money supply, paving the way for much higher inflation.

Source: Federal Reserve.

What Is the Government's Credit Limit?

Anyone with a credit card understands what a credit limit is. Does the U.S. government have a credit limit? Most people, including investment bankers and government leaders, don't even ask the question. They seem to implicitly assume that there is no credit limit and the government can just keep borrowing forever at record low interest rates. They probably know this can't possibly be true, but like so many other false assumptions underlying the bubble economy, they don't really think about it.

However, this is probably the most important question of all in determining when Phase I (the Bubblequake) will become Phase II (the Aftershock), and the bubble economy will finally fully pop. We will reach our credit limit when foreign investors stop or dramatically reduce their lending to the U.S. government because they are concerned about the risk of not being repaid with dollars that have the same value as the dollars they are lending. This will be heavily driven by the onset of inflation and the fear of higher inflation rates.

So, the credit limit is not the same as the debt ceiling, which can be raised by Congress at any time. The credit limit is the point at which it becomes very difficult for the government to sell bonds due to investor fears of inflation or default. Of course, the Federal Reserve could easily move into the bond market, as it did in 2009 and 2010, and purchase massive amounts of bonds—thus preventing a failed Treasury auction—but that will fuel the fires of inflation. The end result is the same as not being able to sell bonds because the inflation the Fed creates in the process will drive away foreign investors, as well as domestic investors. It will also become increasingly difficult and eventually impossible to sell fixed-rate bonds in such a high inflation environment. Once the government can sell only adjustable rate bonds, such as Treasury Inflation Protected Securities (TIPS), the Treasury market will effectively die as a means for raising funds for the government, and we will have hit our credit limit.

At some point, this kind of astronomical debt is going to scare the people who have been lending us the money, especially foreign investors.

Keep in mind that the $14 trillion we have already borrowed is effectively a bad loan. We have almost never paid down the debt, much less pay it off. All we seem to do is add to it enormously. That bad loan is going to scare foreign investors from investing more money into the world's biggest bad loan. They don't think of it as a bad loan now, but that perception can and will change dramatically over time.

Think Like a Foreign Investor: How Much of This Will They Take?

As we write this in early 2011, many people—including many foreign investors—are still expecting to see a significant recovery soon. Some believe the recovery has already started. How long this optimism will last depends heavily on how much money the Federal Reserve will print and the federal government will borrow (as described in Chapter 3).

When investors became disillusioned in 2009 and 2010, the Fed came to the rescue with money printing to boost the stock market and stimulate the economy. This cheered investors greatly in 2010 and may continue to cheer investors well into 2011. The problem, as we have said again and again, is that this stimulative money printing is clearly not sustainable and in time will have to end. And even worse than merely ending, this short-term stimulus will create a very big long-term problem: inflation.

As inflation nears 10 percent, investor optimism will start to seriously evaporate and a significant minority of foreign investors will begin to reduce their U.S. dollar exposure. What looks okay now will look much worse when inflation begins.

What Is the Repayment Plan for the National Debt? 10 Years? 15 Years? 20 Years?

Well, as everyone knows, there is no repayment plan. What a country! Borrow all the money you want, and you don't even need a repayment plan!

This question is like asking what our credit limit is. It's very useful for understanding our national debt. So, since we don't have a payment plan, let's create one. Let's keep the math simple. If we assume our debt is $15 trillion (which it will be by 2012) and our annual payment is $500 billion, then it would take 30 years to pay it off, assuming we don't do anything sneaky like borrowing more money during those 30 years.

(continued)

Thirty years is not a particularly aggressive payment schedule, but let's see how easy that would be to accomplish.

To make that payment, we would also have to eliminate our deficit of $1.6 trillion. For ease of calculation we're going to round that to $1.5 trillion. So, we would need $500 billion plus $1.5 trillion, or $2 trillion in total, in taxes to start on the 30-year road to paying off the debt. Currently, we are bringing in about $2 trillion in taxes—about $900 billion in individual income taxes and about $1.1 trillion in Social Security and other taxes.

So, we would need to increase all taxes by 100 percent or income taxes by 200 percent to begin a very, very slow road to paying off the debt. This is not politically or economically feasible. And, again, that is assuming we don't increase our deficit and don't have any interest rate increases above the incredibly low interest rates we are paying today. By any measure, that is a toxic asset. There is no hope of paying it off.

Of course, right now none of our lenders care if we can't afford to pay back our debt because, for now, we can keep rolling it over and refinancing it. However, at some point, foreign and domestic investors who are supplying all this capital are going to say, "Enough is enough!" Most people like to say this will be our grandchildren's problem. But why? In reality, investors do not have to wait another generation to stop lending us the money. It can happen at any time.

Any loan you cannot afford to pay off or successfully refinance is likely to default. That will happen just as soon as investors, especially foreign investors, see the reality of the situation, and that perception of true reality starts to affect the value of the dollar. In the end, it will be like a giant Ponzi scheme that's destined to fail. As Bernie Madoff so plainly put it when he was arrested, "I knew this day would come eventually." The same will be true for our monstrous national debt with no repayment plan.

The Hidden Dollar Bubble Won't Fall until the End, Then It Will Pop Very Quickly

The dollar bubble will remain relatively hidden until the end, but when it starts to blow up, it will look a lot like the financial crisis of late 2008, meaning it will come on very quickly. Unfortunately, the financial crisis of 2008 and 2009 was relatively small compared to the coming dollar crisis. When it hits, it will be too large for central banks to solve, as just explained. The reason it is stealthy is that prior to the final dollar bubble pop, much effort will have already been taken to prop up the dollar, and much is currently being done. So it will take a long time for big problems to appear on the surface, but when they do, it will be like a fire that firefighters can no longer control. It is not uncommon for foreign currency crises to come on quickly and dramatically. What is very uncommon is for it to happen to the United States. In fact, it will be a once-in-history event.

The Debt Bubble's Achilles Heel: The U.S. Government Is the Largest Holder of Adjustable-Rate Debt in the World

One of the biggest problems with rising interest rates is that the interest costs for the U.S. government are starting to go up. The United States is the largest holder of adjustable-rate debt in the world. It's not technically adjustable-rate debt, but it functions as such because most of this debt is short term, and therefore it has to be regularly refinanced at whatever is the current interest rate. As Figure 4.4 indicates, almost 40 percent of our government debt has a maturity

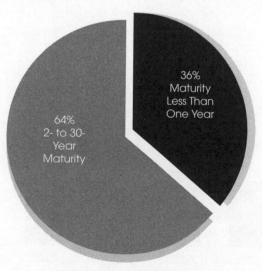

Average Maturity: 4.3 Years

Figure 4.4 Federal Government Debt Maturity Distribution
U.S. government debt is very short term forcing frequent refinancing which makes it effectively adjustable rate debt.
Source: U.S. Treasury.

of less than one year, according to the U.S. Treasury. The average maturity of all our debt is 4.3 years. As interest rates rise, the government is forced to pay out more and more interest on its debt every time it has to refinance this short-term debt. This is the same problem that hits homeowners when their adjustable-rate mortgages rise. When interest rates go up significantly due to inflation and increasing risk, debt service could fairly quickly consume a large part of our government's income.

As Figure 4.5 shows, our interest costs are low right now. If they rise, our interest costs can quickly consume over half of our tax income. Remember, we only bring in about $2 trillion in taxes. If interest rates go back to where they were in the early 1980s, almost all of our taxes would go just to pay interest costs alone. This is the big difference between the $1 trillion debt that we had over two decades ago and the $14 trillion debt we have today. This current debt is much more dangerous because we are becoming increasingly vulnerable to rising inflation and rising interest rates, just like the homeowner who has an adjustable rate mortgage.

The risk of rising interest rates fueled by inflation is greatly compounded by the Federal Reserve's recent massive increases in the

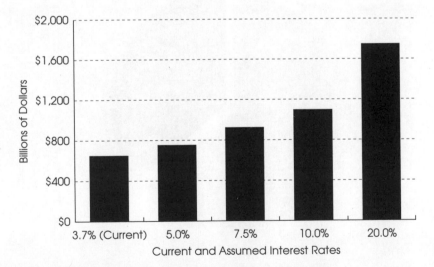

Figure 4.5   Interest Costs of U.S. Government Debt
Even small increases in interest rates can dramatically increase the interest costs on such a massive government debt.

Source: The Foresight Group.

money supply, which will cause rising inflation over the next two to four years. Rising inflation will cause rising interest rates, and high interest rates will make it increasingly hard and then impossible for the federal government to pay its debt or to borrow more—finally popping the massive government debt bubble.

The Government Debt Bubble Pops

In the short term, massive money printing by the Fed (see Chapter 3) will likely continue to boost the stock market and help temporarily stimulate the economy. However, in the long term (likely in the 2013–2015 range), a heavy price for this temporary stimulus will have to be paid. Rising inflation will put downward pressure on the dollar, thus reducing investment from foreign investors in dollar-denominated assets, especially bonds, but also stocks and real estate. Eventually, especially after inflation passes 10 percent, foreign investors could actually take their money out of the United States, which would sharply reduce the available capital inside the United States.

To calm the markets, boost liquidity, and keep the outflow of investor capital from driving interest rates up even further, the Fed will be forced to print even more money to purchase the bonds that foreign investors, as well as domestic investors, are no longer purchasing. However, at that point, the Fed's medicine will rapidly become poison, as more and more investors fear inflation from the Fed's money printing operations. Sharp declines in stocks, bonds, real estate, and the value of the dollar, due to rising inflation, will create a greater sense of perceived risk among lenders, which will further reduce capital availability and further push up interest rates. Real interest rates—the difference between the inflation rate and the interest rate—will eventually soar, with the perceived risks and the real risks of lending increasing rapidly.

In this downward spiral, the Federal Reserve will launch additional bursts of money printing as it has done in the past, but to a much, much greater degree, in an attempt to stimulate the economy and keep it alive. This will of course create ever-increasing amounts of inflation. The exact inflation rates will be changing constantly and will not stay at one level for any length of time. Fortunately for the investor, the exact numbers at any given time will not be relevant. What will be relevant is knowing what is going on and what will happen next.

The combination of high inflation, rapidly rising interest rates, and rapidly rising perceived risk (and real risk) of any lending will quickly put the U.S. government, the world's biggest borrower, in a position it has never been in before. Unlike in the past, when the U.S. government could ride to the rescue of Bear Stearns or AIG when investors, lenders, and counter-parties had lost confidence, this time the U.S. government will increasingly find itself needing to be rescued, and unfortunately, the government cannot rescue itself.

At this point, the world will start to perceive high risk in U.S. government debt. Even if the government pays much higher interest rates, as it will have to because interest rates and inflation are rising rapidly, there will be an even faster increase in perceived risk for government bonds. U.S. government bonds are supposed to be AAA. But just like AIG or mortgage-backed securities, U.S. government bonds will increasingly be viewed as toxic assets. As we already saw in 2008, assets can go from being AAA to XXX in a relatively short period of time. As with AIG and mortgage-backed securities, once these assets go toxic, trading starts to freeze up very quickly, and these assets cannot be sold. It will also become increasingly difficult and eventually impossible to sell fixed-rate bonds in such a high inflation and high fear environment. Once the government can only sell adjustable rate bonds, such as Treasury Inflation Protected Securities (TIPS), the Treasury market will effectively die as a means for raising funds for the federal government. Instead, we will turn, once again, to printing even more money, with the Federal Reserve purchasing massive amounts of bonds with printed money, further fueling the fires of inflation.

Long term we will need to solve this high inflation problem in the same way that many governments have successfully fought high inflation: spending cuts and tax increases. These massive spending cuts and tax increases will ultimately help the government bring inflation back into the low double digits. Although that is high by current standards, it is more acceptable long term and certainly much better than the devastating multihundred percent inflation that could be incurred prior to the massive spending cuts.

What about the option of selling all our gold to pay off our government debt? Sounds promising until you run the numbers: Assuming the federal government owns about 9,000 tons of gold, which is what the published figures indicate, and it was willing and able to sell all of it, that would bring us only about $400 billion or so, at current values. Clearly, that is not a solution. We just have way more debt than we have ways to get out of debt. Eventually, our debt party will be over because we will not be able to borrow any more money, and we will not be able to pay any of it back.

Despite concerns about a collapse of the financial system, the U.S. government will definitely be able to maintain enough liquidity to maintain the payments mechanism. This will allow normal payment processing to occur within the United States and outside the United States. But, clearly the government will not be able to borrow money, since it will have ruined its "credit rating." The old debt will mostly have been inflated away, and the little remaining debt will likely be defaulted on or paid off with another burst of printed money.

The government debt bubble will be no more.

Money from Heaven Is the Path to Hell

We have said before that we think the government will likely have to hit the wall before the decision to cut spending and reduce our debt is made. It is a lot like General Motors, which had high expenses, declining revenues, and too much debt. GM, once the world's greatest company, chose to hit the wall instead of changing its ways, and we seem to be following the same path.

That wall appears when the government hits its credit limit and can no longer borrow the money it wants to spend. Of course, we also predict that the government will try to extend its credit limit by printing money—something General Motors could not do. Printing money will help extend our credit limit by making the market for our bonds more receptive in the short term.

We may say we want to cut the deficit but clearly we do not. When the bipartisan deficit commission report came out in the fourth quarter of 2010, recommending ways to cut the deficit, the report didn't even get enough votes to be formally presented before Congress. So much for any interest in deficit reduction.

In November 2010, Federal Reserve chairman Ben Bernanke started printing more money with QE2, extending our credit limit in the short term. And not long after, he announced on *60 Minutes* that he

(continued)

might even print more than $600 billion if he thought the economy was growing too slowly. Just a few days after Mr. Bernanke's TV announcement, the president and Republican congressional leaders agreed to a package of spending increases and tax cuts that lets both sides add to the debt as each would like. So much for bipartisan interest in cutting the debt. There does seem to be, however, plenty of bipartisan interest in adding to the debt.

Congress felt it really needed to borrow a lot more money to deal with current economic problems. But, what if we have economic problems in 2011 or 2012? Are we just going to borrow more money then, too? As long as the government can continue to borrow and print money, that will be the easiest way out of the situation.

Congress seems to view our ability to borrow and print money as "Money from Heaven." What it and many voters don't realize is that when the government hits its credit limit, it doesn't just mean we cannot borrow more in the future. It means the government's entire past debt comes due. The entire $20 trillion or $25 trillion—or whatever the number is when we finally can't borrow more—will be due because we won't be able to refinance our debt any longer. And we are constantly refinancing our debt because we can't pay off even a little bit of it. The catch is when you can't refinance it, no one will lend you any more money. Your loan has been called due. Game over.

The Fed can print lots more money to make up for the loss of our lenders, but at that point it creates so much inflation that it not only destroys all dollar-denominated asset values, it could virtually destroy the economy.

In the end, all the "Money from Heaven" gets very real and every bit of it will be "paid back" almost entirely from a massive loss of value in all our assets—and much of the world's assets—caused by massive inflation and ultimately, a U.S. government debt default. "Money from Heaven" will have created the path to Hell.

Aftershock: All the Bubbles Fully Collapse

With the dollar and government debt bubbles fully popped, and interest rates and inflation very high, unemployment will soar, the U.S. stock market will crash even further, the real estate market will be decimated, consumer discretionary spending will dry up, and the number of banks in business will be greatly reduced. The dollar will be worth a fraction of its peak value relative to other currencies, and gold will be a stellar investment for many years to come (see Chapter 7).

Most Americans (who don't follow our advice in Chapter 6) will lose most of their money, but they won't starve in the streets. In fact, because we have so much wealth to begin with, the United States will be in better shape than other countries (see Chapter 5), although life in the post-dollar-bubble world will be quite different than it is today.

One of the most striking differences will be the dollar itself, which will no longer buy nearly as much in imported goods. Like all the other bubbles, once the dollar bubble pops, it will not reinflate any time soon. The only way to make it go up again is to increase the demand for it, and that simply will not be possible. Remember Lehman Brothers? Being big and powerful is not enough; you also have to be a good investment.

Dead dollars, we are sorry to say, don't bounce.

Where Did All This Begin? When Could It Have Been Stopped?

With so many interacting bubbles first driving up and then pushing down the U.S. and world multibubble economies, it may seem impossible to know what caused what. But based on our analysis, we believe there was one critical moment that got everything started. That critical moment came back in 1981 when the U.S. government decided to start running large federal budget deficits. This big deficit spending sowed the early seeds for the coming asset bubbles in real estate and stocks. Big deficit spending boomed the economy, attracting U.S. and foreign investors to jump on the surging investment returns of a blue-chip (normally slow growing and secure) stock market on its way to 1,400 percent growth. The dollar soared, stocks kept climbing, private debt and discretionary spending rose tremendously, and real estate prices went intergalactic before plummeting back to Earth and, well, the rest is history.

When could we have stopped it? We've had a lot of internal discussion about increased deficit spending and at what stage we passed the point of no return. Our best estimate is that by the time we surpassed $200 billion in our annual federal deficit, it became politically infeasible to turn back. The economic pain that would have come from halting this level of deficit spending and moving instead to a budget surplus to pay down the accumulated federal debt, would have been simply too enormous to sell to voters. And honestly, given all the positive effects of easy, high-deficit spending induced economic growth, it would have been politically challenging to change our course even at $100 billion in deficit spending. It was just too tempting, too easy, and too profitable to walk away from the chance to grow our way out of our economic problems with deficit spending, especially when the eventual negative consequences would not be felt for decades. Like mall-happy teenagers with someone else's credit cards, it was just too irresistible. Yes, for two years in 1999 and 2000 we did run a small surplus, but it was insignificant in reducing the total debt and quickly became a large annual deficit again when the dot-com boom went bust, and large increases in spending were added to the budget.

Of course, credit-crazy teenagers can't get too far without outside support. In this case, we had plenty of help from foreign investors who were more than willing to help finance the government debt. If they hadn't done so, the "crowding-out effect" from the government's borrowing so much money would have pushed interest rates up too high for us to be able to easily finance our deficit spending domestically. This would have forced us to deal with our underlying economic problems sooner. Instead, foreign investors loved lending us money and buying U.S. assets. Without these investors, popping our relatively small bubbles back then would have involved a whole lot less pain than what we are about to face.

Not that we are blaming foreign investors. Investment money always flows toward opportunity. But, once you decide to borrow so much from foreign investors, you have made a game-changing decision in the way you manage your country's economy. The enormous negative consequences of this decision for the U.S. dollar will kick in fully in perhaps as little as two or three more years. We are about to see the same thing happen to the dollar that happened to home prices—home prices rose higher and then fell harder than anyone had ever seen before. We've never seen a dollar problem like this before because we've never before borrowed so much money from foreign investors to fund our government deficits and to help inflate our asset bubbles. And hence, the consequences for the dollar will also be like nothing we've ever witnessed before in history.

The Six Psychological Stages of Denial

As the dollar and government debt bubbles pop in Phase II (the Aftershock), people will naturally be very upset. We believe there will be six distinct psychological stages in which individuals, businesses, and governments will first ignore, then react to, and ultimately solve the economic problems. Each of these psychological stages performs the function of keeping people feeling as comfortable as possible while avoiding making any more changes than are absolutely unavoidable at that point in time. Change is threatening, inaction equals safety, and comfort comes from avoiding any changes that might threaten the benefits of the status quo. But the consequences of inaction also create pain, so eventually some actions are taken.

Over time, as the U.S. and world economies worsen, complete denial and inaction will not be entirely possible. Still, people will strive to ignore what is happening and do the least they can because the many benefits of the old multibubble economy are hard to give up. Our understanding of the underlying *psychology* of coping with and resisting change is one more thing that sets us apart from all the other bearish analysts. We know that at each stage of the falling economy, there will be a deep longing to return to the past and get back to the good times. Actually, the really good times are still ahead, but first we will pass through six psychological stages of coping with the current Bubblequake and coming Aftershock.

Although these stages are distinctly different, there will be some overlap between them so we may be experiencing multiple stages at the same time.
The six stages are:

1. Denial
2. Market Cycles
3. Fantasized Great Depression
4. Back to Basics
5. Imagined Armageddon
6. Revolutionary Action

First Stage: Denial   This is the stage in which the United States has been firmly planted for quite some time. This is the "Don't worry, just go shopping" phase of dealing with (or more correctly, not dealing with) the reality of our vulnerable multibubble economy. Regardless of the facts, in the Denial stage people firmly believe that home prices cannot drop any further, the stock market has already hit bottom, and the mighty U.S. dollar will always be king.

The big advantage of the Denial stage is that people do not have to take any unpleasant actions at all. We don't have a problem and therefore we don't have to change. But this stage involves more than simply ignoring the problem. In the Denial stage, we actively keep our multibubble economy pumped up and expanding. Governments, businesses, and individuals continue to borrow their way to prosperity, regardless of the future price tag. And even when things start going bad, the Denial stage just won't let the party quit. We continue to buy homes we can't afford until we can no longer get mortgages, and run up more and more debts we can't easily repay until we can get no more loans. And we continue to entrust our retirements and other investments to Wall Street even when stock prices have far outstripped an economic basis because we want to believe in Tinker Bell.

It can be very comfortable to live in denial—in a big, multibubble economy that has only begun to fall. In the Land of Denial, there's no need to recognize economic bubbles before they grow too large. After all, this is the United States of America, the biggest, most powerful economy in history. *Everything is fine.* And besides, if things really start to look bad, we can always turn to our next stage of dealing with our economic problems, which is to rely on our abiding faith in repeating market cycles.

Second Stage: Market Cycles   In the *Market Cycles* stage, an increasing number of individuals, businesses, and financial analysts come out of denial and begin to notice that something is wrong. They can see home sales falling, consumer spending slowing, jobs being lost, credit drying up, and stocks on the decline. They may even be able to recognize an individual falling asset bubble, like the declining real estate bubble. But few people at this stage will recognize any yet-unpopped economic bubbles, let alone be able to see an entire multibubble economy. Instead, they will explain the falling stock market, the failing real estate market, and the overall economic downturn in terms of historical up and down market cycles. While not as cozy as the Denial stage, the Market Cycle stage provides some significant comfort, too, because every "down" cycle is guaranteed to be followed by an "up" cycle.

The key comfort advantage of the Market Cycles stage as the multibubble economy begins to fall, is that we don't have to take any scary new actions. We can take actions similar to those we've taken before, even much bolder actions, but nothing fundamentally different that would deeply change the status quo. In fact, the actions are taken to preserve the status quo to the extent possible. Many individuals and businesses will just wait passively and tough it out thinking that, sooner or later, the economy will automatically improve. It always did before, right? Even world-class economists hold tightly to this outdated faith in repeating market cycles. The current recession may be deeper than we hoped, but just hang in there—it's bound to turn around soon.

When the unrecognized multibubble economy does not turn around soon but continues to fall, the next stage in the unfolding Bubblequake begins as people worry that maybe things really are different this time; maybe (can we even say it out loud?) the economy is heading into another, full-fledged Great Depression!

Third Stage: Fantasized Great Depression   During this stage, considerable fear starts setting in. Consumers and businesses significantly cut spending, more jobs are lost, banks further restrict lending, and the federal government ramps up spending money like there's no tomorrow. The words "another Great Depression" increasingly work their way into the national conversation, and the government begins taking unusual steps, like massive government spending to stimulate the economy. The psychological advantage of this stage is the comfort we get from seeing the government run big deficit spending—supposedly it worked in the past, and we can sit back passively and wait for it to work again.

But in fact, there is no Great Depression on the way. What we have instead is something new, a multibubble economy on its way down, so all the government spending to stimulate the economy does not have the intended positive effects that it would have in an actual depression. Instead, massive federal deficit spending just sets us up for an even bigger fall down the road, when both the dollar bubble and the government debt bubble eventually burst in Phase II, and no one wants to lend us any more money. At that point, printing dollars will be our only option, creating significant future inflation.

Fourth Stage: Back to Basics   With everything getting significantly worse and worse, the next stage in the ongoing process of dealing with our failing multibubble economy will be the urge to get *Back to Basics*. The impulse in this stage is to figure out what went wrong in the past and try to set it right in the present. If we can just rectify our previous mistakes, we will be okay, and the way to rectify those mistakes isn't to create a whole new financial and economic structure, but go back to where we were before all this mess happened—go back to basics. In the Back to Basics stage we will see federal and state governments beginning to enact tough regulations that would have helped protect us *in the past* from some of the problems we now face, such as defaults on subprime mortgages and the dangers of credit default swaps.

But at this late date, these measures will do little, if any, good to undo our current problems. Such attempts will be the equivalent of installing highly sensitive smoke detectors and fancy sprinkler systems, *after* the house has already burned down. Certainly none of that will help us rebuild. Instead of protecting the current economy in any meaningful way, going Back to Basics with tough backward-looking regulations will do little to reverse the damage that has already been done, and it won't put us on a course toward future recovery. The psychological advantage of this stage is the comfort people get from returning to the past and making as little fundamental change as possible so they can feel safe.

Fifth Stage: Imagined Armageddon   These backward-looking actions won't help us in a falling multibubble economy. With the dollar bubble popping, more and more people out of work, and the economy continuing to deteriorate, we are likely to next enter the stage of *Imagined Armageddon,* in which many people may come to think everything is hopelessly going to hell. Feeling angry, helpless, and scared, some people may imagine horrible scenarios of unlikely wars, long breadlines, sharply rising crime, and other calamities that simply will not occur. The invalid analogy to this stage was the earlier rise of fascism and World War II. The psychological advantage of this unpleasant stage is the opportunity to feel like passive victims in order to avoid the discomfort of having to make real decisions that bring about real change. It's hard to know how long this non-productive stage could last or what short-term consequences it would create. Politically and socially, it's bound to be a difficult time.

Sixth Stage: Revolutionary Action   Finally, after other actions have been tried and failed, the nation will enter into the final stage of dealing with the collapse of the multibubble economy, in which we will give up the last vestiges of comfort in the past and take major steps toward *Revolutionary Action.* This will include big changes to improve global financial stabilization, increase economic productivity, prevent asset bubble formation, provide targeted stimulation, and create sustainable capital generation.

The truth is, we could potentially make any and all of these changes at an earlier stage, including right now. But politically, such radical changes will be impossible to implement until we absolutely have to. Eventually, people and governments will face reality and figure out the changes necessary to get us out of this mess. We'll certainly be there to help. It will be a very exciting time.

Is There Any Scenario for a Soft Landing?

Yes, but it would have had to occur many years ago, back when the government debt bubble was still under $1 trillion, and before the rise of the real estate bubble, the private debt bubble, and the stock market bubble. In other words, we could have created a softer landing for America's multibubble economy back when the mother of all bubbles, the government debt bubble, was still manageable. Even when the bubbles grew larger, we still could have ended the problem, but with a not-so-soft landing. But at this point, now that the bubbles have grown so large and are so interconnected, the fall will be far, and the eventual landing will be anything but soft.

The Hamptons Effect

Rising bubbles created a rising bubble economy and plenty of bubble-money wealth. If you have a big, expensive house in the Hamptons, and a grand lifestyle to go with it, you are keenly aware that a collapse in the stock market, real estate market, and the other asset bubbles would mean an end to the good times you have come to think of as permanent. Naturally, that isn't too appealing. Therefore, you have a powerful incentive not to see the bubbles or the bubble economy, and instead to believe in wishful thinking that assures you everything is, and will continue to be, all right.

We call this "The Hamptons Effect." Wealthy people, stockbrokers, and asset managers have a deep need to keep believing we don't have any bubbles and to keep investing in the stock market. The Hamptons Effect is part of the reason for the stock market rallies over the past year and it drives plenty of other irrational decision making, as well. It is part of the Denial Stage we told you about. The bigger your house, the more denial you need to sleep at night.

CHAPTER

Global Mega-Money Meltdown

IT'S NOT JUST AMERICA'S BUBBLE ECONOMY, IT'S THE WORLD'S BUBBLE ECONOMY

A popular fairy tale gained favor in early 2008, proposing that the rest of the world, especially China, had magically decoupled from the naughty U.S. economy. Regardless of whatever foolishness and financial problems we happen to get ourselves into here, China (and to a lesser extent, the other emerging markets) would continue to be a reliable hotspot for investment profits. Even more magical, these burgeoning economies might actually help buffer the rest of the world, and even the United States, from the full impact of the U.S.-led recession.

Unfortunately, by the end of 2008 it became fully evident that this de-coupling myth could not be further from the truth. It was just another failed attempt at wishful thinking and economic cheerleading. In fact, when the U.S. housing bubble, stock market bubble, private debt bubble, and discretionary spending bubble all began to burst in late 2008 and 2009, the speed at which the rest of the world fell into deep recession was staggering. In the fourth quarter of 2008, GDP in the United States declined by 6.2 percent on an annual basis; in the UK it declined by 5.9 percent; Germany declined by 8.2 percent; Japan declined by 12.7 percent; and South Korea declined by a staggering 20.8 percent. By comparison, during the Great Depression, U.S. GDP fell by about 25 percent. Both Germany and Japan had accelerating declines in the first quarter of 2009 with

Germany falling at an annual rate of 14.4 percent and Japan falling 15.2 percent. Mexico actually topped the list in the first quarter 2009 with a 22 percent decline. As the U.S. economy reduced its imports of goods from overseas, particularly in the fourth quarter of 2008, the rest of the world's economies, joined at the hip to ours and each other's, simply fell off a cliff.

Now that the U.S. economy is no longer declining, those economies are also no longer declining. The myth of Chinese decoupling is growing again, now that China is showing very high growth as are the countries that export heavily to China, such as Brazil and Australia. However, that growth is heavily driven by various government stimulus policies (see the sidebar titled "Now That's Stimulus!"). The Chinese government became extremely worried when tens of millions of Chinese were put out of work due to declining exports. The government panicked over worries of potential political unrest and launched massive stimulus programs, to promote real estate and infrastructure construction funded by massive money printing, which is helping to stimulate their economy in the short term.

But that certainly does not mean China's economy is decoupling from ours. The United States and other economies are so tightly linked, and the impact of the U.S. Bubblequake and Aftershock will be felt so deeply around the world, that we almost titled our first book *The World's Bubble Economy*. But our book targeted a U.S. audience, so we accepted a less encompassing title. Nonetheless, just as we predicted in *America's Bubble Economy*, when the U.S. multi-bubble economy started to fall, the world's multibubble economy had little choice but to fall, too. And as we continue to fall, the rest of the world will end up in even worse shape. We should add that the world is starting to take notice of what we are saying. In spring 2011 *Aftershock* was published in both Chinese and Korean language editions.

The United States Will Suffer the Least

The U.S. economy is by far the most flexible, diverse, and stable economy in the world. We have the biggest, strongest economy, and we are less dependent on exports than most of the rest of the developed world. Therefore, the United States will naturally suffer the least in the current Bubblequake and coming Aftershock. This may seem unfair because we started most of these problems by inflating so many bubbles in the first place. On the other hand, many economies around the world benefited handsomely from our seemingly virtuous upward bubble spiral. They also actively supported it by lending us the money and not complaining when the many bubbles began to rise. So it's only logical that now, during our vicious downward bubble spiral, the rest of the world will suffer, as well. And, fair or unfair, because other economies were never as strong as our own, even at the height of the bubble party, the rest of the world will suffer more than we will during each stage of the multibubble bust.

After the United States, Western Europe will suffer the second least, followed by Japan, and then Eastern Europe and Russia. Developing nations, such as India and Brazil, will suffer more, and the underdeveloped, poor countries of Africa and elsewhere will do quite badly indeed. China will be hit very hard, and much of the country will be pushed back into rural poverty (more details later in this chapter).

Think of the World's Bubble Economy in Two Categories: Manufacturing and Resource Extraction

We can better understand why and how the world economy will suffer so badly if we analyze the economy in terms of two broad categories: manufacturing and resource extraction. Manufacturing can be further divided into two subgroups: (1) High-end manufacturers, primarily Germany and Japan, and (2) Low-end manufacturers, primarily China and other Asian Tiger nations. India is similar to low-end manufacturers because it provides low-end service exports.

Low-end manufacturers are directly affected by America's multibubble economy, both on the way up and on the way down, for the simple reason that we are the world's largest importer of low-end manufactured goods. So when the U.S. economy goes up, many other countries' economies go up.

There is an additional multiplier effect in terms of job creation. For each job created to produce exports sold to the United States, roughly two more jobs are created in support of those jobs. This is true not only of nations, but of cities and regions, as well. Any job that produces a good or service that is exported from a region also produces secondary jobs to support those people in the export industry, such as jobs in medicine, government, and housing.

These multiplier effects are extremely important to the export-driven economies of China and the other Asian Tigers, like Korea, Taiwan, Hong Kong, and Singapore. Because of these multiplier effects, a large increase in exports can create a massive economic boom in an export-driven economy. Of course, the very same thing is true in reverse: A big export decline can cause a massive decline in an export-driven economy.

The United States also drives the economies of the second sub-group of manufacturers, which produce high-end manufactured goods, especially Germany and Japan. The United States imports both consumer goods, such as electronics and automobiles, and industrial goods, such as machine tools and construction equipment. This provides a big boost to the Japanese and German economies, not only because of the exports themselves, but also because of the same job multiplier effect described previously.

In addition, it is important to realize that the low-end manufacturing countries such as China, import enormous amounts of high-end machinery from Germany and Japan to produce their manufactured goods and to build their economies. This demand helped Germany become the world's largest exporter in 2008. Obviously, this helped further boost the German and Japanese economies.

A side note that emphasizes the growing importance of China in the world economy is that China became the world's largest exporter in 2009 with $1.2 trillion in exports, ahead of Germany with $1.16 trillion in exports, according to the CIA *World Factbook*. In 2010 China also became the world's second largest economy, ahead of Japan. Although it may damage Germany's bragging rights, China's growth has increased Chinese demand for German products and made it one of the best performing economies in Europe—a small light in an otherwise dismal European economic picture. The only problem with China's recent growth is that, as we mentioned earlier, unlike in the past, China's growth is currently being heavily driven by government stimulus, not exports, which at some point, will fail.

Back to the larger picture: What happens when the virtuous spiral of massive imports and massive exports starts to go into reverse? As U.S. demand for low-end manufactured goods declines, so does the demand for German and Japanese high-end goods from China and the Asian Tigers. When the lack of demand from low-end manufacturers like China is combined with the lack of demand for high-end German and Japanese goods from the United States, Germany and Japan will see their economies truly devastated.

It will happen quite rapidly because the prices of foreign goods will soar as U.S. inflation climbs and dollar-denominated asset values fall. Remember, most of these items imported by the United States are discretionary. They are part of that discretionary spending sector that was discussed in Chapter 2. U.S. spending on imported nonessential items, from luxury 600-thread-count bed sheets to entertainment electronics, will collapse as inflation rises, the dollar bubble pops, and we move deeper into the global mega-depression.

The other big group in the world's bubble economy includes countries that have large resource extraction industries. This group benefits nicely from growth in both the low-end and high-end manufacturing nations and also from America's multibubble economy. Nations within the resource extraction group include both poor and wealthy countries such as Australia, Russia, Canada, and nations in the Middle East, Africa, and South America. Interestingly, this group also includes China, which is now heavily involved in both low-end manufacturing and resource extraction.

Naturally, economies that rely on resource extraction are especially impacted by the rising and falling demands for their various minerals, oil, lumber, grains, and other resources by the booming manufacturing economies of the world's bubble economy. The benefits to these resource-producing nations are double-boosted by both greater quantities of exports and much higher prices for their resources as demand rises. These higher prices can propel a normal economic boom into a hyper boom, creating enormous job growth, highly valued companies, and billionaires just about everywhere there is a mining shovel operating.

What do you think will happen to these resource-extraction economies when demand drastically declines? The double-boost of growing exports at higher and higher prices will easily turn into a double-downer of falling exports and falling prices. At the same time we will be importing far less, we will begin to export far more than we do today, because the dollar will have fallen and U.S. goods priced in dollars will be relatively cheap. This will also hurt other resource extraction economies, because cheap U.S. goods will compete with their goods for export to other countries.

The United States produces quite a few resources itself. However, the United States has a very diverse economy and will not feel the effects of either the resource boom or bust to the same extent as other countries.

America's Bursting Bubble Economy Will Bring Down Both Groups of Exporting Nations

On the way up, America's multibubble economy fueled the expansion of the world's bubble economy. As each economy expanded, it stimulated and expanded other economies, not only because the United States imported many goods and services from around the world, but also because many other nations have been trading back and forth in a positive feedback loop of economic stimulus. Europe and the more developed economies bought from the underdeveloped and developing countries, and those countries, in turn, bought from other countries.

The popping of America's bubble economy will rapidly pull the plug on every exporting nation in this complex web of interdependence. Given that America's bubble economy has a heavy discretionary spending component, and given that we already have quite a lot of big capital goods in place that will keep us going for a while (like cars and refrigerators), it will be relatively easy for American consumers to drastically reduce their purchases of imported goods (now at sky high prices due to the falling dollar) as the U.S. economy heads deeper into recession. And in any case, after the dollar bubble pops, the costs of imports into the United States will soar astronomically.

Salt in the Wound: Not Only Will Foreign Investors Suffer as Their Domestic Economies Fall, They Will Also Lose Their Huge Profits from U.S. Investments

While the U.S. multibubble economy was booming, domestic and foreign investors from around the world made tremendous profits on their U.S. holdings, including their investments in U.S. stocks, bonds, Treasuries, real estate, and other dollar-denominated assets. As the bubbles pop and these assets lose value, the once-rising profit tide will rapidly flow in reverse, leaving foreign investors with tremendous losses. The economic consequences of this worldwide evaporation of wealth cannot be overstated.

More Salt: Other Governments Have Large Debts As Well

In addition to being hit hard by a huge downturn in exports, many of these export-dependent countries, like Germany and Japan, have built up large government debts of their own during the last two decades. And, just like the United States, they are now rapidly adding to those deficits with big stimulus packages in the hope of saving their economies. These growing government deficits in the exporting countries will only add to their economic problems later. When their economies hit the Aftershock, their people and economies will be hit harder because their governments are strapped for cash with huge debts, and they will not be able to fund social welfare programs at anywhere near the current, accustomed levels. It will be a real shock, especially to Europe, but also to Japan, to have governments that move from being perhaps overly lavish in their benefits in the past to being much stingier in the future.

How the Bursting Bubbles Will Impact the World

Although all the economies of the world will suffer as the current Bubblequake recession deepens into the coming Aftershock megadepression, some regions will do better than others. Similar to reactions to flu, those who are healthier and stronger before trouble hits tend to hold up better under stress. Here's what we see ahead.

Europe and Japan

As mentioned earlier, the U.S. economy will fare best in the Bubblequake and Aftershock, followed by the countries of Europe and Japan, which have larger shares of their economies devoted to exports than we do, and so will be hit harder when their exports radically decline.

At the same time, Europe and Japan will have to continue to import some goods from other countries, although far less than before. Much more than the United States, Europe, and Japan will continue to import food and energy. To keep manufactured imports to a minimum, these countries will enact protectionist tariffs to protect what remains of their manufacturing industries, and higher taxes on food and energy, slowing the flow of imports into their countries. This will naturally decrease other countries' exports to Europe and

Japan even further than they will have already fallen, adding to the already negative downward spiral for the overall world economy.

Because their export industries will be so hard hit across the board, Europe and Japan will suffer very high unemployment, again with that multiplier effect mentioned earlier, in which each lost job that is directly related to exports is coupled with several additional jobs lost that are indirectly related. Stocks will do quite badly, and real estate values will crash. The European welfare system and many labor protections, currently far more generous than ours, will become increasingly difficult for their governments to afford and will decline to U.S. levels.

But despite this grim picture, some governments in Europe, such as France, Germany, the Scandinavian countries, and Switzerland will not need to default on their debts, but the U.S. government will. Japan will not need to default either. Ironically, although the U.S. economy will do better than these other economies in the Aftershock, we will be forced into default, and they will not. That's because these governments did not depend so heavily on large amounts of foreign capital that will suddenly disappear. Like the United States, these countries will print money out of necessity and suffer extremely high inflation, just as we will. But the value of the euro and the yen will hold up relative to the dollar, because Europe and Japan won't have the massive outflow of capital that we will experience, as investment money pulls out of the United States and flows back to home countries. Europe and Japan will be further protected from the need to default on their debts, because inflation will help reduce their debts, as it will reduce ours. However, U.S. inflation will be much greater than in other countries, because we printed so much more money. Our dollar will be crashing faster and deeper because foreign capital will be leaving.

Massive outflows of capital from the United States into Europe will cause the dollar bubble to pop and the U.S. government to default on its debt. Some governments in Europe (France, Germany, the Scandinavian countries, and Switzerland) will avoid having to default on their debt for three reasons. First, massive inflows of new capital into those European countries and Japan when U.S. and foreign investors sell their U.S. assets and buy euro-denominated assets will keep more capital available for European governments. Second, as many governments seek stimulus spending to save their economies, there will be a smaller and smaller money pie. The U.S. government

Europe Faces a Debt Problem, Not a Euro Problem

Europe is facing a massive debt problem. Whether that debt is denominated in euros or drachmas (the previous Greek currency) doesn't matter. It's still debt. If Greece could get rid of their debt by just dropping the euro, they would have done that a long time ago. And if Greece could pay off its debt to French and German banks by converting back to drachmas, the banks would have agreed to that a long time ago. But the currency isn't the problem, the debt is. That is part of the reason that despite a huge increase in the European debt problem since we wrote the first edition of *Aftershock*, the euro has actually risen about 10 percent relative to the dollar. The euro has been volatile and will undoubtedly see more volatility, but the bottom line is that getting rid of the euro will not solve Europe's debt problem. If only their problems were that easy to solve.

will gobble up a big share of this smaller money pie, going into debt further and faster than some countries in Europe, which will help keep those European governments from running up massive increases in their debt. Third, investors who buy those European government bonds will encourage those European governments not to go too far into debt because they will be worried about a possible bankruptcy.

China

China has had unbelievable growth in the last two decades, and under other circumstances you might expect China to do fairly well despite a global economic downturn—but not in a global *bubble economy*. Much of China's recent growth has been driven by America's and the world's bubble economies. While the economies of some of the poorest countries, such as in Africa, will be in far worse shape, none will suffer the pain of crushed expectations more than China.

In addition to tremendous decreases in their exports and the resulting collapse of the part of their domestic economy that was supported by those exports, China will be hit again, because it has been actively supporting the U.S. dollar for many years, a position that will prove to be particularly devastating to its own finances when the dollar bubble finally pops.

On top of the massive decline in Chinese exports, as well as China's losses due to holding so many falling U.S. dollars, China will also endure a bursting bubble economy of its own. The rapid growth of the Chinese economy created a series of co-linked Chinese bubbles that will have no choice but to burst with devastating force. Their falling bubbles in real estate, stocks, and banking will be particularly dramatic. Construction and related industries, which have grown so rapidly in the past few years, will see huge declines (see sidebar "Now That's Stimulus!"). This will contribute to massive unemployment in China and inflation as the government is forced to print more currency.

These economic shocks will cut deeply into China's economy. When the United States, Europe, and Japan drastically cut their

Now That's Stimulus!

In response to the big decline in Chinese exports in 2008, the Chinese government told their government-run banks to greatly increase their lending. In response, banks lent out $640 billion in just the first quarter of 2009—almost as much as they had lent in all of 2008! This massive increase in lending (primarily for real estate and infrastructure construction) was heavily financed by government-supplied printed money.

According to Lombard Street Associates, a macroeconomic consulting firm in London, the Chinese have been increasing their money supply by more than $120 billion per month. Compare that to our Federal Reserve, which is increasing the U.S. money supply by $85 billion per month as part of its QE2 program of buying bonds. Remember, our economy is much larger than China's (their economy is about one third the size of the U.S. economy) so the relative increase in China's money supply is huge.

The popping of the construction and real estate bubbles will greatly magnify the misery caused by the collapse of their export economy when the Aftershock hits. Right now, it might seem as if all is well with China, but China has a bubble economy and, like all bubbles, most people won't be able to see it until it finally pops.

All of these difficulties will create a populace that is much more supportive of political change in China. Hence, the next Tiananmen Square is likely to have more widespread support than last time, and the Chinese government will have a much more difficult time controlling it.

imports from China, China will experience their great boom in reverse. Unlike in the United States, Chinese citizens are not so used to prosperity that they can't easily return to lower consumption, like eating less meat, for example. And when Chinese consumers do pull back, their still-fragile economy will collapse. In fact, after a while, the Chinese stock market and banking system could suffer a semi shutdown for a period of time. There will likely be a massive migration out of the depressed urban centers and back into the countryside, with widespread poverty and eventual malnutrition because there is no safety net.

A Closer Look at China's Current Bubble Economy: This Dragon Is More Smoke Than Fire

Eye-catching statistics coming out of China indicate the Chinese economic bubble, especially their real estate bubble, is pretty big. For example, the average sales price of an apartment in Beijing is 57 times the average worker's annual income according to SouFun Holdings data reported in the *Wall Street Journal*. In the United States, at the height of our real estate bubble, the average price of a house was barely four times the average worker's income. According to the State Grid Corporation of China (SGCC), a power grid corporation owned by the State Council, 65.4 million houses in 660 cities across China have had zero electricity consumption for six months in succession, indicating that they are unoccupied. This is largely due to overbuilding and the inability of Chinese to buy homes at current prices.

Many investors are buying Chinese homes waiting to flip them at higher prices. These investors consider empty homes to be gold in the bank. They are also being richly rewarded. *Monthly* increases in 2010 prices have been between 5 percent and 10 percent in many major cities, including Shenzhen and Beijing. Of course, all Chinese statistics are suspect. It's hard to know exactly what's going on over there. Some people say that all U.S. statistics are suspect, too and, there is some truth to that. But, we'd like to think that Chinese statistics are even more suspect.

Nonetheless, the fundamentals for China don't look good. After seeing exports decline by nearly 25 percent and millions of people move from urban areas where export workers were being laid off back to rural areas where there were no jobs, the Chinese government panicked and began a massive loan program thorough their government controlled banks. In the first quarter of 2009, Chinese banks lent more money than they lent in all of 2008, heavily with printed money (just as our Federal Reserve prints money). For a variety of reasons, Chinese lending is front-loaded to the early part of the year, but that figure is still telling.

Construction and Real Estate Are Driving China's Bubble Economy

In China, land is owned by the government. Local governments can sell this land to real estate developers and pocket the proceeds. So sales of land have now become a critical source of revenue for many local governments. It is also a critical source of money for corrupt government officials. Hence, there is a big incentive for governments to sell land and encourage more development even if there is no need for it. And, with rapidly rising prices and easy credit, developers are more than happy to buy the land and build under the assumption that prices will continue to soar even if they cannot sell the land or real estate immediately. As an added incentive, the developers may be pocketing some of the money gained through corruption.

The Chinese construction and real estate bubbles have been key drivers of the recent growth in China's bubble economy, even more so than these equivalent bubbles in the U.S. bubble economy. Possibly as much as half of China's bank lending is to property-related businesses. Even large industrial manufacturing companies are setting up real estate development divisions to fatten their profits in the real estate boom. And all of this is in addition to massive government infrastructure construction spending that has been thrown on top of real estate construction spending.

Some sources say that construction now accounts for almost 30 percent of the Chinese economy. By comparison, at the height of the U.S. real estate bubble, construction made up about 15 percent of our economy. At the peak of their real estate booms, construction represented only 20 percent of the economies of Spain and Dubai.

Another sign of a China bubble is that Chinese real estate investors are starting to play lots of little financial games to maximize the amount of money they can borrow to buy more real estate. It sounds a little like the loose lending practices and liar loans of our own real estate bubble.

With so much incentive to build, plus very easy lending and lots of government corruption to incentivize government officials to encourage building, it seems like a situation ripe for an historic real estate bubble. And, of course, that real estate bubble is powering the rest of the Chinese economy's massive current growth.

The Greatest Economists and Government Planners in the Universe?

Despite the evidence of China's bubble economy, many people still say that all the growth in China is just a result of its outstanding government economic policies. In fact, some would have you believe that the smartest economists in the world are running China's economy to perfection. It is truly unsettling that so many people believe that a Communist party-controlled government bureaucracy could really run an economy better than a free market. Few people seem to be concerned that this government bureaucracy could be making some of the worst economic decisions that any government could be making right now.

Where has all this respect for a huge and corrupt government bureaucracy come from? Probably the same place support for all bubbles comes from—*cheerleaders*. Investment analysts and economists are hoping against hope that the Chinese are experiencing economic progress rather than a bubble and it will help pull the U.S. economy out of its downturn, even if all the evidence points toward a massive Chinese bubble.

Is China's Bubble Starting to Pop?

There are a few early signs. For example, lending in the first quarter of 2010 was down 43 percent from the first quarter of 2009 according to the Chinese central bank. China's GDP is slowing somewhat. And lending (made possible by money printing) is also slowing.

There is also some scattered evidence that China's real estate bubble may be starting to pop, at least in some cities. According to the market research firm Dragonomics, real estate prices in nine major Chinese cities fell 4.9 percent in April 2011 from a year earlier.

However, we haven't seen enough nationwide evidence to think that a big pop is underway yet, although the economy is clearly slowing down. And even once it starts, it can take time to really affect the economy. Our home prices peaked around the summer of 2005, but the big impact on the economy wasn't felt until 2008, although real estate was clearly in trouble in 2007. Of course, like its stock market, China's real estate market could also be much more volatile than the United States going from dramatic growth to dramatic decreases more rapidly.

Why Does All This Matter to Us?

It matters to us because China's growth has been one of the few bright spots in the world's bubble economy. It has helped drive forward the economies of countries such as Brazil, Australia, and Germany, which are big exporters to China. Everyone wonders how Germany can have significant growth while the rest of Europe is struggling. Germany is the world's biggest exporter, and a lot of those exports go to China. Co-author Bob Wiedemer will always remember watching a Chinese businessman and a German businessman at a trade show in Guangzhou, China speaking to each other in English. It emphasized how important a trade partner China is to Germany and, as a side note, how important the English language is as a universal common second language.

So, China is not only spurring a lot of growth in other countries, including exporters in the United States, but it is also boosting the hopes of professional stock market investors for a stronger United States and world economy. If China's economic growth slows significantly, the U.S. stock market will take a hit. Growth in China's GDP is already expected to fall from 11 percent last year to around 9 percent this year, and that slowdown has already started to bother the U.S. stock market.

However, we wouldn't expect a wholesale popping of China's economy to happen in 2011 because the government can do a lot to keep it alive for a while longer—but the next few years could be a different matter. Growth of only 5 percent or less would be a big shock to the stock market. At that point, people will more clearly see that China's massive growth was, in the face of falling exports and a downturn in the rest of the world's economy, really just a government-induced bubble.

Such a slowdown would also be a big shock to the commodities markets, which have been driven heavily by China. Almost the entire growth in demand for oil since 2005 can be traced to China and to countries that supply China with materials. The same is true for many other commodities as well, such as steel and copper. Even some growth in the price of agricultural commodities, such as corn, can be traced to China and, in particular, its growing demand for more meat in their people's diets.

As we have mentioned earlier, such a slowdown in commodities prices or the stock market could also affect gold. Gold is having a very good run now but we still think it is vulnerable to a very large downturn in commodities or the stock market, although there are increasing signs of decoupling.

China has long been a country of mystery. Exactly when and how the Chinese bubble will pop is also somewhat mysterious. But, there is no question that the country is currently on an unsustainable path and that the bubble will pop. This dragon is blowing more smoke than fire.

The Middle East and Elsewhere

With the exception of Israel, which will react more like Europe and Japan, the Middle East will look a lot like China in many ways. The big problem for the Middle East is oil. The massive decline in economic activity worldwide will dramatically decrease the demand for oil. Plus, the world's largest consumer, the United States, will be faced with skyrocketing prices for imported oil because the dollar has fallen. So, demand from the United States, which will be declining because of the terrible economy, will take an even bigger hit because of the high price.

Although exploration for oil will dramatically decline, it will take many years for supply to decrease enough to match up with rapidly falling demand. The collapsing demand will ultimately push oil down to the $10 to $25 (in 2011 dollars) per barrel range.

Such a dramatic decrease in income will devastate the Middle East, especially because some of these countries are already significantly poorer than the United States, Europe, and Japan, even before the world bubble economy bursts. Like China, the Middle East will suffer massive unemployment. And like China, the global mega-depression will likely accelerate political turmoil, especially in the Kingdom of Saudi Arabia. The monarchy there could quite possibly go the way of the monarchy of Iran, since there is already considerable underlying tension in the Kingdom.

The Green Economy Won't Produce a Lot of Green

Although there may be some good green technologies in the works, as the economy goes down, so will investments in the green economy. In fact, the investment climate for green tech/clean tech will turn increasingly negative as we go through Phase I, given the falling stock market and returns on investment. In such a down market, good investments will be taken down along with the bad. Also, demand will fall as the economy falls, as there is less spending on capital goods and construction. A final blow will hit when the government debt bubble pops in Phase II since government subsidies will be eliminated. Subsidies are very important for a lot of green technologies. Some of those subsidies may be eliminated before Phase II, in 2011 and 2012.

Many investors are pumping money into green technologies, and no doubt some will succeed in making money. Some even seem to hope it will be the next financial bubble. We think the clean tech investment boom will be the Bubble That Never Will Be.

Long term, we will need to greatly improve the productivity of our energy sector, just as we will need to improve the productivity of other sectors of our economy. But, like other sectors of our economy, this will involve far more than just new technologies.

Outside of the Middle East, many other countries will also suffer. When the world's bubble economy falls, the already very poor countries of Africa and Asia will be truly devastated. With commodities and mineral exports slowing to a trickle, citizens of the poorest countries will face a real struggle for basic survival. However, it is quite likely that when localized famines and epidemics start to grow larger and larger, the richer, more developed nations, like the United States, will eventually step in and help. We won't have all the money we did before, but we will still likely have the money and political will to help other countries who desperately need survival support.

If the World's Bubble Economy Is Hit Harder Than the U.S. Bubble Economy, Won't That Be Good for the Dollar?

No! This is the most common misconception about the value of the dollar. Even if the rest of the world is pretty well devastated economically, and it will be, the value of the dollar will still fall relative to the euro, yen, and other major currencies. That's because the value of a currency is *not* a reflection of whose overall economy is better relative to the others, but a matter of *supply and demand* (see Chapter 4).

If people see a risk that the dollar will decline in value due to inflation (rising supply) or to other investors becoming disenchanted with the poor performance of their U.S. investments (falling demand), they will stop buying dollar-denominated investments, thus reducing the demand for the dollar and further reducing the dollar's value.

That initial concern about the dollar becomes a self-fulfilling prophecy because as a small number of investors stop buying dollars, the dollar will fall, causing other investors to become more concerned and stop buying dollars. At some point, the market can change quickly from people merely reducing their purchases of dollars to a full scale panic where they try to sell off whatever dollar-denominated investments they still have, causing a traumatic collapse in the dollar's value. Unfortunately, the majority of investors will not be able to sell their dollars fast enough to get out, and their investment money will go to Money Heaven (see Chapter 4).

However, the dollar, despite its collapse in value, will still be one of the most widely traded currencies simply because of the size of the U.S. economy and the size of its imports and exports. As such, the dollar will retain its role as a reserve currency. Even the much-maligned euro will continue to function as a reserve currency, as well.

If the Rest of the World Is Collapsing, Won't That Be Good for Gold?

Yes! Gold will especially benefit from the collapse of economies around the globe because it is a favorite safe haven investment for people in Asia and the Middle East. Those countries buy most of the gold in the world. In fact only 10 percent of the world's total gold is purchased by the United States. India, on the other hand, represents almost 20 percent of the world's gold demand and will be eager to get its hands on more as insecurity rises. Demand for gold has been exploding in China partly due to fear of inflation. It now represents nearly 20 percent of world gold demand, according to the World Gold Council. So, it is important to view gold from a global

A $100,000 Toyota Camry?

An important side effect of the dollar bubble collapse is that the price of imported goods will soar. Imported cars, for example, will be priced so high that the United States will no longer buy a significant number. This is the market's way of restoring trade balance after so many years of imbalanced trade. Some things we will have to import, such as oil, but it will be very expensive. Hence, gasoline prices in the United States will easily reach $12 to $15 a gallon (on an inflation-adjusted basis, in 2011 dollars), while the price for oil plummets around the world due to the huge economic slowdown and the drop in demand.

Other goods will need to be imported because we no longer have the facilities to make them, such as toys, clothing, and some electronics. Again, they will be expensive but we will still buy them, since, even with higher prices it will be hard to beat the imported prices, when the alternative is to create new factories in the United States with very high cost capital and with relatively high cost labor.

The lower dollar will make our exports much cheaper for other countries, and we will do a booming business in exporting necessities, such as coal and wheat. However, most other goods will be hard to export because the demand will have collapsed, and other countries will likely use import restrictions to protect the remaining companies in their countries that still produce those goods.

Coal is an especially good export for the United States because many countries don't have it, yet will still need it to produce electricity, even during the depths of the economic downturn. Plus, we have an awful lot of it, and it will be dirt cheap for other countries to import because of the collapsed dollar.

perspective and not a U.S. perspective. The rest of the world looks at gold as a very viable and particularly safe investment. People at every economic level often own or want to own gold. It is much more favored culturally around the world than it is in the United States and even Europe.

Instability in Asian and Middle Eastern economies will encourage investors in those countries to buy a lot more gold, further accelerating the rising gold bubble. Yes, gold is another bubble on the ascent, and eventually it, too, will fall. But that is a very long way off and, in the meantime, you might as well learn how to profit from its coming meteoric rise (see Chapter 7).

International Investment Recommendations

Our detailed investment suggestions are offered in the next two chapters, but for those of you who just can't wait, here's your executive summary:

Our best advice for U.S. investors looking to invest in foreign markets: In the short term, there may be ways to profit, if you are sophisticated about these kinds of investments, and you very actively and correctly manage them. However, in the long term: *Stay away!* Both the low-end manufacturing and high-end manufacturing economies and the resource-driven economies we just discussed will not recover until America's economy recovers. And since America's economy won't recover until after the dollar bubble pops, there is no reason to invest overseas for many years.

Obviously, there are always exceptions but, in general, investments will not do well because overseas economies will be in much worse shape than the U.S. economy. They are simply more dependent on exports, not as diverse, and not as flexible as we are. Plus, they invested heavily in the U.S. economy, which is about to cost them dearly.

Our best advice for foreign investors looking to invest in their own markets: If the long-term investments in your countries are not good for U.S. investors, they certainly aren't any better for you. Short term there are opportunities, but it is a bubble, so you have to be aware of that. Even long term, there are always individual exceptions but, in general, when economies nose-dive, normal stock and real estate investments in your home countries will lose you tons of money. Gold and certain currencies, such as Canadian dollars, Swiss francs, Norwegian krone, and even euros, in the form of short-term debt instruments, offer easy outs for those looking for returns above normal interest rates. Shorting stocks will also be quite profitable for those willing and able to move into that arena, as many foreign stocks will be plummeting just like U.S. stocks, only faster in many cases.

Our best advice for foreign investors looking to invest in the U.S. markets: Given that the value of the dollar will fall significantly, low-cost investments in the United States will eventually become quite profitable for foreign investors. In fact, this is where a great deal of money will be made in the next couple of decades and, unlike the bubble money of the past, which will largely disappear, the money made by smart foreign investors in the United States after the dollar bubble pops will last because it's not bubble money.

The biggest challenge is timing. Most foreign investors will think that U.S. investments have hit bottom when, in fact, they still have a long way down to go. By jumping in too soon they will lose an enormous amount of money. A simple rule for anyone interested in purchasing U.S. assets is to refrain from investing until *after* the dollar bubble pops and stabilizes.

PART

II

AFTERSHOCK DANGERS
AND PROFITS

CHAPTER 6

Covering Your Assets

HOW NOT TO LOSE MONEY

For most people, the advice we are about to give you on how not to lose money in the Aftershock is far more important than any of our good investment ideas (offered in the next chapter) about how to cash in on it. We understand that no one likes to hear this. Most of us find *making* money far more interesting than simply not losing it. But knowing how to protect yourself is absolutely crucial to surviving and thriving in the months and years ahead, so please don't skip this part. If you only pay attention to one page in this book, this should be the one.

Let us say at the outset that this chapter discusses protection strategies *for the long term*. In the shorter term, these protective steps are not immediately necessary. There is no immediate crisis or need for panic. But there is a real need to know what is coming and to learn now how to protect yourself from what is ahead.

For the long term, there are three simple rules for where *not* to invest as the dollar and other bubbles fall:

Rule #1: Get ready to exit stocks.

Rule #2: Stay away from real estate until after the dollar bubble pops.

Rule #3: Stay away from long-term bonds and all fixed-rate investments (including whole life insurance and annuities).

153

We said three *simple* rules; we did not say *easy*. After years of investing in stocks, real estate, and fixed-rate investments, we know that the idea of pulling out of these bulwarks of wealth building may feel counterintuitive and just plain wrong. Here's why you have to bite the Bubblequake bullet and do it anyway *before* the dollar bubble pops.

This Is Not a Down Market Cycle; It's a Big Multibubble Pop, Pop, Pop

As we've said many times, we are not in the middle of a down market cycle. The economy is not merely fluctuating back and forth between an "up" business cycle and a "down" business cycle. The overall U.S. and world economy is fundamentally *evolving*, and therefore we are not going backward to whence we came. Instead, we are going forward to where we have never been before. At this moment in history, forward involves the bursting of a series of interconnected economic bubbles. On the way up, these expanding bubbles created tremendous wealth both here and around the globe. On the way down, these bursting bubbles will destroy a very impressive amount of wealth, as well. How much of *your* wealth will be destroyed in the months and years ahead is entirely up to you. Ignore the problem, or react as you may have in the past, and things could get away from you rather fast.

Each falling bubble will put increasing downward pressure on the others, creating a combined, cascading, multibubble fall. Hence, our key advice during the Bubblequake and Aftershock is to purge your mind right now of the false idea that if you just wait long enough, economic gravity will somehow disappear and the asset values that are currently falling (like stocks, real estate, etc.) will defy gravity and automatically return to an "up cycle." These popping bubbles are not going to float back up just because we want them to!

People who tell you otherwise are simply trying to cheerlead the economy. As you may recall from the discussion in Chapter 4 about the psychology of how people react to changing economic conditions, we are currently in the Market Cycles stage of psychology regarding the evolving economic collapse. In the face of the evidence, people can no longer say everything is fine, so the next best way to ignore reality is to say we are experiencing a "down" market cycle. We know beyond any doubt that this is no more than cheerleading because these same experts who are now insisting we will return to an up cycle soon, never once said a word about a coming *down cycle* back when stocks and real estate were soaring high. Yet now we are supposed to believe that an automatic and reliable up cycle is inevitably on its way. It's all just part of the broader attempt to cheerlead the economy and keep investors relaxed. Just be patient, they say. Everything will get better soon. The economy (and your particular stocks, bonds, real estate, etc.) will be just fine.

Please don't fall for this! Multiple, linked, collapsing bubbles cannot and will not magically reinflate.

"I got out of tulips after the market collapsed, but I'm slowly getting back in. Especially pink ones."

Long Term versus Short Term

Before we dive into the details of our three rules for protecting assets, we want to be very clear about the difference between the *long term* (most likely beginning sometime between 2013 and 2016) and the *short term* (prior to 2013). In the long term, rising inflation will eventually top 10 percent and higher. Eventually, interest rates will rise even higher. We believe that not long after inflation exceeds 10 percent, investor psychology will significantly change enough to fully pop all the bubbles, including the dollar and government debt bubbles. Prior to that occurring, in the short and medium term, inflation will be less of a concern and investor psychology will still be relatively good regarding most U.S. assets, with the exception of U.S. real estate, which will generally continue to decline.

Therefore, the long term is *not* the same as the short term. In fact, in the short term we may see the exact opposite of what will occur later, depending on how aggressively the federal government fights to stimulate the economy and save the dollar. As we have already pointed out, many of the government's actions designed to stimulate the economy in the short term will only make things that much worse in the long term when the dollar and government debt bubbles finally pop. But in the short term, they can have a lot of temporary, short term benefits that many people will confuse with a recovery (which we certainly are not having).

Some of the most powerful *short-term* benefits of the actions by the federal government include directly boosting the stock market, as evident by the huge stock rally of 2009 after Federal Reserve began its massive money printing operations called quantitative easing (QE), in which the Fed purchased $1.7 *trillion* worth of Treasury, Freddie Mac, and Fannie Mae bonds. The almost direct correlation between QE and the rise of the S&P 500 is shown in Figure 6.1.

The Fed stopped its bond purchases in April 2010, and the stock market promptly ran into trouble. Less than two months later, the May Flash Crash occurred, followed by a negative summer for the stock market. Things were looking down for stocks. But, for Federal Reserve chairman, Ben Bernanke, that was no problem. Uncle Ben (Uncle Sam takes your money; Uncle Ben makes your money) had the solution and announced another round of massive money printing. If QE1 worked wonders, maybe QE2 would work even more wonders—and it did.

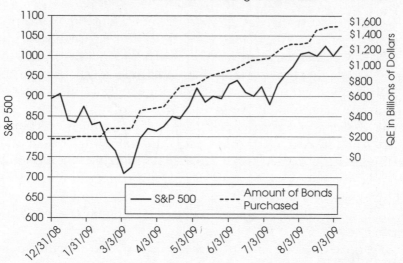

Figure 6.1 Correlation of Quantitative Easing (Fed Money Printing) with S&P 500
When the Fed Prints Money, Investors Listen
Source: Federal Reserve and Standard and Poor's.

As can be seen from Figure 6.2, almost as soon as QE2 was announced, the stock market headed back up in an almost unbroken line through the end of the year and continued to go up into the early part of 2011. The market would have finished *down* 15 percent or more in 2010 (as defined by the S&P 500), but with Uncle Ben's magic money printing machine, it finished *up* 11 percent. If Ben keeps printing money in the second half of 2011, it's quite likely that the stock market will continue its upward march, or at least not have a major collapse.

So when you read in the sections that follow about our long-term rule for protection in the stock market, keep in mind that in the case of stocks, the long term and the short term are not the same thing. Of course, no one knows exactly what the Fed will do next or exactly how it (and many other changing factors) will impact the market in the next several months, so we can't give you a rule for the short term, other than to say anything is possible and if you are in the stock market now, be prepared to get out quickly when investor sentiment changes. Better yet, you could play it safe and get out *before* investor sentiment changes. Just be aware that if you choose to do so, you may miss out on more of the potential upside

Figure 6.2 Growth of the S&P 500 after Ben Bernanke Announced His Second Round of Money Printing in Late August 2010
The stock market thinks you can never print too much money—printed money is Miracle-Gro for stocks

Source: Standard and Poor's.

before the Fed's medicine (money printing) becomes a poison (causing inflation) that will eventually pop the stock bubble. This can be hard to time, so if you have already gotten out of the market, don't worry; you have protected your assets, which is most important.

In regard to real estate, our long term rule is the same as our short term rule regarding real estate: *Stay away!* The section below on real estate will explain why.

And our long-term rule regarding bonds and other fixed-rate debt is not dramatically different from our short-term rule. In the long term, stay away. In the short term, stay away or proceed with caution. Fixed-rate debt offers only low returns and faces very high risk as interest rates rise, which will surely happen as inflation rises. If you want to own fixed-rate assets in the short term, chose those that mature in 5 years, or less, because they will fall less sharply than longer-term debt, and be prepared to get out of these quickly when interest rates start to go up. Even a small increase in interest rates means a big drop in asset value.

Much more on all of this is offered in the sections that follow. We just want to make sure that you understand that the short term and the long term are *not* the same. *This economy is evolving.*

Rule Number One: Get Ready to Exit Stocks

Just after the financial crisis and stock market crash in late 2008, coauthor Bob Wiedemer had dinner with a friend. After a few drinks, the man revealed that he had recently made one of the biggest financial mistakes of his life. A fan of our first book, Bob's friend admitted he only half-believed our 2006 predictions in *America's Bubble Economy* about the coming Bubblequake, and therefore, he sold only about half of his stocks prior to the 2008 crash. For sure, this guy saved himself from what could have been twice the loss by selling half his holdings near the market peak. But he felt terrible having not sold the other half, too.

Let Bob's friend spare you his learning curve. Despite the stock market rally in 2009 after the big crash, stocks are vulnerable to a crash or a series of smaller downturns, and will eventually fall much further than the crash of late 2008.

As we said before, the long term and the short term are not the same.

In the short term, more massive money printing by the Federal Reserve could continue to support the stock market and could even push it higher in 2011 and beyond, assuming there are no Black Swan events that spook investors. In fact, if the Fed wanted (and if there was enough political support for it, which there may not be), continued massive money printing could potentially push the Dow back to its 2007 all-time high of 14,164 or higher. (See the Appendix

Since the Financial Crisis of 2008, the Only Time the Stock Market Has Gone Up is When the Fed Prints Money

That's right. Since the financial crisis began in late 2008, the stock market has only gone up when the Fed has printed money via QE. The stock market began its rebound from the financial crisis lows in March 2009 with the beginning of the first round of money printing (QE1). That ended on April 1, 2010 and only *five weeks later*, the market faltered and we had the May Flash Crash. The market continued to struggle through the summer of 2010 and only began climbing again when Ben Bernanke announced that the Fed would soon print more money (QE2). It will be interesting to see what happens after QE2 ends on June 30, 2011. Past history has shown that when the bubbles start to pop, the stock market needs a lot of printed money support if it is going to go up.

on possible market manipulation for further thoughts on how high the market could go.)

However, *in the long term*, inflation and interest rates will climb, and the stock market (and all our asset bubbles) will fall. Again, if we did not already have a multibubble economy on the way down, big economic stimuli, like massive government deficit spending and massive money printing, might do the trick of jump starting some real economic growth. But we do have a multibubble economy on the way down, and big stimuli funded by more massive government borrowing and more massive money printing are only going to make things much worse in the *long term*, when inflation rises, investors lose their appetite for buying our debt, and the bubbles fully pop.

When to Exit Stocks?

In the *short term*, the answer depends on your particular investment style, goals, and risk appetite. Some people have already exited the stock market completely, and that's fine. (In about five years, you will be very happy you did.)

If you want to own stocks for a while longer to take advantage of any potential additional upside, in large part driven by massive money printing by the Fed, please be aware that at any time things can change very quickly, depending on what the government decides to do. It can also change due to events in the Middle East, Europe, China, no or slow economic growth, rising unemployment, more bad news for real estate, or any wildcard events that may occur. Most people will stay in the market and will lose money when it falls because they don't think it is a bubble; they think it's a bull in a downturn. It will be quite difficult to tell when the market has topped out and is going down long term. As they say on Wall Street, nobody rings a bell when the market peaks.

This new investment environment takes very active, time-consuming, and complex portfolio management. Unless your financial advisors have the correct macroeconomic view of what is going on (very few do), you will essentially be flying solo. Therefore, you will need to watch the news, have the correct macroeconomic view of what is occurring, and know how to apply it to your particular investments. (Our newsletter and other services can help with that. For details, call (800) 994-0018 or go to www.aftershockeconomy .com.)

Please also be aware that eventually the short term will evolve into the long term, and at some point you will want to exit stocks before they begin to drop significantly. The fall may occur in a few stages with some stabilization between the drops, or all at once. There is an increasing possibility of a catastrophic collapse that could happen very quickly. Once the market starts to rapidly crash, it will become increasingly difficult to sell your stocks because there will be so few buyers. If everyone is running for the gates at the same time, most people can't get out.

One action the government might take to try to slow down this financial death spiral is to halt stock market trading. At a certain point, market declines could be very large—like a Flash Crash that doesn't rebound. Hence, government and market officials may decide that the best option is simply to close the market for a few days or a week to let investors settle down and get their confidence back. They might make changes to limit high frequency trading as an excuse for closing the market. Blaming the market's decline on high frequency trading or some other technical issue is certainly a lot better than blaming it on a fundamental lack of confidence. These market stoppages—there may be several—might even work short term, but more likely, they won't and they certainly won't work long term. The downward spiral will simply resume after the stoppages since the fundamentals won't have changed.

Ultimately, automated selling may be completely blocked. In addition, after a market stoppage, selling may be limited when it re-opens and there may even be incentives for buying stocks. Shorting stocks may also be limited or stopped completely.

Given that it is nearly impossible to time these market declines perfectly, you will likely either get out of the market a bit too early or get out a bit too late. Which would you prefer?

How Long to Stay Out of the Market?

As a general rule, once the stock market begins to crash, stay clear of all stocks, until each one of the interconnected asset bubbles has fully popped, especially the dollar bubble. There are a few small exceptions to this rule (see Chapter 7), but in general, *get out* and *stay out* of your stocks until after the dollar and government debt bubbles fully pop and inflation stabilizes.

Only the correct macroeconomic analysis can give you this kind of accurate road map over several years. What macroeconomic analysis cannot do is tell us what any individual stock will do week to week or even month to month. As we said, in the *short term*, stocks could continue to hold up and even move up further. But the overall *long-term* trend is down. Stocks could drop sharply at any time with little warning, and then for a while, could come back up. As the market goes down in stages, resist the temptation to throw money away on what may look like bargains. Do not get lured back into stocks *until after the dollar bubble has fully popped*, if you still have any interest in investing in stocks at that point (most people won't). Also, asset purchases may be a better investment at that point, which we will discuss in detail in a later book.

We discussed the timing of the dollar bubble pop in Chapter 4. It could happen as early as 2013, but more likely in 2015, 2016, or even later, depending on what the United States and other governments do in the fierce fight to save the dollar. These actions will only delay, not prevent, the dollar fall. As mentioned earlier, it is very hard to predict exactly when the dollar bubble will pop because it is so heavily influenced by additional money printing by the Fed, and by the willingness and ability of governments, like China, to intervene in the foreign exchange markets, and, most importantly, by foreign and domestic investor psychology. When the expected recovery does not occur, it seems reasonable to assume that massive money printing, massively growing deficits, and rising inflation and interest rates will all have increasingly negative effects on investor sentiment over time.

Another factor that makes precision timing difficult is the real possibility that the stock market is occasionally manipulated by certain powerful forces (see the Appendix).

You don't have to leave the market all at once, but you should do it over a reasonable period of time. In the short term, stock prices

This "Recovery" Is 100 Percent Fake

That's right. The recovery is fake. It is *completely* a result of massive increases in government borrowing. The cheerleaders like to tell you that the economy has rebounded. We had government stimulus earlier, but now they say that the Animal Spirits have taken over and the recovery is running on its own. Ha! The recovery is *only* stimulus. Let's look at the numbers:

In 2007, the GDP was $14.0 trillion.
In 2010, the GDP was $14.6 trillion.

That's a net increase of $600 billion. Now let's compare that to the increase in government borrowing:

In 2007 the US government borrowed and spent $163 billion.
In 2010 the US government borrowed and spent almost $1.4 *trillion*.
That's a net increase of over $1.2 trillion.

That means the entire increase in our GDP can be attributed to the increase in government borrowing and spending. In fact, the increase in government borrowing and spending is almost *two times* the increase in our GDP. Therefore, the economy is doing very poorly indeed. Without massive increases in government borrowing and spending, there would be no "recovery" at all.

As additional evidence of how much the U.S. government has increased its borrowing, in February 2011 we borrowed $222 billion. That's almost 40 percent more in just one month than we borrowed in *all* of 2007.

will go up and down, but long term they most definitely will go down, down, down, so you should sell them within some reasonable time frame, depending on your personal views, how much you believe our macro view, and how close to the edge you are willing to push it. This same advice applies to the stocks in your 401(k) plan or other retirement accounts. Within what you believe is a reasonable timeframe; begin to move your money out of stocks and into cash.

The next chapter offers ideas about what you can do to make money during the coming Aftershock, but right now, you need to wrap your mind around this very difficult to accept idea: In the long term, *stay away from investing in stocks*. This is also true for U.S. investors looking to invest in foreign stocks and for foreign investors looking to invest in the United States or in their own countries. *Stay away!*

While it is true that profits can be made in any market as long as it is moving either up or down, trying to survive and profit in this stock market will take an extraordinary amount of time-consuming, active, and complex management, with precision timing and a good dose of plain luck. Very few people will do it successfully, and even those who do may not be able to do it again, as things keep changing. The only exception to our no-stocks rule is if you are extraordinarily talented and have a whole lot of time on your hands, or if you are working with a very sophisticated money manager who closely follows the macroeconomic analysis of *Aftershock* and can actively—and correctly—play the ups and downs.

Rule Number Two: Stay Away from Real Estate Until After the Dollar Bubble Pops

Unless you find an exceptional bargain that you can realistically flip fairly quickly to a ready and qualified buyer, investing in real estate is not a good idea until after the dollar and all the other bubbles burst. Despite what the cheerleaders want you to believe, real estate prices have not hit bottom. All real estate now is basking in the glow of ultra-low mortgage rates, which won't last indefinitely.

As inflation and interest rates rise (see Chapter 3), mortgage rates will rise, too, shrinking the already small pool of able buyers even smaller and growing the already large pool of real estate inventory even larger—further driving down prices. As inflation and interest rates go up and eventually the dollar bubble falls (see Chapter 4), the overall economy will sink and unemployment will rise, pushing real estate prices even lower—much lower than most people can imagine today. As much as rising interest rates will harm the stock market, they will be even more toxic to the real estate market because high interest rate mortgages and tough credit requirements will put home buying out of reach for most Americans.

So any rah-rah advice you get about grabbing cheap real estate now before home values go back up is just plain wrong. Stay away from real estate! Do not be tempted by past profits you may have made or wish you had made. Now is not the time. Rest assured there will plenty of *real* real estate bargains in the future.

That said, we all have to live somewhere, so where should it be? In general, from a financial point of view, now is a good time to rent rather than to buy, so if you haven't bought a home yet, keep renting and feel free to skip the next section about what to do if you currently own a home or other real estate.

What to Do with Owned Real Estate

As we have already said, real estate values are not going to significantly recover, even if they move up slightly in some areas of the country in the short term. Over time, with rising mortgage rates and growing unemployment, real estate prices will continue to fall, and will certainly crash once the dollar bubble pops. So if you own a primary residence, vacation home, investment property, commercial real estate, or farmland, the coming months and years will likely present some challenges. Here's what we recommend and why.

Vacation Homes, Investment Properties, and Commercial Real Estate

Unless you have very compelling attachments to or very strong sentimental interests in any vacation homes, sell them now. You can always just rent when you go to your favorite vacation spots. Even if selling a vacation home now will result in a financial loss, it will not be as much as you will surely lose later. Ditto for investment property and commercial real estate. *Sell them all now* before prices fall even lower. We are nowhere near a bottom in real estate values. Now is the time to get out.

Later on (after all the bubbles pop), if you have the means, you will be able to buy vacation homes and other real estate very, very cheaply, but only if you don't lose all your money in the collapse.

So be practical and wise, and resist the cheerleaders. Later you are going to look like a genius.

Your Primary Residence

For your primary home, the situation is trickier. Many people have a sentimental attachment to their homes and may not want to sell them to capture their equity before their values fall further. In addition, it may not be easy to find an equivalent rental. As we said before, strictly from a financial standpoint, you probably should sell your home now and rent instead, but we understand that for many people it is difficult. None of the authors have sold their primary residences. However, if you are planning to move or retire in the near future, by all means, speed up that process and sell your home now. Don't wait for home values to pick up significantly in the near future. They won't.

Get Fixed

If you are going to keep your home, make sure you have a *fixed-rate* mortgage, not an adjustable-rate loan. If you have an adjustable-rate mortgage, we suggest you try to refinance to a low fixed-rate mortgage. Mortgage rates are at historic lows. No one knows exactly when interest rates will begin to significantly rise, but it could be sooner rather than later. If you can, move now to lock in a low rate before it's too late.

With a fixed-rate mortgage, the monthly payments on your home will be dramatically reduced by high inflation when the dollar bubble pops. Of course, so will the value of your home, but at least you will have a good, cheap place to live for as long as you wish. Just the opposite will be true for anyone holding an adjustable-rate mortgage. The rapidly increasing monthly payments will quickly make repaying the loan difficult if not impossible. So refinancing from an adjustable-rate to a fixed-rate loan is absolutely essential.

What about refinancing an already fixed-rate mortgage? That only makes sense if you can lower your current mortgage interest rate by at least 0.75 percent. If your saving will be less than that, it is probably not worth the trouble and expense to refinance.

Pay It Off Faster or Slower?

Once upon a time, accelerated mortgage repayment made a lot of good sense because it got you out of debt and out of paying interest that much sooner. But not so going forward in this popping-bubble environment. It may seem counter-intuitive, but you do not want to pay off your low-interest, fixed-rate mortgage any faster than is minimally required. Remember, high inflation is going to all but wipe out this kind of debt for you in the not too distant future because you will be repaying your mortgage with "cheaper" dollars. However, you do have to be able to make enough money to pay your mortgage payment each month or you'll risk losing your home.

Pull Out Equity?

Rather than paying your mortgage off faster, there is a very good argument to be made for paying it off even more slowly, given that inflation will rise and therefore each year you will be repaying this loan with cheaper and cheaper dollars. High inflation will essentially make your fixed-rate mortgage payment close to free because it will be tiny compared to the number of dollars you will have as the value of the dollar drops and your income goes up more or less with inflation, assuming you still have a job or inflation-protected assets to sell, such as gold.

If you share our point of view on this, you may want to consider extracting some of the equity from your home to invest elsewhere (see next chapter), to the extent that you feel comfortable and agree with our forecasts. This clearly has risks—the big one being difficulty in paying your monthly mortgage payments if you do not save and properly invest the excess proceeds from your home. But, as soon as high inflation hits, you will be able to pay your fixed-rate mortgage payments with cheaper and cheaper dollars.

What about pulling out equity with a "reverse mortgage," in which a buyer pays you each month for your property, while you remain in your home? Under normal circumstances, a reverse mortgage can be a good idea for some people, especially later in life. However, under current and future circumstances, reverse mortgages are a very bad idea because inflation will eat away at the value of your fixed payments. Even if your payment is tied to the official inflation rate, it is very likely that the bank or mortgage buyer you are dealing with will go under. In time, even government guarantees of reverse mortgage payments will not be honored (once the government is out of money), and you will not get another penny for your property.

Rather than a reverse mortgage, consider selling your property and investing that money for protection and growth before and after the dollar bubble pops.

What to Do If You Are "Underwater," Facing Foreclosure, or Cannot Make Your Mortgage Payments

As we already mentioned, the best plan is to refinance to a low, fixed-rate mortgage that will lower your monthly payments to an amount you can manage. If you cannot refinance, walking away from the house can be a good idea if your income does not depend on your credit score or you don't have high-value assets that could be jeopardized, based on the laws in your state.

If you are underwater (owe more than the home is worth) or you are facing foreclosure, be on the lookout for any mortgage bailout programs you may qualify for in the next couple of years. On the other hand, it is not a good idea to throw good money after bad and for many people who are underwater in their mortgages, walking away might be best, depending on your individual situation.

Even if all else fails and you cannot refinance, don't qualify for any bailouts, and simply cannot make your monthly mortgage payments, you do not necessarily have to abandon your property immediately. Even now, it can take a year or longer from the time you stop paying your mortgage until you are evicted. After all the bubbles pop, it will take much longer to be forced out of a property because the courts will be so backed up. So keep paying your mortgage as long as you can, and if you must stop paying, you can stay in your home as a squatter. When the dollar and government debt bubbles pop, banks will be overwhelmed and foreclosures will become increasingly harder to enforce. You will probably be able to stay in your home as a squatter for longer than you think. But not forever. Eventually, squatters will lose their homes, too. But at that point you may also be able to rent your home from the bank or government very cheaply and avoid eviction. We are moving into a very dynamic situation that we have never seen before in the United States, in which many actions will become possible that would not be possible today.

There are also some delaying tactics you can use to put off foreclosure for as long as possible. For example, you can claim that records are not accurate and ask for depositions; both will buy you time. Or try negotiating with whoever owns the mortgage note by offering to make a partial payment each month to bypass or delay foreclosure. Keep in mind that banks do not like to foreclose on a property if they can avoid it because they will most likely have to sell the property at a loss and then show that loss on their books. Also, foreclosing costs the banks money and time they would rather spend elsewhere. So if you get in trouble, don't immediately assume that you cannot cut a deal of some kind, such as a loan modification, refinance, or temporary partial payment. It's worth asking. Banks won't even talk to you unless you are behind on your payments, so you have to be a few months late before you can make your request. On the other hand, if you are underwater, it gets a lot harder to get the bank to modify your mortgage because it is no longer fully collateralized by the home's value.

In general, we recommend doing a short sale (selling the property for less than the balance due on the mortgage) rather than a foreclosure if the bank will allow it. However, in a short sale, the difference between what you owe on the loan and what the home is sold for can be counted by the IRS as a gain to you that may be taxable (check this with your CPA or tax attorney).

The key is to not give up easily. You can fight foreclosure and the government does have programs to help you do that. In a blatant plug for a sibling's book, if you find yourself in a foreclosure situation, you should take a look at *The Homeowner's Guide to Foreclosure: How to Protect Your Home and Your Rights,* Second Edition by James Wiedemer (Kaplan, 2008). Jim is a real estate attorney who practiced during the foreclosure crisis in Houston in the mid-1980s and knows foreclosures well. It's a good book that gives you excellent detailed information on how to fight foreclosure.

What to Do with Commercial Real Estate

If you have commercial real estate that is bringing in money, keep running it until it goes under—assuming your mortgages are not personally guaranteed loans and are owned by a corporation. If they are personally guaranteed loans, it would be wise to sell now or as soon as possible, rather than waiting for the bubbles to pop. Also, if you have significant equity in your commercial property you should sell to capture that equity before it is lost.

If you wait too long, it will get hard to sell at a decent price and you may find yourself throwing good money after bad, in a losing attempt to just hang on until things get better. (Every situation is different. Please call us at (800) 994-0018 if you want to discuss yours.)

What to Do with Farms and Farmland

As with primary residences, unless you have a strong personal attachment to your farmland or are actively using it in some way, the best thing to do from a strictly financial point of view is to sell your farmland now, while land values are still relatively high compared to where they are going in the future. If you are attached to your farmland, think through your individual situation carefully and try not to make an entirely emotional decision. Are you near an urban center where you can get a reasonably good price if you sell now, or are you in an economically depressed rural area? Are you ill and unable to work on or fully enjoy your farmland? Have you been planning to sell your land in a few years due to retirement or other change? If so, better to sell now than to put it off.

If you love owning farmland, remember that, just as with houses and other real estate, farmland will get very cheap in the future and you will be able to buy farmland for much less than you can sell it for today.

Working farms are businesses, not merely real estate. As we are already starting to see, food and crop prices will rise significantly with inflation. When the dollar bubble pops, the buying power of the dollar will fall relative to other currencies, making U.S. crops cheaper for foreigners to buy than food grown in other countries, so demand for our food exports will rise, making U.S. crops profitable. So the farmland that produces those crops will create a significant income. That income could be high and if you don't intend to sell the land because it is part of the family, then your future farmland income will be good even if high interest rates lower the value of that land. If you don't plan to sell your land, who cares?

High interest rates will make the cost of borrowing money to buy farmland high, and with credit not flowing, loans will be hard to get. Adjustable-rate mortgages on farmland, as on all real estate, will go sky-high with rising interest rates, pushing some farms into foreclosure. Like commercial real estate, working farms that are underwater in their mortgages may not be worth fighting to keep, depending on your unique situation.

If you have a working farm or some other reason why you wish to keep your farmland, your best bet is to refinance any adjustable-rate loans to low fixed-rate loans as soon as possible. As with your house, you have the option of pulling some or all of the equity out of your property to use for more profitable investments elsewhere (see Chapter 7).

The main thing to keep in mind is that real estate values across the board are not coming back to their past bubble highs, so don't make the mistake of hanging on at all costs because you "just know" things are going to turn around soon. Even when real estate values do begin to recover (long after all the bubbles pop, including the dollar bubble), they will not return to pre-bubble pop prices, in terms of inflation-adjusted dollars.

Our national house party will definitely be over.

Rule Number Three: Stay Away from Long-Term Bonds

When inflation and interests rates rise, asset values across the board will fall, and the dollar and government debt bubbles will finally pop (see Chapters 3 and 4). Foreign investors will no longer lend us money, and much of our bubble wealth will have gone to Money Heaven, which will greatly constrict the supply of capital and further raise the price of borrowing money, pushing interest rates higher. That will leave the government with little choice but to print even more dollars, causing even higher inflation and higher interest rates.

Even before the dollar and government debt bubbles pop, just a moderate rise in interest rates will have a terrible effect on bond prices (see sidebar). As inflation continues to rise, higher and higher interest rates will devastate the value of all fixed-income securities.

Here's a good way to think of the relationship between rising interest rates and falling bond prices, and how the risks of short-term, mid-term, and long-term bonds compare to each other. Imagine a very long seesaw. On one end of the seesaw is interest rates, and at the other end is bond prices: As interest rates go up, bond prices go down. But because this is a very long seesaw, the long-term bonds that are out at the far end of the seesaw go down in price the most, while short-term bonds that are much closer to the fulcrum, don't go down as much. Short-term and mid-term bonds are at less risk than long-term bonds to movements in interest rates, although all bond rates will fall as interest rates rise significantly.

Moderately Rising Interest Rates Equal Sharply Falling Bond Prices

Think U.S. Treasury bonds are a safe investment? Sure, the U.S. Treasury may not default on bonds in the next couple of years, but bonds can still lose a lot of value if inflation shows up and forces interest rates to rise. To give you some idea of how much a Treasury bond can lose with relatively small increases in interest rates, we offer you the following example. Let's assume you just bought a 10-year Treasury bond that is earning 3 percent. If the interest rate rises from 3 percent to just 4 percent, your bond loses a whopping 12 percent of its value. Here's what happens if interest rates go even higher than 4 percent:

Interest rate	Lost bond value
5%	18% lost
6%	25% lost
7%	31% lost
10%	46% lost
15%	63% lost

But even these less-risky bonds will be tricky because you will need to sell them well before all bond prices drop. The other problem is that short-term bonds are not especially profitable, due to their very low interest rates. Ideally, if you want to invest in bonds and other fixed-rate investments in the short- to mid-term, you need to be very aware of when to pull out or have a money manager who understands the coming Aftershock and knows what to do and when to do it.

What about Municipal Bonds?

Municipal bonds, which include state, local, and special tax districts for baseball stadiums, etc. are increasingly in the news. Analysts are comparing Greece to California. But so far, the threat to municipal bonds is still relatively small. Most of the trouble muni bonds are having now is due to special circumstances that are compounded by the slow economy. It is true that the muni bond default rate has more than doubled recently, but if your bond holdings are in a diversified bond fund, these defaults will have little impact. So far, there is not a major threat.

Although the short-term outlook for municipal bonds is okay, the long term outlook is not. State and local governments have taken on a massive amount of debt that they can only pay if the economy recovers. In fact, the amount of debt states owe has more than doubled in the past 10 years from $1.1 trillion to $2.3 trillion. Some states, such as New York, are now borrowing from their pension funds to fund general expenses. Those problems are already pressuring muni bonds, in many casesmaking them unattractive investments. More importantly, if the economy does not significantly improve, and it probably won't as the bubble continue to pop, many state and local governments simply won't be able to service their debt putting much greater downward pressure on muni bonds. Later on, when there is any major threat of default by a major state or local government, the Federal government will almost certainly bail out the muni market before it becomes a significant crisis. Guaranteeing debt and opening a borrowing window at the Fed for states and localities could avert any major meltdown in the muni market. That will work for a while. But the problem is, the ability of the federal government to continue to bail out defaulting municipalities is not limitless. At some point, they won't be able to do it anymore.

So, short term, there is no need to panic about your municipal bond holdings, but given that we know how this movie ends, why wait for the long term to begin exiting these investments? There is nothing wrong with beginning to trim your muni bond portfolio now. We sent out an alert to our newsletter readers in June 2010 suggesting they begin to move out of munis. That would have been a good move. Moving temporarily into U.S. Treasuries is a viable short-term option, but only in the context of a properly managed and diversified Aftershock portfolio.

Where's the Best Place to Stash Cash?

The cash you get from selling your stocks, real estate, and fixed-rate investments obviously has to go someplace. Right now, you are pretty safe with just about anything short-term, such as money markets, short-term government bonds, and so forth, although these have very low interest rates and don't pay very much. However, as we move deeper into the recession and closer to the dollar bubble pop, you will need to be much more careful about where you put your cash.

Keeping cash in money market funds of banks and corporations that may fail is clearly not a great idea. Your money market accounts are likely heavy with Treasury bills. But, when the dollar bubble pops, even short-term U.S. government debt will be problematic, which means you should be moving heavily towards precious metals, such as gold and silver (see Chapter 7), and similar inflation-driven investments, such as some foreign short term debt instrument, as pressure on the dollar and government debt increases. These types of investments have to be carefully watched and need very active and very competent management. Clearly, this is a dynamic situation. We are no longer in a "set it and forget it" investment environment, which is why we have a variety of services, including our money management partner, to help you negotiate the changing economy with the least amount of risk (please call (800) 994-0018 or go to www.aftershockeconomy.com for details).

How Long Do I Have to Follow These Three Rules?

We know that as the collapsing multibubble economy falls, the last bubble to burst will be the government debt bubble. As we explained in Chapters 3 and 4, the exact timing of when the dollar and government debt bubbles will pop is hard to nail down. It could occur as early as 2013 but much more likely in 2015 or 2016. Rising inflation and rising interest rates will be key to kicking things off. When inflation and interest rates are high enough to significantly impact investor psychology, particularly foreign investor sentiment, there will be a significant decrease in the amount of foreign capital flowing into the United States. Instead of borrowing massive amounts of foreign money, we will have to print massive amounts of money, further pushing up inflation and interest rates, and further devastating U.S. asset values. Therefore, you have to follow our Three Rules until after the dollar and government debt bubbles fully pop, or you will very likely lose a lot of money.

Letting Go Is Hard to Do

We understand that quitting stocks, bonds, and investment real estate is not easy. It's tough to just give up on investments that we have come to know and love, investments that have provided so well for us in the past—so supportive and so comfortable. It's almost like giving up on Mom and Dad. These investments have served us so well over the past few decades; how can we just walk away? Everybody invested in stocks, bonds, and real estate, and usually everybody did very well. The world just doesn't seem right without them. And if leaving Mom and Dad isn't bad enough, moving to alternative investments may feel like moving to an orphanage. Actually, you can make much more money with alternative investments (see Chapter 7) than you could with stocks, bonds, and real estate in the past, but that will be much harder to do than in the relatively easy glory days of the rising real estate and stock markets. Also, few investors will join you in the alien world of investments that go up when the economy goes down. It just won't feel the same as the rising bubble economy.

In most economic situations, reading what *not* to invest in is pretty useless because you probably wouldn't invest in it anyway. You would invest in typical stock mutual funds and some basic real estate just like everyone else. However, in a bubble economy, what not to invest in can be one of the most important financial decisions you make in your lifetime. That's because the losses on stock, bonds, and real estate can be so large. At this point, especially with the dollar bubble yet to pop, you have to be very careful about what investments you hold.

There was a great line in the old television show *M*A*S*H* that essentially said, "In war, there are two rules. Rule #1 is that young men die. Rule #2 is that doctors can't change Rule #1." The same logic can be applied to this falling multibubble economy:

Rule #1: No matter what happens, all bubbles eventually pop.

Rule #2: No amount of optimism can change Rule #1.

Being optimistic about your stock, bonds, and real estate investments will not change their future value. We have to deal with the reality we have, not the reality we want.

If you are still not convinced that we are in the middle of a bursting multibubble economy, please re-read the first half of the book. On the other hand, if your head says, "This book makes sense" but your heart says, "I want my bubble back!" then take a few deep breaths or have a few stiff drinks or take a nap but, whatever it takes, get over it and get on with your new life in the new economy. Don't spend too much time wishing for the good times to magically return. They won't. It's time to wake up and change your thinking. You still have time to protect yourself. In a few years, you are either going to look like a genius or you are going to be kicking yourself for waiting until it is too late. It's really up to you.

What to Do If You Sort of Believe Us, but Not 100 Percent

You don't have to believe us entirely to start protecting yourself now. You needn't change your investments completely and all at once, but you do need to change and you need to continue to change as our analysis starts looking more and more correct to you. Hindsight is 20/20, but times like this call for more than hindsight. Right now, what you need is foresight. We are trying very hard to offer that to you. Listen to what we are saying, and keep your eyes open for evidence that what we are predicting is in fact actually happening. In time, you will believe us partially, and then you will believe us fully. The sooner that happens, the better it will be for you.

"I want my bubble back."

If you think we are completely wrong, we advise you to wait until you see real estate values going back up again for at least one year before you invest. Waiting at least a year before buying real estate will be easy because prices move slowly, and you won't miss much by holding off for a while. With stocks, we suggest a slow withdrawal from the market while it is going up. You can never lose money making a profit. The more you don't believe us, the more slowly you should go. Think of it as diversification.

On the other hand, if you think we might be partially right and also partially wrong, then do what Bob's friend did and only take half our advice. That would certainly be a prudent course of action for any reasonable person. For example, you could sell 10 to 30 percent of your stocks with every 1,000-point drop in the Dow. You may later end up like Bob's friend, wishing you had done more, but better to do half than do nothing. More sophisticated investors can employ a hedge strategy, increasing their hedging as they see the stock market and overall economy continuing to go down.

Even if you don't believe us fully now, try to be very open to changing your mind. If what we are saying seems to become increasingly true, then increasingly move in the direction of our suggestions. This show's not over by a long shot, and you still have time to adjust your positions. Moving gradually may mean you could take some losses, but that's okay. It's not always smart to go 100 percent with any one way of thinking. Just keep your eyes and your mind open. And be sure you make adjustments along the way.

What Else Can I Do to Protect Myself?

In addition to the three big rules (stay away from stocks, real estate, and long-term, fixed-rate investments), there are a number of other actions you can take to avoid losing money in the current Bubblequake and coming Aftershock, including those outlined in the sections that follow.

Dealing with Credit Cards, Student Loans, and Other Debts

Many credit card balances are adjustable-rate loans. Even fixed-rate credit cards have clauses in their contracts that, under certain circumstances, allow interest rates to increase. When interest rates go up with inflation, so will adjustable-rate credit cards, making interest on your debt very expensive. So the sooner you can get out of adjustable-rate credit card debt, the better. If the credit card balance is relatively small in proportion to your income level and wealth, pay it off now or as soon as you can. If necessary, cut back where you can and make as large a monthly payment as you can manage, so you can get out of credit card debt as soon as possible.

However, if your credit card debt is quite high relative to your income and assets, you might want to consider not paying your credits cards at all. When the bubbles pop, many credit card companies will go out of business. In fact, with the new credit card laws going into effect, credit card companies will go out of business even faster when so many people cannot make their payments. After the bubbles pop, you will likely still owe your credit card debt balance to the government but at that point, who knows when they will get around to collecting it, and in any case, high inflation will rapidly destroy the debt. They will have many other emergencies to deal with first. Not paying your credit card debts will significantly harm your credit score, but after all the bubbles pop, credit scores are going to be pretty lousy all around, and few people will have the need for a high credit score.

The same goes for most other debts. Don't pay off debt and leave yourself with little rainy day savings. Also, save some money to take advantage of the investment ideas in the next chapter. As with home mortgages, if you can, refinance all adjustable-rate loans to fixed-rate loans, including any home equity lines of credit, car loans, and personal loans. Lock them in now at the lowest fixed rates you can get.

What about student loans? To pay or not to pay depends on your situation. If you have a job or think you can get one, keep paying your student loans so you can maintain your credit score and be able, perhaps, to buy a car to get to work. But if you have no job and don't expect to get one anytime soon, your credit score may not matter as much to you. Student loans come with very aggressive collection actions, so be prepared to be pursued. But if you can't pay, you can't pay. You can talk to the lender about possible deferment or restructuring of the loan, or you can just let it go. Even people who are paying back their student loans now may find themselves stopping that later, when they make less income. As we mentioned before, after the bubbles pop, credit scores won't be as important as they are today because many Americans will have very poor scores. Even the U.S. federal government will have a very poor credit score!

1. If you need a car to get to work, that is the first loan to focus on repaying. If your car is repossessed and you cannot get to work, you will not be able to borrow money to get another one.

Also, if you have an expensive car loan, consider downgrading to a cheaper car and car loan as soon as possible.

2. A distant second is the house. Normally repaying your mortgage would be a very high priority, but in this case repaying the mortgage is not as high a priority as repaying your car loan because they will repossess your car almost immediately but not your home (see the earlier section in this chapter on mortgages).

3. The last priority is to pay off all other debt, credit cards, vacation time share, student loans, etc., if possible. Whether to pay or not to pay depends on your income and assets, as well as the loaner's ability to collect. For example, a loan for a vacation time share will not be easy to collect on, and if you have to let something go, that could be a good choice. Unless you have significant income or assets, it does not pay to worry too much about your credit score in the global megadepression ahead because there won't be much money to lend, and interest rates will be ridiculously high, so you won't want to borrow or won't be able to borrow.

Reduce Spending

One of the hardest steps to take to protect yourself, your family, your business, and your future investments is to reduce spending—not starting next month or next year, but right now. Not many people like downgrading or contracting their lifestyles without a really good reason or future reward. Luckily, you have one: The less you spend, the more money you will have available for some of the investment ideas in the next chapter. Not only that, as the recession continues and the economy does not recover, you will need some cash on hand for emergencies, such as losing your income or your home. Cutting spending is the quickest way to put some money aside. Please start today.

Some people find it helpful to begin by listing all their expenditures for a two-month period to see where the money is going. Then go through the list, item by item, and reduce what you can. Shop for a cheaper telephone, cell phone, TV, Internet, and other services. Eat out less often (a big money drain for many people). Cut down on entertainment shopping. Think about creative, lower-cost vacations. Perhaps even consider reducing your mortgage payment by renting out part of your home, if that is possible.

Don't look at it as a loss. Cutting spending is a positive step toward maximizing your future prosperity. With the extra funds, you can cover a rainy day and also invest in assets that will grow in value while the dollar declines (see next chapter). You will also be able to sleep better as well! Think of all the great bargains you will be able to buy when most people will be broke.

Most people will experience two stages of cuts: small spending cuts now with only moderate impact, and much bigger spending cuts later, with more dramatic impact. The more of this you can do sooner, the more funds you will have for investing in growth assets during the bust.

Hang onto Your Job

While you are looking at ways to cut spending, it is also very important that you give some thought to how you can up your odds of holding onto your job. See Chapter 8 for details about which careers and employment will do relatively better than others. But keep in mind that even if you are in one of the "safer" job sectors, like healthcare or education, that doesn't guarantee you work. Many positions even in these sectors will be cut and some people in safe positions will be replaced. Consider spending some time now making yourself more marketable in a safer job sector, or adding skills within your chosen field, or looking for ways to make yourself irreplaceable in your current job. If you decide to change jobs, don't quit your current employment before getting your next position lined up.

What about Retirement?

For those approaching or in retirement, the coming multibubble pop could not happen at a worse time. After a lifetime of working hard, raising a family, accumulating wealth, and planning for one's golden years, it may feel like the plug is being pulled on all your expectations. And for those who don't yet know what is about to hit, the shock will be even more unexpected.

Putting some real gold into those "golden years" will take a new kind of retirement planning—with new knowledge, courage, and actions that very few financial planners can help you with. We plan to devote an entire chapter to this subject in our next book, *The Aftershock Investor.* For now, here are some key points to think about for your Aftershock retirement.

Estate Planning and Gifts

For tax reasons, it is usually better to give gifts to children and others now rather than later as part of one's estate. However, in the new, upside-down world of bubble-popping retirement, it may be better to give those gifts later, for a variety of reasons. For example, when asset values are way down, there will be less to tax. However, taxes will go up eventually, so you will only have a small window to take advantage of this.

Giving gifts now that can be wisely protected and grown is also a good idea. For example, selling assets and buying gold to give to others, rather than dollars, stocks, bonds, or real estate, would be an especially thoughtful gift. Overall, gold will increase in value for quite a long time to come, especially as the dollar, stocks, bonds, and real estate all fall in value.

Whole Life Insurance and Annuities

Whole life insurance companies will not hold up well in the coming bubble pops, and in any case, the value of whole life policies in a highly inflationary environment will be minimal. Given that all life insurance policies will take very big losses when inflation climbs to and passes 10 percent, it does not make good financial sense to own any whole life insurance. If you are an active breadwinner with a dependent family to protect, you should buy term life insurance, not whole life. Whole life insurance is much more expensive than term policies and they will lose all or almost all their value during high inflation and the real estate, bond, and stock bubble collapse.

If you already own whole life insurance, consider getting out now, before inflation begins. Depending on your whole life policy, you may be able to take a lump sum payment, borrow against the cash value of the policy, or simply take the penalty, and cash out. Check to see what your options are. Some loss now is better than an even bigger loss later.

The story with annuities is not much better. Like whole life insurance, all annuities will lose money. Unfortunately, annuities are even harder than whole life insurance policies to get out of. It is possible to cancel, but it is difficult and time-consuming so you may want to start now. Once again, there will be penalties for getting out, but better to lose some now than lose more later.

As with all our advice, move only as fast as and to the extent that you feel we are right. As inflation moves up, it will get easier and easier to see things from our point of view. Just don't wait too long to take action. Make your moves well before inflation goes to and beyond 10 percent.

401Ks, IRA, and Other Retirement Accounts

Retirement accounts are tricky to deal with as we near 10 percent inflation because they often contain stocks and long-term bonds that will do very poorly in the years to come, but may not be so easy to get away from now. To the extent that you can control these investments or turn them into "self directed" accounts, you may want to begin slowly moving into what we consider good Aftershock investments (see next chapter), specifically gold and short-term bonds.

You needn't panic now, but to the extent that you believe our macro view, you can begin to get out of your more risky holdings. If you are not entirely sold on our point of view, wait until you are pretty sure we are right. You will lose money the longer you wait, but you will gain peace of mind. At some point you are probably going to believe us. Whenever that is, make sure it is well before inflation goes to 10 percent. With our continued guidance, you can anticipate macroeconomic changes before they entirely take down your investments.

What about taking the penalty and getting out now? We never like to recommend that people take penalties, but if you don't have many options, it may be better to take part of your retirement account assets and put it into assets that will eventually perform better than cash, stocks, and high-risk long terms bonds. If you move into gold, make sure you hold onto it for a while, despite its volatility. Gold may fall temporarily but in the longer run it will rise quite significantly.

In the case of corporate pensions, such as defined benefit plans or defined contribution plans, your only viable option is to get out as quickly as possible because you cannot control the investments and most will be lost when the bubbles fully pop. These are not easy to get out of. Some plans offer a lump sum payment. Take it as soon as you qualify for it. Other plans allow you to borrow against your assets in the plan. Do that, if you can. If you can't get your money out soon, plan to not have it later.

In our next book we will devote an entire chapter to retirement investment issues. For now, here are our general recommendations:

- Sell investment real estate as soon as possible.
- Refinance all adjustable-rate debt to fixed-rate loans.
- Reduce exposure to most stocks.
- Seek high-dividend paying stocks.
- Gold will be less volatile and far less risky than the S&P.
- Short and medium-term bonds, and inflation-adjusted Treasury Inflation Protected Securities (TIPS) will be okay for a while, but be prepared to get out quickly.
- Consider active management for your Aftershock portfolio for maximum protection and growth.

What about Bankruptcy?

In early 2009, we saw a personal finance article suggesting that readers not wait too long before filing for bankruptcy. It suggested declaring bankruptcy to get rid of credit card debt while you still have a job. The article also advised readers to not use up all their assets paying a mortgage that was too expensive or underwater. In fact, the article suggested just letting the mortgage go unpaid because the foreclosure process could take a year or more to complete. During that time, while you were no longer paying credit cards or a mortgage, but still had income from a job, you could put some money away.

At the time, we were a little surprised to see such bleak, hard-nosed advice in a personal finance column, which is usually much more upbeat. It was a sign of the changing times. We agree with the advice. Better to face reality and plan for the future, than keep running full steam ahead down the wrong track. Try not to be emotional, just realistic.

The first thing you need to know about bankruptcy is that, after all the bubbles pop and unemployment shoots up, many, many people will declare bankruptcy. It may feel lousy, but truthfully, it will be a logical course of action for many people. Also, at that point, virtually no one will want or be able to get more credit anyway, so bankruptcy won't be that terrible. There won't be much money available to borrow, it will be hard to borrow it, and even if you can qualify to borrow money, the terms will be very unattractive.

However, after the Aftershock hits, banks will be so devastated that lenders probably won't be too aggressive about collecting debts. So, you may not want to declare bankruptcy at that point since banks may not be doing much about debts for a while anyway.

Prior to the Aftershock, you may want to do a strategic bankruptcy if that will free you to make some strategic investments that you would otherwise not be able to make because of your debt.

Also, well in advance of filing for a bankruptcy you may want to transfer any assets out of your name and perhaps into a trust fund for your children. If this route interests you, the sooner you do it, the better. Please check with a bankruptcy attorney regarding the details of the law regarding the timing of asset transfers. If the transfer is too close to a bankruptcy filing, it can be considered a "fraudulent conveyance."

Remember, Your Net Worth Is Not Your Self Worth

It's never a good idea to equate your personal worth with your net worth, but in a booming, multibubble economy on the rise, it may not cause you too much harm. On the other hand, in a bursting multibubble economy on the way down, this bad habit may come back to haunt you. Most people will see their net worth fall dramatically in the months and years ahead. Reading this book can help minimize your losses and maximize your gains, but please don't focus so much on your wallet that you forget what really makes life so worthwhile. We are not being corny when we remind you of what you already know: *It's not really about the money.* It may seem like money buys happiness, especially when the money is rolling in. But remember, the potential for happiness is actually always available to us because it comes, not from money or from things, but from other people. We need to remember this when money is flowing in our lives, and even more so when it is not.

As much as this book focuses on money, and as much as everyone will be terribly focused on money over the next few years, the best advice you may get won't be financial. Be sure to focus on your family and friends. Your family will need your support, and your friends may need you now more than ever—and you may need them more as well. Mutual support is the key to a good life in both the best of times and the worst of times.

Look for what makes you happy and find your glass half full. You don't have to ignore reality, just be sure to see what is real and what is not.

In the Bubblequake and Aftershock, do your part to help by making sure you don't judge people by the size of their wallets but by the size of their heart and the quality of their character.

Cashing in on Chaos

BEST AFTERSHOCK INVESTMENTS

There are enormous amounts of money to be made during the Bubblequake and Aftershock—far more than during the three decades of the bubble years, because the bubble money is not sustainable and its loss will be very harmful to the economy. In fact, we predict that far more "real" (nonbubble, sustainable, and non-economy-damaging) money will be made in the Aftershock than in the last three decades combined. Of course, it won't come close to matching the total amount of *bubble money* made during the past three decades, but most of that money will soon go to Money Heaven along with a lot of real money. Money that goes to Money Heaven is not coming back.

Plenty of Profit Opportunities, but They Will Feel Quite Uncomfortable, Even Scary at Times

Gone are the days when you could just sit back with a glass of wine or a six-pack of beer and watch TV, knowing that by the end of the year your house would be worth 10 to 20 percent more than at the start of the year even though you didn't lift a finger to improve it.

Gone are the days when you could just buy a set of stocks or mutual funds that everyone else buys and watch them rise 1,400 percent in 25 years, or if you chose higher-growth stocks, watch them grow 2,500 percent or more. No need to be a stock-picking genius or a high-risk, high-judgment venture capitalist to make ridiculously high returns. In fact, for most investors, it was better if you didn't use any judgment at all and just chose index funds, as John Bogle, the founder of Vanguard Funds (the second largest mutual fund company in the United States), correctly advised. Back then, you could just sit back and watch the stock market automatically take your investments to tremendous heights while you did absolutely nothing.

Those were the good old days. That's over now. Today, good judgment and taking risks are critical to making money and will be even more so in the future. In fact, good judgment and taking risks will be critical to simply holding onto your money in the future. Without smart thinking and some risk-taking, your money will go straight to Money Heaven, along with just about everyone else's money in the coming years. This journey is not for the faint of heart.

"We were wondering if __now__ would be a good time to panic?"

Invest Where Most People Do Not, and Be Very Smart About It

The highest returns on investment in the past have often been made by people who spotted trends or new ideas *before* everyone else. In fact, they often invested in ideas that other people roundly criticized. That's investing the old-fashioned way. Old-fashioned investing says

it is important to invest in opportunities before other people see
that they are good opportunities because that's when you get the
best prices. But seeing something early is not enough. You could
invest in a lot of things other people don't see and lose a whole lot
of money because you might be seeing a bad investment. Being con-
trarian is necessary but not sufficient for success in the Bubblequake
and Aftershock; you also have to be *smart* and see a *good* investment
before others see it.

To our thinking, there are three rules to smart investing in the
treacherous future investment environment:

Rule Number One

Correctly judge the macroeconomic environment. If you
don't, even your most well thought out investments will be
crushed. We have made a strong case in Chapters 1 through 5
for what the future macroeconomic environment will be like.
If you don't correctly judge the future environment, you will
likely lose most of your money—as will most everyone else.

Rule Number Two

Invest for the long term. Even if your macroeconomic analysis is spot-on, it is hard to make correct short-term judgments
(less than a year). Investor psychology, government actions or
inactions, and unusual political events can have major impacts
on the short-term course of the financial markets. Even more
annoying is that certain events or actions may have little positive effect on the economy. However, they will have a major
positive effect on financial markets because investors mistakenly *hope* that those actions will have a major positive effect on
the economy, such as quantitative easing (QE, a.k.a. money
printing) by the Federal Reserve.

Rule Number Three

Go against conventional wisdom in fundamental ways. There
is a lot of talk in the business world about disruptive technologies or unconventional thinking. In truth, unconventional
thinking is rarely very unconventional. The terminology is
more of a marketing gimmick than reality. It is easy to think
you are being unconventional when, in fact, you are only

being unconventional on the surface and not in any fundamental way.

This is true for investing, as well. You may think you were being unconventional, for example, if you jumped back into the stock market in December 2008 when almost everyone else was getting out, but in fact you were being very conventional. You may have appeared unconventional on the surface, but fundamentally you were supporting the very conventional wisdom that says stocks are always a good long-term investment. They're not. Being unconventional *in a fundamental way* means realizing that, at this stage of the evolution of our economy, stocks are a bad investment for the long term.

Remember, in the future, far more long-term money will be made during the Bubblequake and Aftershock than in the rising multibubble economy of the past. However, post-bubble money will be harder to make, very scary to try to make, and it will require a fair amount of skill. For that reason, much more long-term money will be made in the future post-bubble economy than in the past bubble economy.

Also, be aware that the government and many financial professionals have a vested interest in spinning any news in a positive light for stock, real estate, and other investments helped by the bubble economy. Keep a level head and look at the economic fundamentals of what's really going on with the economy, and don't focus on the latest spin. There is plenty of news out there that gives you the real economic picture and many financial journalists who have at least some degree of skepticism of any spin.

Best Short-Term and Long-Term Aftershock Investments

In the short term (the next one to three years), massive money printing by the Fed will likely continue to support the stock market, keep interest rates low, and sustain investor and consumer confidence—keeping the bubbles from popping fully.

In the long term, this massive money printing by the Fed will create rising inflation and rising interest rates. As inflation reaches and exceeds 10 percent, investors will get increasingly concerned and eventually will lose their appetite for the dollar and dollar-denominated assets across the board, causing all the bubbles—including the dollar and government debt bubbles—to pop.

In the Short Term, the Key Is Protection, Protection, Protection!

From now until inflation exceeds 10 percent and all the bubbles eventually fully pop, the main name of the game is protection, protection, protection! Of course, investment growth is always good, too, and there are ways to do that, as well, but in the coming rising inflation environment, not losing money to inflation is critical. That means not holding too much cash as inflation rises, and choosing investments that will not lose value as inflation creeps up and the dollar slides down.

Failing to protect assets in the short term will leave you fewer funds available to cash in later on the dollar and stock bubble pops, a major wealth growth opportunity.

Please see Chapter 6 for how not to lose money in the run up to and beyond the Aftershock, including the section on "Where's the Best Place to Stash Cash." For additional, updated information about investing in the short and long term, please see our newsletters and website www.aftershockeconomy.com, as well as our forthcoming book, *The Aftershock Investment Guide: A Crash Course in Staying Afloat as the Economy Sinks*, to be published in late 2011 or early 2012.

In the Long Term, the Key Is to Take Advantage of a Falling Stock Market and a Falling Dollar

Once inflation passes 10 percent and investors begin to seriously lose confidence in the dollar, stocks, bonds, and other dollar-denominated assets, it will be time to shift the focus from big protection to big profits. At that point, the stock market will be falling, and the dollar will be falling, relative to other currencies, due to rising inflation and high and rising interest rates.

Falling stocks and a falling dollar will create enormous opportunities to make money while other investors will lose their shirts. Such is the power of Rule Number One: having the correct macroeconomic view.

Smart Investing for a Falling Stock Market: Shorting Stocks Using LEAPS

We love LEAPS! Long-term Equity AnticiPation Securities, or LEAPS, follow Rule Number Two: Invest for the long term. In the case of shorting stocks, that means you should never short short-term; you should always short long-term. LEAPS do this perfectly by allowing you to short stocks for one- to two-year periods. However, it is important not to buy LEAPS too soon because you don't want them to expire before the stock and dollar bubbles begin to pop.

LEAPS are long-term stock options. Most options are for much shorter periods of time. You buy *put* options when you want to short a stock, and you buy *call* options when you want to buy (or go long) on a stock. You buy LEAPS exactly as you would buy options, but the short-term volatility risk is lower because they expire over a longer period of time. LEAPS, however, are not offered on every stock that is optionable. So don't expect to find them in the option chain on all optionable stocks.

If you are not comfortable dealing with options, then LEAPS are not for you. However, if you are comfortable with options and would like to learn more about the technical details of buying and selling LEAPS, we recommend you go to the Chicago Board of Exchange website on LEAPS, which is www.cboe.com/products/leaps.aspx or go to the Options Industry Council website at www.optionseducation .org/basics/leaps/default.jsp.

Smart Investing for a Falling Stock Market: Shorting Stocks Using Bear Funds

Bear funds are an easier way for most people to short a falling market. They will not provide the returns of LEAPS but they are much easier to use since you can purchase them like mutual funds. These funds usually short indexes such as the S&P 500 and can use leverage to even "double short" the market. This means that if the S&P index falls 10 percent, the fund should increase in value by roughly 20 percent.

However, these funds are reconciled on a daily basis, which means they may not track long-term trends as closely as LEAPS. In fact, some leveraged funds have done very poorly in tracking long-term trends.

Be very careful on the timing of shorting the stock market with bear funds, because if the stock market is not yet falling and instead goes sideways for a while or goes up for a while, bear funds will obviously do very poorly.

Also keep in mind the very real possibility that at some point during the Aftershock chaos, the government could limit or even

The Future for Good Hedge Funds Is Brighter Than Ever

The opportunities for hedge funds to make money in the Bubblequake and Aftershock are enormous, but they can't do it by copying what worked in the past. Hedge funds, like individuals, will have to change. They will have to move strongly against what most hedge funds are doing. Instead of succeeding by doing what everyone else does, they will have to fundamentally challenge conventional investment wisdom—just as people have always had to do to make a lot of money in business in the United States.

Long term, they will also have to become more entrepreneurial, meaning no more "2 and 20" (2 percent management fees plus 20 percent of the upside). Instead, fees will more likely be 1 (or even 0.5) and 30. They will have a much higher upside, but a minimal or limited management fee. In the future, hedge funds will have to make their money only when their investors make money. They will share in their gains and losses.

Most importantly, they will have to have, by sheer luck or by correct analysis, the *right* macroeconomic view of the global economy. They will have to be right when almost all of their competitors are wrong. This is nothing more and nothing less than what has worked so many times before in American investment management.

ban the use of LEAPS and shorts in an attempt to stabilize a rapidly falling stock market. Such government intervention has happened before and will most likely happen again.

For this and other reasons, it may be wise to work closely with financial advisors or asset managers who are in close alignment with the correct macroeconomic view of what is occurring.

Smart Investing for a Falling Dollar: Buying Foreign Currencies

A very obvious way to profit from the falling dollar in the Aftershock is to buy foreign currencies that will rise relative to the falling dollar. Foreign currencies may also lose buying power compared to their previous values due to rising inflation in their own countries, but they will not be as inflated as the dollar. Therefore their values will not fall as deeply as the dollar. So, *relative to the dollar*, these currencies will do well.

The major foreign currencies, such as the euro, yen, Canadian dollar, and Swiss franc can be easily bought and sold using exchange-traded funds (ETFs). For example, the euro ETF trades under the symbol FXE (a Rydex Investments product). Each share of FXE sells for the price of 100 euros. You can buy this ETF just like a stock through your normal brokerage account.

The other ETFs are FXF for the Swiss franc, FXC for the Canadian dollar, FXY for the yen. Clearly, each one is affected by their government's policies, so they don't move in tandem. A most obvious example is the euro, which is affected whenever the European debt crisis flares up.

Many people are interested in the euro because it is so important and has lately been very volatile. We have also found many people simply don't like the idea of a multinational currency and so, don't like the euro. We think the euro zone will likely see significant economic problems among its members. However, despite these problems, we expect the euro to survive the coming Aftershock and in the long run, rise along with other foreign currencies as the dollar falls. In the meantime there could be some significant volatility due to what will be an ongoing European debt crisis.

As always, timing is everything. Buying and selling currencies can be highly risky, and we don't recommend highly active currency trading unless you really know what you are doing. Even then, you may lose money if you sell when you should hold, or hold when you shouldn't have bought in the first place.

Please also be aware that changes in the value of currencies relative to each other will be manipulated by central banks, which adds an additional level of volatility and risk. Also, central bank manipulation can be effective in the early stages of a major foreign exchange collapse but can fall apart suddenly when market pressures become greater than the central banks can handle. This means you may be running up against significant manipulation against your positions until the central banks can't manipulate anymore and then the price moves very quickly and very massively in your favor, but only during a very short window. The key is not to miss that window because that's where most of the money will be made.

If you want to diversify the risk of being involved in any single currency, you can buy an ETF called UDN that rises when the dollar falls against a basket of currencies known as the U.S. Dollar Index.

You can also buy foreign currencies through bond funds that invest in foreign corporate or government debt. These are fine currency investments in that they also pay interest and diversify your foreign currency holdings. However, like any U.S. long-term corporate or government bonds, they will lose their value when interest rates rise. So, be careful with bond funds because when interest rates rise, their values will fall significantly. Hence, you will need to exit them before interest rates climb. Like any bond fund, you also have to be careful about default risk, especially with debt-troubled European counties and some emerging markets.

One other issue to be aware of is that if inflation is significantly higher in other countries than the United States, the value of the dollar in nominal terms would rise. However, the inflation adjusted value of the dollar would still be falling. To offset the effect of inflation on your currency investments, you will need to invest in short term debt instruments of that currency rather than just the currency itself. As we just mentioned, not long term debt, but short term debt.

Again, this is only an issue when inflation begins to hit in other countries, but it is an important issue. You can't invest in currencies at that point; you will need to invest in short term debt instruments of those currencies so that you will receive interest that offsets the rise in inflation.

Smart Investing for Rising Inflation and a Falling Dollar: Shorting Fixed-Rate Bonds Using ETFs

There are ETFs that short fixed-income bonds, such as Treasuries. When interest rates rise, fixed-income bonds fall in value making these ETFs an excellent investment opportunity. One option is the ETF that trades under the symbol TBTF (a ProFunds Group product), which tracks the inverse of the daily performance of the Barclays Capital 20+ Year U.S. Treasury Index. A more aggressive option is TBT, which tracks two times the inverse of the daily performance of the Barclays Capital 20+ Year U.S. Treasury Index. This allows you to "double short" long-term U.S. Treasuries.

ETFs can be highly volatile, so you need to be a long-term player who won't panic and sell at the wrong time. These investments are only for the relatively sophisticated. In addition, like bear funds, they are reconciled daily, which means they don't always follow long-term trends.

In addition, the Treasury market is a highly manipulated market because the Federal Reserve, in the short term, can have a big impact on interest rates by buying bonds. Hence, you have to factor in moves by the Fed to buy bonds and thereby artificially drives up the price of bonds, which will lose you money if you are shorting bonds. The Fed has used its power to drive down interest rates and thus push up the price of bonds in the past and will likely do so again. Also, investor psychology can play a big role in the short term, as with other investments. Once inflation approaches 10 percent and higher, psychology will change, and the Fed will eventually run out of bullets.

Be Careful with Commodities (Other than Precious Metals, Such as Gold)

Investing profitably in commodities, such as copper and oil, will require a good macro awareness of changing trends in supply and demand, and these trends will be changing rather dramatically over the next few years, as we have described. So, for now, with the world economy rebounding somewhat due to massive government stimulus both here and in China, which is one the largest buyers of commodities in the world, commodities have been rising. However, if China's economy should happen to crash before ours (due to their real estate bubble popping, massive money printing of their own, and other issues), we will certainly see demand for commodities begin to fall, and therefore commodity prices. And as the dollar falls deeply, collapsing economies around the globe will put heavy downward pressure on the demand for all industrial commodities, which will further depress prices.

Interestingly, when the dollar bubble begins to fall significantly, commodity prices will increase dramatically *in dollar terms*. And the demand for U.S. commodities will rise because in nondollar terms, our commodities will look like bargains. For example, the price of non-U.S. oil will eventually fall as low as $10 to $20 per barrel, as worldwide demand declines with the overall world economy. But in the United States oil will eventually cost $100 to $150 per barrel due to the drastic decline in the value of the dollar. Meanwhile, demand for U.S. coal will rise because it will be cheap in nondollar terms and other countries will want to buy it.

In general, commodities will go down in value when the economy goes down. However, as we just mentioned, this downturn is different because of the dramatic fall in the dollar. The low-value dollar makes commodities imported into the United States more expensive. Even if the commodity is produced in the United States, it will rise to the imported price level because it could be exported. The low-value dollar makes U.S.-produced commodities low-priced in foreign currencies and hence, good exports. U.S.-produced commodities will often cost much less than anything produced by other countries. So expect demand and prices for U.S.-produced coal, grain, and beef to be very good.

Again, there is a limit on this export growth because some of these commodities, such as lumber and copper, will see demand fall precipitously worldwide due to their use in producing capital goods. However, both coal and grain will see solid demand since they are used heavily for production of necessities—food and electricity. In terms of U.S.-produced commodities, we see the brightest future for coal since many countries have a current need to import it and will continue needing to import it in the future to produce electricity even in the Aftershock. However, even necessities will feel some downward pressure. For example, grain prices will rise, but it will be a limited rise because the demand for beef and other meats will fall worldwide (a lot of grain is used to feed cattle). Also, grain's price now is highly influenced by ethanol requirements in gasoline, and those requirements could easily be reduced if grain prices are very high due to high exports.

Exactly how the twin forces of a cheap dollar and worldwide mega-depression will affect exports of U.S.-produced commodities is a complex issue. One thing is certain, though: dollar prices of U.S.-produced commodities will be high. It's equally certain that world prices in nondollar terms will be quite low due to the worldwide drop in demand because of worldwide recession.

For investors, these twin forces will produce a great deal of volatility. Increasingly, a commodities play will become a dollar play. Commodities are always volatile and the popping of the bubbles and the impact of the falling dollar will make them even more volatile. It won't be a market for the faint of heart or the inexperienced newcomer. It's like going from Class I rapids to Class V. On the following pages we describe the specific impact of the popping of the bubbles on specific classes of commodities.

As the Bubbles Pop, Gold Will Not Be Treated as a Commodity; It Will Be in a Class by Itself

We want to point out that, as the bubbles pop, gold will not be treated as a typical commodity. This has often been true throughout human history and will remain true through the popping of the bubbles. Gold holds an unusual position in the minds of many people around the world as a store of monetary value. Even in the United States, until the twentieth century, it was the most common mode of monetary commerce. Hence, it is not really a commodity in the same sense as wheat or zinc or oil.

For this reason, long term, it will act very differently from other commodities in terms of its price. Other commodities are driven by commercial demand. Gold will be driven by demand for it as a store of monetary value. In the short run, before the bubbles pop, it may at times follow the price of other commodities as they go up and down. But as the bubbles start to pop, its attraction as a traditional store for monetary value will set it increasingly apart from commercial commodities. Yes, the demand for gold as jewelry will fall since jewelry is a discretionary good, but that loss of demand can be more than offset by a big increase in investment demand. Furthermore, a great deal of gold jewelry that is purchased in Asia and the Middle East is often for investment purposes since it can be easily resold if the money is needed.

We will talk about gold at length later in this chapter.

Other Precious Metals, Such as Platinum and Silver

Let's look at a couple precious metals other than gold that are getting a lot of attention.

Silver is a bit of a hybrid. It has significant industrial demand, primarily in electronics, which accounts for about 50 percent of its usage (its traditional industrial use in photography is quickly evaporating). Like gold, silver also has investment demand because it has long been used as a secondary store of monetary value. In the same way as copper, when the bubbles pop, there will be a big decrease in industrial demand, as well as a big decrease in demand for silver jewelry as discretionary spending declines.

However, there will likely be a significant increase in the investment demand for silver. Historically, silver has more or less tracked gold trends up or down.

But recently, it has been much more volatile than gold. Despite that volatility, silver was up 66 percent in 2010, while gold was up 26 percent. Long term, silver will likely do very well, but the safe bet and likely the highest long-term return in investment metals is gold. Rightly or wrongly, the world does tend to see gold as Number One ("as good as gold") and silver as Number Two (like the silver medal at the Olympics). However, it would be good to have some silver in your precious metals portfolio. It is referred to sometimes as the "poor man's gold" because it is easier to buy especially as gold gets more expensive. Hence, it is likely to shine brightly when there is both a worldwide mega depression and a huge loss of confidence in normal financial investments.

Another precious metal that gets a lot of attention is **platinum**, which is in a similar position to silver, in that it is a hybrid metal with both strong industrial demand and investment demand. However, much of the industrial demand is from catalytic converters in the automobile industry and, since autos are a capital good, it will see an unusually sharp decline in demand once the government debt bubble pops. Because of that, platinum is likely to be harder hit than silver, so we would recommend staying away from platinum as the last two bubbles (the dollar and government debt) begin to pop. Despite a big drop when the last two bubbles pop, platinum will still do well over the long term, just not as well as gold.

Commodity Metals, Such as Copper, Nickel, and Zinc

Metals, such as nickel, zinc, and especially copper, have huge industrial demand, especially in a rising bubble economy. Even now, China is holding up the demand and prices for these metals. Conversely, as the bubbles begin to burst, the industrial demand for these metals will fall precipitously, and there is little investment demand for these metals.

So the advice regarding commodity metals is simple. You can play with them for a while and, if you are a good and/or lucky trader, you can make some money; but as the bubbles start to pop, get out. When the bubbles pop worldwide, commodity metals prices will fall dramatically. But, fairly quickly, the falling dollar will counteract the fall in worldwide prices for commodities *produced in the United States.*

Oil and Natural Gas

The price of oil during the coming Aftershock will be a tale of two cities—one where the price is very high, and one where the price is very low. In the United States, the price of oil will be high; in the rest of the world, it will be low. This is one of the more unexpected effects of the popping of the bubbles, but it makes perfect sense. The price of oil has been driven up by the economic growth engine of the world—the U.S. economy—and as that economy hits a major downturn, the world economy will decline, and so will the price of oil. This is especially so because much of the recent growth in oil prices is from Asian growth, which is highly dependent upon massive exports to the United States. When those exports drop substantially, the Asian economies will fall dramatically, and so will their consumption of oil. However, in the United States, where we have to buy oil with dollars that have declined substantially in value, the price of oil will be very high.

Falling demand for oil and lack of capital to drill new oil wells, particularly in unstable countries where most of the world's remaining oil now resides, will cause a collapse of drilling other than in the United States, Iran, and Iraq. The rest of the world will not have enough capital to drill (because capital will no longer be cheap). So as oil demand falls and supply in Iran and Iraq increases, oil prices will fall.

Because we import about two-thirds of the oil we consume, even in the Aftershock we will still be dependent on foreign oil to meet all our needs. The foreign oil coming in will be expensive because we will be paying for it with dollars, and that will make U.S. oil expensive, as well, helping to support the price of oil in the United States, even though overall demand will be falling.

Natural gas will continue to be in demand in the United States and, like oil and coal, will be more expensive in dollars as energy prices rise.

Coal

The world consumes a lot of coal now and demand for coal will continue for quite a while because there won't be as much competition from other forms of energy in the depressed world economy. Subsidies for alternative fuels will dry up, and demand for coal will remain strong, at least until economies rebuild and alternative energy sources become more economically viable.

Who will fulfill the steady demand by the world for coal? U.S. coal will be relatively cheap for the world to buy because the dollar will be down against other currencies, and therefore U.S. coal will take over a larger share of the world coal market.

Because demand for U.S. coal will rise, production will be profitable and will produce lots of new jobs. The current problems with coal, both mining it and burning it, will be gradually solved. We will continue to move toward environmentally sensitive strip mining of coal, and in time develop and employ more advanced pollution controls, as well as carbon sequestration to deal with carbon dioxide and global warming.

Coal will be one of the few industries that will do well in the United States after the bubbles pop. Once we develop alternative energy sources, coal will decline, but will still be used in the creation of synthetic fuels in the future.

Gold Is a Great Aftershock Investment Because It Takes Advantage of a Falling Dollar, a Falling Stock Market, and a Falling World Economy

Let's get something clear right up front: We are not gold bugs. Like most smart, reasonable people, we don't jump on bandwagons based on wishful thinking or a habit of seeing only doom and gloom. Traditionally, the warning to "Buy gold!" has been the longtime mantra of the chronically pessimistic. More recently, however, an entirely new, much more optimistic crowd is starting to buy gold, too. And for very good reasons.

As other asset values decline, people will want to put their money somewhere. They will want to buy something, preferably something of rapidly rising value that has a long tradition of acceptance and demand during difficult times. That is gold. As demand continues to rise for gold, and then rapidly rises when the other bubbles pop, the price of gold will shoot up. The rising gold bubble is your very best bet for profits during the Bubblequake and Aftershock.

Gold is not inflation or interest rate dependent, unlike stocks, bonds, and real estate, so gold is one of the few remaining assets that will not be brought down by rising inflation and interest rates. Quite the contrary, investors worldwide will pile into gold as a flight to safety, when those other assets fall. In time, this will create a gold bubble, as more and more money rushes into gold, and gold prices explode.

Will the rising gold bubble eventually fall? Of course it will, after many years. But why not go for the ride? Compared to other assets, such as stocks and bonds, the amount of gold now available in the world is relatively tiny. Surely, more gold will be mined in the future to satisfy growing demand, but rapidly increasing demand will far outpace supply, pushing up the price. Huge and growing demand, plus relatively tiny supply—you do the math.

As we have already said, we are not gold bugs. In fact, gold just might be the silliest of all investments. Think about it. People spend tons of capital, time, and effort to haul a bunch of rock out of the ground at enormous expense and smelt out tiny bits of gold from the rock, melt them together, and then do absolutely nothing with it—just put it in a vault. How much sillier can you get?

But in the coming years, silly gold will be a truly smart and truly spectacular Aftershock investment. Huge amounts of money will be made—*and lost*—in gold. Gold is a rising bubble on its way to becoming one of the biggest asset bubbles of all time. Second only to the fall of the dollar bubble, the bursting of the gold bubble many years from now will be quite impressive, as well.

Gold is an excellent investment for these crazy times because it takes advantage of *both* the falling stock market and the falling dollar, as well as the overall falling world economy. Gold is an investment opportunity that is custom made for the crazy times ahead. Silly times call for silly investments? Well, sort of.

Here are some not-so-silly reasons why gold will be a super-smart investment in the Bubblequake and Aftershock:

- The gold market is very, very small compared to the stock and bond markets. Even a small shift of capital out of these markets and into gold will dramatically boost its price. And a large inflow of capital into gold will have a very huge, positive effect, indeed.
- Dollar-based investors receive a double benefit by buying gold. That means if you buy gold with dollars you are taking advantage not only of the price rise in gold, but also the fall of the dollar. As an example, if gold goes up four times, and the euro goes up two times against the dollar, your net increase is eight times.

- Gold has significant potential for being an illegal tax avoidance technique. Once the bubbles collide, tax rates in the United States and around the world will increase dramatically, and incomes will decline. The combination means that interest in tax avoidance, even if illegal, will skyrocket. Holding physical gold has been and will be a very effective way to avoid taxes around the world. We, of course, do not advocate illegal tax avoidance, but there's no denying that others will find this appealing, further boosting the demand for and the price of gold.

- The gold market is much more of a world market than U.S. stocks and bonds. Foreign investors can buy stocks and bonds, but in many countries buying gold is easier. Hence, gold has a much greater world demand. For example, India is the world's biggest consumer of gold, buying 20 percent of the world's gold output annually—about twice as much as the United States. On the other hand, India is not a large consumer of stocks and bonds. There's not a stockbroker on every corner of town, but there is a gold dealer. Therefore, the ease with which worldwide investors can buy gold will also heighten its appeal.

- Gold is viewed much more positively as an investment in the Middle East and Asia than it is in the United States. Hence, for those countries, which are the biggest consumers of gold, its acceptability as a good investment will push up the price of gold when their economies tank even worse than the U.S. economy.

- It is very difficult to rapidly increase gold production. Gold mining will not be able to keep pace with demand for many years. When demand for gold goes up, so will the price.

- Gold has traditionally been seen as an inflation hedge in the past, and in this case will be an extraordinarily good hedge against inflation in the near future, so high inflation often drives gold purchases. Inflation will be very high in the United States and also in major European and Asian nations.

- All of the world's stock and bond markets will be under severe downward pressure. Some stock and bond investors, especially in the Middle East and Asia, will move out of stocks and bonds and toward higher gold holdings over the next few years, driving up the price.

- Just as we predicted in 2006, as the world's banking system comes under increasing stress, gold is having, and will continue to have, increasing appeal.
- Gold closed out 2010 with its tenth consecutive year of increases. And that is before all the economic problems the world will face ahead, which will be the main drivers of gold's upward rise in the future.

What if the Environment for Gold Turned Positive?

As gold has rapidly reached new heights, we are often asked if gold has "topped out?" You know it's kind of funny how, no matter what the price of gold, conventional wisdom always says that gold is at its peak. However, the stock cheerleaders would always have you believe that stocks are poised to move up past the next hurdle or poised to rebound, whereas gold gets questioned, again and again, at every upward step it takes. You would think this would have gotten a bit old by now, since gold has gone up *every year for the last 10 years*, now up more than 400 percent since 2000, whereas stocks, as measured by the Dow, are actually down 5 percent since 2000, and down almost 20 percent in inflation-adjusted dollars. But hardly anyone ever asks us if stocks have "topped out."

Nonetheless, the question always comes up when gold has a good run, as it has had lately. The reality is that gold may have peaked temporarily, in the short term. It certainly has gone up very fast, and we could easily see a correction. However, the Fed is throwing plenty of fuel on the gold fire by printing massive amounts of money to stimulate the economy.

While always a volatile asset, the long-term outlook for gold is as golden as it gets. Think about this: If gold has done this well in what we can call a generally negative environment for gold (low inflation and low investor fear), what would happen in a generally positive environment for gold (with high inflation and high investor fear)? Over the past decade, we have had low inflation, a pretty stable dollar, and two of the big alternative investments to gold—stocks and bonds—have done okay, and yet gold is up over 400 percent. Imagine how well gold would do if the environment for gold turned positive, with significantly rising inflation, or the dollar beginning to falter, or a big downturn in the stock or bond markets? What would happen to gold then? Admittedly, those are not likely short-term events, and some of that is already baked into the current price of gold. It may even be a couple years before we see any of that, but when it does happen, what would be the effect on the price of gold? If the price of gold can go up 400 percent in a negative environment, how much would it go up in a positive environment?

Part of the reason we may not see big problems in the stock and bond markets for a while is that the Fed may purchase a lot of bonds with printed money. However, that alone would be enough to keep gold on at least a moderate upward path.

Trying to time the short-term outlook for gold is a tricky business. Among the tricky factors is the real possibility of central banks manipulating the price of gold when they feel it is necessary. The U.S. government will not especially like to see gold rising rapidly while stocks, bonds, and real estate fall. The federal government could decide to use some of its multithousand-ton stash of gold to lower the price of gold by either selling gold or simply loaning it out. (For more on the potential manipulation of gold prices, please see the Appendix.)

It is hard to know exactly what actions will be taken in the fierce fight to save the dollar and the economy. What is more clear is that, at some point, the environment for gold is going to turn quite positive, and when that happens, watch out. Gold's golden days will have arrived.

How to Buy Gold

There are many ways to buy gold—some good, some not so good. We think the three best ways to buy gold are:

1. Buy physical gold from a local coin dealer or a reputable online dealer.

   When buying physical gold, we suggest buying gold bullion coins since they have the lowest premium over the spot price of gold. The easiest coins to trade are the Canadian Maple Leaf, American Eagle, and South African Krugerrands. Coins are usually one ounce in weight, but also come in smaller half-ounce and tenth-ounce sizes. We suggest buying one-ounce coins since they have the smallest markup. You can buy these from local coin shops, but they will be a bit more expensive per ounce than buying online. However, there are no shipping and insurance charges at the coin shop. Some states may charge sales tax or, like Maryland, may require that you buy at least $1,000 worth of gold in order to be tax exempt. You can find local coin shops in the yellow pages or online. Getting to know a local coin dealer now may help you later when you want to sell some coins.

Many people prefer to buy bullion online or by phone. You can simply type "gold bullion" into the search bar of your favorite Internet search engine and investigate your options. Online outlets and retail stores require certified checks or cash to buy gold, or will ask you to wait until your check clears your bank before they ship or let you pick up your gold. Keep in mind that retail coin stores often charge a higher sales commission than a gold ETF, often $30 or more per ounce.

One of the problems with physical gold is that it can be lost or stolen. Hence, we suggest you keep it in a safe-deposit box at a bank or in a lockable safe at home.

2. Buy Gold ETFs.

Gold ETFs (exchange-traded funds) are traded like stocks on the New York Stock Exchange with the price tracking one-tenth of the price of an ounce of gold, making them a very quick and convenient way to buy and sell gold.

Appearing on the scene first in the fall of 2005, gold ETFs now hold more than 1,200 tons of gold. There are two major gold ETFs, and they are very similar. One has the symbol GLD and is a product of State Street Global Advisors. The other has the symbol IAU and is a product of iShares. Just like stocks, gold ETFs can also be bought on margin.

One issue with GLD and IAU is that they are not backed 100 percent by physical gold. They are 100 percent backed by gold, but some of the gold is "paper gold." The ETFs still reflect very closely the price of gold, but if you want an ETF that is 100 percent backed by physical gold, you could look at PHYS. The downside to PHYS is that it trades at a premium to the spot price of gold. You pay a premium when you buy and you may not get the entire premium back when you sell—it depends on the market.

GLD and IAU are perfectly fine ways to invest in gold in that they are low cost and highly liquid with little premium. In the longer term, it may be wise to move to an ETF that is backed 100 percent by physical gold or holding physical gold yourself. But, for now, GLD and IAY are an excellent way to invest in gold.

3. Buy Gold Using a Gold Depository.

An alternative to buying physical gold or gold ETFs, is to buy gold from a gold depository. With a gold depository, you have ownership of the gold without necessarily taking physical possession, although at any time the gold can be shipped to you. As soon as you buy it, they sign legal ownership over to you and deposit it with a separate legal entity. If the depository were to go bankrupt, the gold would still be yours.

Gold depositories solve the problems of gold storage and safety and also give you the opportunity to buy gold on margin, with the maximum percentage of the allowed margin determined by the federal government, like margin on a brokerage account. Usually, it's between three and five times the amount of the gold paid for, depending on the volatility of the price at that time. That means you can use $10,000 to buy $30,000 worth of gold. You can also buy gold ETFs on margin, but leveraging may be easier and more flexible with a depository. However, gold depositories often have a higher commission rate (and other costs) than you would normally find on an ETF. But those are minor considerations compared to the huge benefits of gold profits and ease of conversion to physical gold.

Monex, in Newport Beach, California, is one example of a gold depository service. All of the authors have used Monex for many years.

What about Gold Mining Stocks?

Gold mining stocks have the advantage of multiplying the profits that a gold mining company can derive from mining gold, so they can rise faster than the price of gold itself at times. Revenues rise as the price of gold rises, but operating costs do not. Therefore, as gold prices go up, gold mining companies can do very well.

However, the downside of gold mining stocks is that they can be affected by three key issues that are unrelated to the price of gold. The first is the overall stock market, which when it falls, will tend to take everyone down with it, at least for a while. The second issue is that each gold mining company faces the same company risks that any company can face. Remember, as Mark Twain said, a gold mine is a hole in the ground owned by a liar. Third, many mining companies, particularly the larger ones, are not pure gold plays. They often get the majority of their revenues from other metals, such as iron, copper, etc., which will be very negatively affected by the Aftershock.

While many gold mining stocks will go down temporarily when the stock bubble fully pops, afterwards many gold mining stocks will do extremely well, in some cases even better than the price of gold.

Confiscation by Inflation

We are periodically asked by our readers about whether they should be concerned about the government confiscating gold, savings, pensions, or other assets in a desperate attempt to deal with their failing financial situation when the Aftershock hits.

Given the legal and political difficulties of outright confiscation of assets we think this is unlikely. However, the government does have a very powerful tool for confiscating assets that we think it will use and that it is well worth being concerned about—that is confiscation by inflation. When the government prints money, it is essentially confiscating certain assets.

The most obvious asset is fixed-rate long-term bonds. This asset's value decreases as inflation increases. Its value can drop dramatically even at small levels of inflation of 10 percent or less. When interest rates rise due to rising inflation, the real value of stocks will decline, as will real estate. The combination of massive declines in the value of stock and bonds is the government's way of confiscating your savings, your pension, and your life insurance. Hence, there is no need to confiscate those assets directly; it can be done indirectly through inflation.

Even if the government wanted to confiscate such assets, a good run of very high inflation will make them much less valuable, so they aren't worth confiscating. Hence, you have little to fear from direct government confiscation of your assets, but much to fear from indirect confiscation by inflation—unless you protect yourself. That's the upside to confiscation by inflation: for those who are paying attention, it's easy to avoid.

So there is a lot of money to be made in gold mining stocks if you are aware of the risks we just mentioned. Long term, when the stock market falls and gold rises, there will be even better opportunities to buy gold mining stocks. You need sophisticated investment research or competent guidance before going into any gold mining stock. By the time the gold bubble is rising rapidly, the stock bubble will have been pretty well deflated, so you will be buying gold mining company stock at low prices.

Gold mining stocks may be more attractive if your investment vehicle allows investments in gold mining stocks, but not directly in gold. But remember, great care is needed to avoid the downward influence of a collapsing stock market on gold mining stocks.

Will Gold Be Confiscated or Become Illegal, as It Was During the Great Depression?

Since the Great Depression, gold's importance to our economy has fallen dramatically. During the Depression it was still very important—in the 1890s almost 90 percent of commercial transactions were consummated in gold. Hence, there was a greater need to confiscate gold. In the current economy, it simply isn't that important. Even with high inflation, the dollar will still be the primary means of trade, even if it is worth much less. In a modern economy like ours, gold won't be a viable means of transacting business. Hence, there is little need for the government to confiscate gold, unlike during the Great Depression.

It's unlikely that making gold illegal in the United States would do any more than hurt smaller, middle class investors who can't easily buy gold globally. Also, any talk of making gold illegal would dramatically increase its price, which would be very counterproductive. Further complicating the situation is the fact that a great deal of gold is already in circulation, making it difficult to outlaw. A large black market for gold among the middle-class could easily develop.

Also, people often forget that, unlike our stock market, the vast majority of the demand for gold is outside the United States. So, the price is very much determined by the international market. Whether the United States makes gold illegal or not is only one factor affecting the price of gold. Since most of the demand for gold is outside the United States, it certainly won't be the most significant factor.

There's no guarantee the U.S. government wouldn't make owning gold illegal, but given the problems just mentioned and the limited positive benefits for the government, we think it is unlikely. In addition, the price of gold would have to rise very dramatically from today's price (making it a very attractive investment) for the government to be concerned.

Instead of confiscation, it is far more likely that the government will put all kinds of restrictive controls on gold, such as barring people from buying and selling it, and taxing its value at a high rate. Also, it should be noted that when the government confiscated gold during the Great Depression, it did pay a market price, although clearly what constitutes a market price can be disputed as it often is when the government confiscates land or buildings.

Another reason gold confiscation is unlikely is because any attempts at confiscation will not be especially effective. If people want to have gold, they will. Gold is easy to own outside the United States and relatively easy to smuggle in and out of the United States.

Leveraging Gold

One thing we've seen in recent years is that leveraging (borrowing money to fund part of the purchase of an investment) can light a fire under the growth of your assets. Hedge funds and private equity funds used leverage to create astounding returns for several years. But that fire can get out of control and burn you, as the hedge funds and private equity funds certainly found out. The same goes for leveraging gold. There is no quicker way to make money in gold, and no quicker way to lose it, than by leveraging it. The greater the price volatility, the greater the risk, because even if you are right in the long term, you can be squeezed out by margin calls in the short term due to sharp short-term declines in the price. The price may jump back to its high very quickly, but you may have lost much of your money in the dip when you couldn't make the margin calls on your highly leveraged gold investment and had to sell your position at a low price.

Because we believe there will be greater volatility in the beginning of the gold bubble, we suggest you keep your leverage more limited. However, as the gold bubble begins to take off with the dollar bubble pop, you should probably increase your leverage.

If you decide to buy on margin, the amount of margin you can get is controlled by the government, as with any brokerage account. But, depending on the volatility of gold, you can leverage three to five times. That means at a three times leverage you can get $30,000 worth of gold for $10,000 cash. There are also significant interest costs associated with leveraging.

Gold now and in the future will likely be highly volatile, so be careful. We can't tell you how much leverage to use since the amount of leverage you can take on is very much a factor of your wealth and willingness to take risks. All we can say for sure is that for most people leverage is like alcohol: Use it in moderation.

The Future Gold Bubble: The Biggest, Baddest Bubble of All

Although gold will perform spectacularly in Phase II (the Aftershock), it is important to recognize that, like the stock market and the dollar, gold too will follow a classic up-down bubble trajectory. The coming gold bubble could easily last 10 or more years, and at its height, gold prices could become truly stratospheric—so high, in fact, we won't even mention our best guess for fear of losing credibility. (Of course, as soon as the Aftershock hits, we will certainly tell you all about it because by then it will all seem much more understandable and believable.)

The reasons that the gold bubble will go up are actually the same reasons the gold bubble will go down, only in reverse. Gold will go up when the other bubbles (stock, dollar, real estate) go down because investors will want to buy something seemingly stable and profitable, while their other assets look increasingly unstable and unprofitable.

In time, however, the instability of other assets will evolve to stability again, and their huge downside risks will transform back to normal upside gains.

However, people will be reluctant to give up on gold at that point, just as they are reluctant to give up on stocks and real estate today. Gold will have been a proven winner, and stocks and real estate will have become proven losers. People will say the reason for gold's rise is a fundamental shift away from intangible assets, such as stocks and bonds (whose value can easily evaporate depending on investor interest and government irresponsibility) and towards more tangible assets, like gold. But that will be pure nonsense. Stocks, bonds, and real estate have much more intrinsic value than gold, and over time, that reality will dawn on investors, who will start selling off their gold to buy investments with an income stream, and the gold bubble will pop—big time.

Bubbles always do.

How far gold will fall depends on a couple of factors. It won't collapse completely because there is some commercial value for jewelry and industrial uses. However, for some period after the gold bubble pops, there will be a huge oversupply of gold, relative to industrial and jewelry demand. That will certainly push the price into the ground. With a huge oversupply and no investment demand, the price of gold will fall well below the cost of production, probably below $100 per ounce (when adjusted for inflation).

In the meantime, we strongly suggest you join us on the wonderful ride up on the gold bubble. You won't believe how high we're going to go.

How Will Other Investment Vehicles, Such as Life Insurance, Annuities, and Collectibles Perform?

Life Insurance and Annuities

As we already mentioned in Chapter 6, term life insurance is fine; whole life insurance is not. Whole life or even hybrid life insurance (combination of term and whole) will do poorly simply because much of the money is often invested in bonds and mortgages, some real estate, and a bit in stocks—all of which will do poorly during the Aftershock. So many whole life insurance companies will go bankrupt. And even government-insured policies will not be protected because in this case the government will not be able to cover these.

Term life insurance is fine since it is not really an investment. However, keep in mind that with very high inflation, the value of the payoff amount will be greatly reduced. On the other hand, the real cost of the annual premium payments will also be reduced by inflation. Also keep in mind that once the bubbles burst, quite a few life insurance companies may go under and not be able to pay their claims. So once the value of the dollar begins to fall, keep a close eye on the health of your insurance company and increase your term life insurance to keep pace with inflation.

Annuities take your premiums in lump sum payments and invest the money in the same investment vehicles as whole life insurance companies do (bonds, real estate) and then they pay you over the course of your life based on their returns. But if those investments are wiped out, those payouts to you are also wiped out, and these companies go under. Under normal circumstances, the government would bail out these companies or the individuals who hold the annuities, but when the bubbles fully pop, that is not going to be possible.

Art and Other Collectibles

When inflation rises sharply and all the bubbles burst, asset values—including fine art, collectibles, and jewelry (other than high-grade gemstones)—will fall to stunning lows. Unless you have a strong sentimental attachment to art or collectibles you own, now—before inflation kicks in and asset values fall—could be a good time to think about selling.

During the summer of 2010, we advised one woman, who called us for advice on this, to walk around her well-decorated house, stop in front of each piece of artwork and each valuable collectible, and ask herself, "Do I really want this?" Surprisingly, just one stroll around her house with pen and paper in hand was all it took to help her make a thorough list of what she was willing to sell and what she felt was hers for life. By selling her valuables at a reasonably good price through an auction service, she was able to invest in gold in a quantity that she didn't think would be possible. Now she feels a lot better about the art and objects she still owns, and she feels great about being better prepared for what is ahead.

For those who love art, jewelry, and other collectibles, this advice may not be so easy to follow. Here's a thought that might inspire: If you have the means, you will be able to buy a wonderful variety of art and collectibles at rock bottom prices when the bubbles pop. Wouldn't you rather sell now for relatively high prices, invest that money, and then be in a position to make some great bargain purchases later, getting a much better and more complete collection in the process? Until the bubbles pop, you would be far better off buying gold as your new "collectible."

Are Diamonds Still a Girl's Best Friend?

Precious gem stones—diamonds, emeralds, rubies, and sapphires—come in two general varieties: investment grade (large, high-quality stones worth many thousands of dollars) and noninvestment grade. As a diversification option in addition to gold and silver, investment grade, high quality gems will do very well in the Aftershock. Of these, diamonds are the easiest to buy and sell, and hold the most value.

During the Aftershock, noninvestment-grade diamonds and other gems will definitely fall in value due to declining demand for jewelry, which is very much a discretionary purchase. Even during the financial crisis there was a big drop in demand for jewelry and some decline in prices for diamonds.

Semi-precious stones, such as amethyst, are not worth investing in because they don't have much value, and their rising price won't be as significant as for the precious gems.

Putting It All Together: Aftershock in Action

So far, we have thrown an awful lot at you. We've told you how we correctly predicted the downfall of the four bubbles that have already begun to pop (real estate, stocks, private debt, and discretionary spending bubbles) in Chapters 1 and 2. We told you how massive money printing by the Federal Reserve will help quicken the fall of the next two bubbles (the dollar and government debt bubbles), bringing down what is left of our bubble economy and creating a mega-depression here and around the globe in Chapters 3 through 5. And in the previous chapter and this one, we have begun to tell you about some of your options for protection (Chapter 6) and even profits (Chapter 7) during these unusual times.

What we cannot tell you in a book is specifically how you can put these macroeconomic Aftershock ideas into action in your own life. We certainly do not want you to panic because that does little good, and we still have some time to get ready for what's ahead. Instead, without knowing your unique situation, we would like to help you with your personal task of trying to prepare in a way that is right for you. Toward that end, here are some ideas about how you might pace some of our recommendations, with the full knowledge that only you can decide if and how fast to implement such personal steps.

When to Get Out of Stocks Selling high is always better than selling low, so one option is to begin to slowly exit stocks while the market is still in pretty good shape. It is true that with the Fed printing massive amounts of money, the stock market could continue to rally. It is also true that this won't go on forever and since it is hard to get the timing perfectly right, you have to decide if you would rather be a bit too early or a bit too late in getting out of stocks.

As we have already mentioned, this may not be too easy with stocks held in retirement accounts, although it is worth exploring your options. For stocks under your direct control, you can slowly move out over the next several months. You may miss out on some short-term profits but you will also miss out on a big part of the coming downturn.

When to Get into Gold   The trouble with trying to decide when to buy gold is that it's easy to feel insecure. Gold is a very volatile asset and often the day after you buy it, the price goes down. Conversely, the day after you decided not to buy it, the price goes up. One thing we have noticed about buying gold—which has risen by more than 400 percent in the last decade—is that each time we buy it we worry that we could have waited and gotten it cheaper, and then after we own it for a while, we wish we had bought more. Whenever you buy gold, as long as it is before the dollar bubble pops, most of the upside will still be ahead. So if this is an investment you want to participate in, try to relax into this investment and buckle in for a bumpy ride.

Rethinking Retirement   If even one-tenth of what we are predicting comes true (and it will be far more), most conventional retirement investments are headed for real trouble. If you have any belief in what we have described in this book, retirement accounts and plans must be revisited, the sooner the better. But you needn't panic because it can be done in stages, with increasing changes made, as you see more and more that we are right, and your confidence in our predictions grows. Even if that takes you until what we would consider the last minute, you can still make some of the moves necessary to protect some of your assets.

Getting Real About Real Estate   On this issue, we simply cannot cut you any slack. In general, the time to get out of real estate (other than perhaps your primary residence that you plan to stay in for quite some time) is *now*. Putting this off while you get used to the idea that real estate is not coming back any time soon could very well cost you dearly. Decide and act now.

Keeping Spending Low and Income High   We already covered this more than you may have liked, but it bears repeating. Cut spending now and hang onto your job for as long as you can. Invest wisely and later you will have the means to pick up a lot of mad bargains when others cannot.

A Final Note on Investing: Dumb Luck Is Still Important

Of course, as in past money-making periods, much of the money in the future will be made through dumb luck. The money will be made by people who didn't really see what was coming but, for a variety of reasons, happened to take one or more of the right actions that lead to a profit.

Gold is an obvious example. Many people will hold gold because they were naturally inclined toward gold for cultural reasons, or to avoid taxes, or because they thought the end of the world was near. These people will make a lot of money in the future. But gold is also a bubble. Hence, many of the people who will make money in gold through dumb good luck will also lose it through dumb bad luck because they won't know when to (or even that they should) get out before the gold bubble pops.

Other people will be lucky if they happen to live outside the United States, and they have the capital to invest in the United States after the dollar bubble falls, and U.S. investments become very cheap for foreign investors. It won't be that they planned it; it's just that they live outside the United States. The dumb luck of living outside the United States when the dollar pops will have to be combined with good judgment in investing in the United States, but there is still a large component of being in the right place at the right time due to plain dumb luck.

■ ■ ■

For more information on current investments please visit our web site at www.aftershockeconomy.com/investments.

CHAPTER

8

Aftershock Jobs and Businesses

THE GOOD, THE BAD, AND THE UGLY

One of the most surprising aspects of writing this book was looking back at this chapter in our 2006 book and seeing how very little of it needed to be changed. Our recommendations passed the test of time, and the economy evolved just as our analysis indicated it would. Basically, we nailed it. Now, four years later, we are going to tell you essentially the same things that we tried to warn you about before. This time, you may find it more relevant to your daily life. Given our unmatched track record for correctly predicting the Bubblequake, you should feel very comfortable about our advice in this chapter on how to find or hang onto relatively safe Aftershock jobs and businesses. Almost all our previous recommendations remain the same, except that we are now able to better refine the timing.

As a reminder, this chapter is no different from the rest of the book in that we give you our best analysis, even if it is not what you want to hear. We don't sugarcoat the truth. Hence, this is not a typical job counseling book that lists the winner jobs and loser jobs because in reality, the job outlook is going to be pretty rough all the way around. There will be jobs and businesses that do better than others, but there won't be many winners. That makes reading this chapter all the more important because even small mistakes can become big problems later. The earlier you see what's coming, the better prepared you can be. This is no minor economic adjustment that we are about to face, so it is critical that you seriously consider the advice in this chapter.

This Ain't Your Daddy's Economic Slowdown

This is not the recession of the late 1970s and early 1980s. What we tend to think of when we hear the term "economic slowdown" is not what we are about to get. This one is going to be bigger, badder, deeper, and last much longer than anything we've seen before. To understand how this will impact jobs, it helps to think of the U.S. economy in three parts:

1. **The Capital Goods Sector**—cars, construction, major industrial equipment, and so forth
2. **The Discretionary Spending Sector**—fine dining, entertainment, travel, high fashion, jewelry, art, and so forth
3. **The Necessities Sector**—basic food, shelter, clothing, energy, health care, and so forth

Typically under normal conditions in an economic downturn, we can expect to see the Capital Goods Sector slow significantly, the Discretionary Spending Sector decline somewhat, and the Necessities Sector to be mostly spared. By this point, you've probably guessed that conditions during and after the bubbles collapse will be anything but normal. If you hope your job or business survives the current Bubblequake and coming Aftershock, or you'd like to gear up for a change, the following insights may shed some light on what to expect in each of the three economic sectors.

Keep in mind that all three sectors will suffer significant job and business losses, with the Capital Goods and Discretionary Spending sectors performing worst, and the Necessities Sector faring better but not much. Conversely, all three sectors will have some safe jobs and profitable businesses, but competition for these will be fierce.

A Caveat on all This Advice

This advice is given assuming all the bubbles, including government debt and the dollar bubbles, have fully popped completely. This won't happen for a while. We may get some popping of the discretionary spending bubble, for example, but the pumping up of the government debt and dollar bubbles could temporarily pump up the discretionary spending bubble again—at least for a while.

That's why we always say: Don't Panic! The final popping of these bubbles will take some time. So, even if all the industries we are about to discuss have risen from their low points of the last couple of years, that is temporary and simply due to substantial government bubble pumping via stimulus spending and quantitative easing (QE) (a.k.a., printing money). These are longer term views and longer term career suggestions. However, since the four bubbles have already popped to some extent, some of what we are about to describe has already begun to occur.

The Capital Goods Sector (Autos, Construction, Major Industrial Equipment, and So On)

Super-high interest rates, coupled with a big economic slowdown, will be very bad news for the Capital Goods Sector. As we discussed earlier, massive money printing by the Federal Reserve's program of QE, both past and future, will drive up inflation and interest rates to unprecedented levels. High interest rates will make borrowing money very expensive for individuals and for businesses. High interest rates will be nothing short of an unmitigated disaster for the Capital Goods Sector, which depends on customers having access to low-cost capital. And sky-high interest rates will add to the reasons why recovery after the Bubblequake will take far longer and be more difficult than in previous recessions.

Most Businesses Will Fare Poorly in the Capital Goods Sector

We won't dress it up for you. The bottom line for business owners in the Capital Goods Sector is not pretty. If you can sell now and get out, you should. No one can predict exactly when the Aftershock will hit, but even if it takes another three years (or more), the marketplace for your business is unlikely to improve much. In fact, the value of Capital Goods Sector companies will decrease substantially as unemployment continues to rise, and the economy continues on its slow growth or no growth track. So if you have a business in the automotive, construction, industrial equipment, or any other Capital Goods industry, the longer you wait to get out, the more vulnerable you will be to very significant losses.

What will you do after you sell? Options include using your proceeds to invest in the huge wealth-building opportunities discussed in Chapter 7 or just holding your proceeds safe and in cash for retirement. But, be careful. As we discussed in Chapters 3 and 6, you will have to be increasingly careful about where you hold your cash. Keep an eye on our Aftershock Newsletter regarding where to put your cash. (You can sign up for a free trial of our newsletter and other services at www.aftershockeconomy.com).

Very Limited Job Prospects in the Capital Goods Sector

As hard as it may be to sell one's business, it can be even harder to quit your job and train for another career. Unlike selling a business, which at least provides the possibility of getting some cash, quitting a job usually means walking away, cold turkey, from a paycheck. And in the Capital Goods Sector of the economy that paycheck may be quite a bit better than jobs elsewhere in the economy. So we are fully aware that you may have no interest in leaving a lucrative job in order to take what may be a lower-paying position.

Still, you might as well know the cold, hard facts: Jobs in Capital Goods industries will be the worst hit by the coming Bubblequake, and there isn't much you can do to protect yourself other than to gear up to move on. Your best bet may be to rethink your career with an eye toward joining an industry that will do far better when the bubbles burst.

Bubble Babies

We all know what Beanie Babies are, but Bubble Babies? A Bubble Baby is a CEO or businessperson who has done extremely well during the bubble economy but won't be able to do nearly as well in the Aftershock. Their CEO skills and ability to get paid sometimes hundreds of millions of dollars have been much more related to riding rising bubbles than leading companies. Bubble Babies have more political skills than business skills. They know how to create the buzz and be recognized as great leaders or great businessmen.

We know who these people are. The question for the future is which of these celebrity Bubble Babies will be able to perform as well during the Aftershock as they did in the rising bubble economy. Who among them will have the real skills required to start or lead a business during the difficult times ahead? Are they Bubble Babies, or are they real businessmen and businesswomen? We'll soon find out.

If a major career makeover is not your style, you may want to consider making a move to a more stable area within your current industry. For example, if you work in the construction industry—which will take a truly terrible hit—you may find that moving into repair-oriented work, rather than new construction, will keep you busy while others sit at home. Of course, many construction workers will also get this idea after the bubbles pop, so the sooner you begin your transition, the better.

Other possibilities include most types of maintenance and repair work, such as automobile repair, which will be in increasing demand, as people buy far fewer new cars and instead hang onto their older cars for as long as possible.

The Discretionary Spending Sector (Travel, Restaurants, Entertainment, etc.)

As the economy continues to fall, Americans are not going to run out to the mall every night after work (if they have work) and squander their limited cash and very limited credit on more high-priced designer handbags or the latest CDs. Discretionary spending is, well, discretionary. And many items and activities we currently enjoy will simply be off our shopping lists after the bubbles pop. This will certainly slow many businesses to a crawl and force others completely out of the game, further driving up unemployment.

But discretionary spending will still hold up better than the Capital Goods Sector of the economy because some people will still have money, and they will keep spending their money, except at a lower level than before. So, instead of discretionary spending disappearing altogether, the people who can still spend will simply buy lower-priced discretionary items. Instead of shopping for designer handbags at Saks Fifth Avenue, for example, they may downgrade to Target or Walmart.

The restaurant business will face this trend as well. Once the bubbles pop, far fewer people and businesses will have money for eating out. That will certainly affect all restaurants. But some people and businesses will have money and will be quite happy to go to restaurants, as long as they don't have to spend as much as they used to. So the restaurant industry will continue to be a huge industry in the United States, but business will shift dramatically toward the lower end. For example, Mexican and Chinese restaurants will continue to survive and increase market share, while seafood and steak houses will be much harder hit.

To a large extent, the same thing will happen throughout the Discretionary Spending Sector. Instead of brand names, we'll buy bargains. We will still want to buy some stuff we don't absolutely need, we'll just buy a lot less of it and at lower prices.

As we said earlier in the book, the Discretionary Spending bubble is popping, and this bubble makes up a large portion of the overall U.S. economy, so when it falls, a whole lot falls with it. That means, once incomes and credit cards are in short supply, a much greater percentage of the U.S. economy is going to feel the pain than ever before. This is an entirely new situation for us. Back in the 1920s, when the nation was much less wealthy and was heading into the Great Depression, discretionary spending represented a much smaller portion of our overall economy. So when the stock market bubble crashed in 1929, and the economy took a major downturn, the large dip in discretionary spending had much less impact because it just didn't make up that large a part of the economy. Other industries took a big hit, but people still had to eat basic food and buy basic clothing, so most of these industries just kept on going.

It's a very different situation today. So much of what we currently buy (and that keeps our economy going), we can easily do without. We may not like forgoing a trip to a high-priced store like Neiman Marcus, where we can select from a huge range of expensive goods, but if we have to, we certainly can and will survive on cheaper items from low-priced stores. We may not like to skip the latest, high-priced fashions, but if we have to, we can easily shop at lower-end and discount stores. We can also survive quite nicely without $100,000 kitchen makeovers, complete with granite countertops and stainless steel appliances. As incomes and assets evaporate, Americans will learn to manage without these pricey pleasures.

If spending on lavish food, clothing, and housing can easily be cut, and if this kind of spending represents a big chunk of America's current economy, then the impact of these changes will be very, very negative indeed. While the Discretionary Spending Sector will be hit less hard than the Capital Goods Sector, the fact that Discretionary Spending has become such a big part of the current U.S. economy means a downturn in this sector will greatly accelerate the coming Aftershock and make our post-bubble recovery quite difficult.

Businesses and Jobs in the Discretionary Spending Sector

We've already mentioned how a slowdown in the Discretionary Spending Sector will harm many businesses in the restaurant, retail, and home improvement industries. The travel industry will take an even greater hit. Leisure travel will be especially stalled, while more Americans visit locations closer and cheaper—such as into their living rooms to watch TV. Major entertainment destinations, such as Orlando and Las Vegas, will hang on due to liquidation of assets and to foreign visitors coming to spend their more valuable currencies in our cheaper playgrounds. Leisure travel by Americans going overseas will face the double whammy of minimal discretionary spending and a dollar that has fallen dramatically against foreign currencies.

Business travel will suffer, as well. Domestic business travel will decrease due to the sharp slowdown in the economy and the cost-cutting mindset that most companies will be forced to adopt. Overseas travel will be hit by high costs and the low value of the dollar, so only the most important overseas business travel will continue. Also, with our imports way down and our exports low due to the global mega-depression, there simply won't be much need for business travel overseas.

Businesses that will survive during these leaner times will include low-end restaurants, low-end clothing stores, discount shops of every description, used clothing and household furnishing stores, and businesses that cater to local or inexpensive travel.

If you own a business in the Discretionary Spending Sector, you might want to give some very serious thought to selling your business now or in the next couple of years. Only the most clever, well-placed, or just plain lucky businesses in this sector will thrive in the coming Aftershock.

If you are currently employed in the Discretionary Spending Sector and are in a position to retrain for another career, this would be a good time to look elsewhere, such as the Necessities Sector.

As a Business Owner, You Don't Want to Be Heading for the Exits When Everyone Else Is

It's always most comfortable to move with the crowd. That way you know you are making the correct decision, right? But as we know, having lots of company is no sign of correct timing. When many

Fierce Competition for Fewer Jobs Will Reduce Pay

Normally, when an economic downturn is relatively short or relatively mild, rising unemployment doesn't go too high or last too long. In this case, job losses will be staggering after the dollar and government debt bubbles pop, and there will be a mad scramble for those jobs that haven't been destroyed. For most people this means it will be increasingly difficult to find a job, any job, regardless of your qualifications and experience. And for those lucky enough to be employed, keeping a job will mean putting up with less desirable working conditions, fewer (if any) benefits, reduced hours, and most of all, reduced pay.

Many jobs will be temporary, part-time, or on an independent contractor basis. And many jobs will offer no pay at all, with lots of people competing for these unpaid jobs (or internships) in hope of perhaps eventually getting paid.

As competition for jobs greatly increases and wages fall, it will not be a measure of your professional worth, but simply an issue of supply and demand. Lots of willing workers (big supply) and not too many jobs (lower demand) equals a lower price paid for your services. After all the bubbles pop, people will accept wage cuts in most jobs for one simple reason: If they don't, somebody else will. (This is not deflation by the way—it's a real price decrease due to rising supply and falling demand. In fact, wages in nominal terms will be much higher than they are today due to inflation caused by massive expansion in the money supply. But income will be lower in inflation-adjusted terms.)

business owners start to realize that they need to sell, it's not a good time to put your business on the market. Lots of sellers and not many buyers will mean prices will go down.

In addition, you are fighting against some demographics. Many of those businesses are owned by aging baby boomers. As they get closer to retirement, they will become more risk-averse and more likely to want to cash out of their businesses and save the money. Yes, they may lose some upside, but they're not 35 anymore and many are nervous about the underlying economy. So, changing demographics will make the number of sellers grow, and the bad economy will make them more likely to sell. Finally, as they start to realize an Aftershock could occur, they will want to sell, but by then it will be too late as prices will have fallen, so that it becomes a wrenching decision to sell at such low prices. At that point, most business owners can't/won't want to sell because prices will be too low.

No need to panic. There is time. But, don't try to time the sale of your business so perfectly that you get caught waiting too long. Your risk is the long term drop in selling price, rather than the risk of having missed out on a perfect high point in the mergers and acquisitions market for small- or medium-sized businesses.

Some Limited Good News: The Necessities Sector (Health Care, Education, Food, Basic Clothing, Transportation, Government Services, and Utilities)

In the job market, the Necessities Sector is the place to be. Historically many of the jobs in this sector don't pay very well, and they will pay even less well after the bubbles pop. But, at least you will have a job, and it will be much more stable and reliable than most other jobs in the postbubble economy. Even at lower pay, Necessities Sector jobs will be a godsend for families with a spouse who used to make more money than his or her mate, but is now unemployed. The lower-paid, still-employed spouse, working as a nurse, teacher, medical administrator, or other Necessities Sector employee, will likely retain his or her job and be able to carry the family through the worst of the downturn.

The Necessities Sector is composed primarily of health care, education, utilities, basic food, basic clothing, and government services, usually run by government or other nonprofit entities. The private companies that supply these government and non-profit entities have the potential to survive, as well. Of course, as things get increasingly negative for the rest of the economy, the Necessities Sector will also take a hit because it currently contains a larger portion of discretionary spending (spending on high-end items within the Necessities category) that will be drastically cut. The difference is that this sector will not do quite as badly as the other two sectors.

Health Care Jobs and Businesses

Health care is currently a very strong element of the U.S. economy, and it will continue to be the best bet in the Necessities Sector after the bubbles pop, but not without a lot of pain. As they lose their jobs, many people will lose their private medical insurance, which will dramatically reduce health care revenues. The government will step in and fill the gap with Medicaid and Medicare, but benefits will be tight.

The loss of so many privately insured people will cause big problems for the health care industry, particularly in health care capital goods, such as radiology machines and hospital construction. However, businesses providing services and supplies to the health care industry will continue to do okay, but will still be hit hard by the large overall decline in health care revenues.

Health care jobs that will do the best include:

- Nurses
- Primary care doctors
- Psychiatrists
- Nurse practitioners
- Physicians' assistants
- Medical technicians, support personnel, administrative staff, and others involved in primary care medicine (not specialties)

Specialists and their supporting staff and services will not do well, with surgeons taking the biggest hit due to falling demand. Elective procedures, such as cosmetic surgery, already had a downturn during the financial crisis. Once the coming Aftershock hits, all medical specialists and their support staffs will see very big declines in income, due to tough limitations on reimbursable procedures and reimbursement rates.

Health Care Could Become 20 Percent of the GDP When the Bubbles Pop

Health care will be one of the safest havens for business owners and workers in the Bubblequake and Aftershock. Currently, the huge health care industry accounts for about 16 percent of the nation's GDP. As other industries decline, especially in the Discretionary Spending and Capital Goods Sectors, the more stable health care industry will naturally take up a larger percentage of our economy. We've seen this before on a smaller scale. For example, during the oil bust in the 1980s, the percentage of the Houston economy represented by non-oil industries grew dramatically.

Add to this an aging population with increasing demands for health care, and it is quite possible that health care could take over a staggering 20 percent of our economy after all six of the bubbles pop, even if we have what could be a 50 percent cut per person in medical care costs, primarily by limiting procedures and reimbursable rates.

That means that not only will the safest jobs and businesses be in health care during the Bubblequake, but also that the nation's hopes for regaining significant productivity growth in the postbubble economy will lie with dramatic productivity advancements in the health care field.

Government Jobs and Businesses

After health care, the next-best positions in the Necessities Sector will be government services jobs, such as police and firefighters. In the Aftershock, as in past recessions, government services will still be needed. However, unlike in past recessions, government services will have to take massive cuts when the government can no longer borrow money after the government debt bubble pops.

In particular, government spending on the defense industry will take a very deep cut. It won't be because people suddenly don't care about defense, but when push comes to shove and Americans have to choose between military spending and kicking Mom off Medicare, they will reluctantly cut the Defense Department before pulling the plug on Medicare and Medicaid. However, funding per patient on Medicare and Medicaid expenditures will also decline dramatically. But we suspect that, along with massive medical benefits cuts, they will drastically cut defense spending. This will particularly hurt government contractors, especially those dependent on the Defense Department for funding.

No one will like any of this, but the days when our government could simply borrow all the money needed to buy everything it wanted will be long gone. Deficit spending, at that point, will no longer be an option. And let's not forget that the government won't be able to borrow money from Social Security taxes anymore because the surplus will be entirely gone. In addition to job losses related to defense, businesses and individuals who supply capital goods or construction services to the government will also be hit. Road construction and maintenance, and transportation in general, will do poorly. As new construction of both roads and buildings plummets, businesses that can make the switch to repair work and related services will fare better.

Education Jobs and Businesses

Along with health care, the demand for public education will continue, so businesses that supply education or health care products or services to the government will benefit from strengthening their marketing and business ties to these areas and increasing their percentage of sales in these sectors.

Jobs in education will be more secure than in, say, the restaurant business (Discretionary Spending Sector), but do not make the mistake of thinking that all education jobs are protected. As many as half of all jobs in education will be lost, as tax revenues drastically drop at both the state and local levels. Jobs at primary and secondary schools will hold up better than those in higher education. Some number of elementary, middle, and high school math and science teachers will still be in demand but many more will go jobless. Music and art teachers will get laid off in droves, along with extracurricular personnel. Seniority and union membership won't matter once all the bubbles pop. Instead, if you want to get or keep a job in education, you'll need to be very good at your job, be willing to teach more classes to more students, and be very loyal to your school's administration.

The picture for higher education will be even tougher. Strong departments in practical fields, like engineering and computer science, especially at top colleges and universities, will suffer less draconian cuts, faring far better than those in "soft" departments (sociology, English, etc.) at liberal arts schools. Don't count on tenure to save you if your department has to take big budget cuts—it won't. And if you are lucky enough to be retained in a strong department, be prepared to teach four classes a semester, for less pay. Not only will your teaching load go up a lot, your research funding and research time will go down a lot, especially funding from internal sources.

Big Opportunities after the Bubbles Pop: Cashing in on Distressed Assets

In nearly every industry in all three sectors of the economy, there will be many opportunities to benefit from falling asset values. Just as high-priced office furniture from bankrupt dot-com companies ended up at auction sales for pennies on the dollar after the relatively small Internet bubble popped, there will be countless auctions of every description all over the planet after the biggest bubble crash the world has ever seen. Opportunities to make large profits by buying and servicing distressed businesses and other assets will actually become one of the good sectors in our postbubble economy.

As always, timing will be key. One of the biggest mistakes many people will make is buying distressed businesses or other assets too soon. In this very unusual economic downturn, involving the fall of multiple bubbles, we will face very high interest and inflation rates that will take a lot longer to come down than anyone might imagine. It will be easy to mistakenly think the worst has passed and the time is right to start buying up distressed businesses and assets, when actually the price of these bargain properties will likely fall even lower. For maximum profits, think years, not months. Many people in the real estate market are making this mistake right now. They think that because an asset has lost 25 to 50 percent of its peak value, it is a bargain. It emphatically is not!

That said, there can be shorter-term flipping investments where a distressed asset can be bought and then resold before the Aftershock hits to someone unaware of the coming Aftershock. Since the Aftershock is still a ways off, profitable distressed investment opportunities can succeed if done this way.

Once the Aftershock hits, the servicing of distressed assets and businesses will be an instant and long-term winner. Bankruptcy attorneys and liquidation/auction houses will obviously do quite well. And so will a whole range of people and companies who will buy, restructure, manage, and resell distressed businesses, and other assets, making huge incomes and profits along the way, including:

- Accountants and financial analysts involved with forensic accounting and distressed properties accounting.

- Consultants, bankers, managers, and others involved in the acquisition, restructuring, and management of distressed businesses and other assets.

■ ■ ■

For more information on jobs please visit our web site at www .aftershockeconomy.com/jobs.

CHAPTER 9

Understanding Our Problems Is the First Step Toward Solving Our Problems

When people start talking about the financial crisis or the very slow economy, there is always a tendency to want to blame someone. The usual suspects are Federal Reserve Chairmen, past and present, individual investment bankers, all investment bankers, Congress, the President, etc. Although all of these people share blame, some more than others, for our economic problems, it is usually only a partial answer. We could change the Fed Chairman, but would that make that much difference? We could put some investment bankers in jail—and maybe they should go—but is that really the heart of the problem? We wish it were so, but it is doubtful that such changes will really turn the economy around.

The culprit we feel that is more important than any of these individuals or groups of individuals is economists. What we are witnessing now is a fundamental failure of the economics profession. Understanding this failure and how to solve it will create a powerful tool for solving our current and future economic problems.

If You Don't Understand Why an Economy Grows, You Can't Understand Why It Doesn't Grow

The fundamental failure of economics goes beyond simply not seeing the crisis before it happened, or not warning of it, or not telling us

231

how to prevent it. The failure is a fundamental lack of understanding of how the economy works. Economists don't really know why an economy grows—whether it be the United States or China or Japan. Hence, they can't tell you why it has stopped growing.

Yes, they can tell you it is growing and where it is growing, but they can't really tell you why. They don't understand growth, so they don't understand the lack of growth either.

Of course, no one really cares if they don't understand how the economy grows, as long as it's growing. Nobody gets mad at economists because the economy is growing 10 percent per year; they get mad at economists when it stops growing—hey, man, we need you to solve this problem, and quick!

Of course, since they don't really know why it was growing, they don't really know how to get growth going again. When it's growing, all a good economist has to do is agree that the economy is growing and will continue to grow, as most economists did. For that, they were richly rewarded with good academic positions, research grants, and other favors.

In fact, we have certainly spent more money on economists and economic research in the past 30 years of the bubble economy than we have for all of previous history. During the bubble economy the resources devoted to economics have ballooned enormously from previous decades, not just in the United States but in Europe and Japan as well.

It's truly been the golden age of economics. The only problem in this golden age is the almost complete lack of major economic breakthroughs from all this economic research. That wasn't true before. We have had big economic breakthroughs in this century, but the last 30 years have been among the least productive of the last 100 years, despite the enormous increase in funding.

You Need to See the Big Picture Before You Start to Focus

This is partly because a lot of money can be spent researching very narrow or obscure issues. In true sciences, like chemistry or geology, these narrow or obscure issues can often be very beneficial in the advancement of, for instance, chemical or geologic knowledge. That's because these additional bits of research are tied very fundamentally to strong fundamental scientific theories of chemistry or geology.

In economics, research on relatively narrow issues is not very useful because it is not tied to a strong overall understanding of economics. When you don't understand the big picture, looking at the little picture doesn't really help.

In geology, if we did the same thing, it would be like having thousands of people study the Appalachian Mountains to understand how mountains form. However, if you don't understand continental drift, even if you put tens of thousands of people on studying the Appalachians, you're not going to understand how mountains form. Beautiful mountains, yes. A lot of well-funded research, definitely. But, breakthroughs in understanding? Not a chance.

Understanding continental drift may involve looking at the Appalachian Mountains, but that's not the focus. The focus is more on fundamental concepts of how all mountains are formed, and what could be driving the evolving nature of those mountains. Which, of course, involves recognizing that those mountains are evolving. Unless you are studying the Appalachian Mountains as simply a springboard for a broader understanding of geology and how mountains form, you will get nowhere. You need to understand the big picture to understand the Appalachians.

It may be comfortable to have thousands of other very focused, very scholarly researchers with you in your Appalachian Mountain research, but it isn't going to get the geology profession any breakthroughs in understanding how mountains are formed. Lots of money spent and no insights gained.

Sounds a lot like the state of current economic research.

But to better understand why economics has hit a brick wall despite the enormous increase in resources being spent on economics, we need to go through a brief history of the breakthroughs in the past. For anyone who wants more than our highlights history of economics, we strongly suggest that you read Robert Heilbroner's book, *The Worldly Philosophers*. It's the runaway best book on the history of economics. It's also easy and enjoyable reading and a great book for noneconomists.

The Key Breakthroughs in the History of Economic Thought

We're just going to review seven major breakthroughs in economic thinking over the past few centuries to give you an idea of how we got to where we are and to guide us in what needs to be done in the future. There were other key insights in economic thought developed during this time, but these breakthroughs basically shaped the structure of economic thought today.

Breakthrough #1: Free Markets

We begin with Adam Smith and the concept of free market competition. His support of free markets and opposition to business monopolies set up by the monarchy was a foundation for modern economic thought. Much of the power of Smith's work is due to his focus on some aspects of property rights (the rights of monarchs to establish a monopoly in a market) and how they are an important part of economics. By focusing on certain aspects of property rights he vaulted economic thought forward. The definition of property rights we use is simply "the way in which society determines who gets what resources."

Smith's most important written work, *The Wealth of Nations*, was first written in 1776, an auspicious time for questioning the wisdom of monarchical rule in the British Empire. He was effectively one of the democratic revolutionaries who helped others to question the value of the monarchy in general and more specifically, in their interference with free markets. To a large degree Adam Smith's work is the start of modern economic thought. He gets an A+ for his work!

What Adam Smith missed was a focus on the evolutionary aspects of economic growth and specifically, the evolution of the forces that were changing property rights, such as the creation of free markets.

Breakthrough #2: More Focus on Economic Evolution and Property Rights

Karl Marx was the second major breakthrough in economic thought, more for what he focused on than for his actual theoretical insights. With his publication of *The Communist Manifesto* in 1848, he continued Adam Smith's focus on property rights but added an evolutionary element to it. He attempted to construct an evolutionary theory of property rights. He just wasn't correct about what that evolution was

Part of the reason that Marx had such difficulties in figuring out the correct evolution is that he couldn't look into the future. His view of economics relied very heavily on Utopian Socialism, which viewed economic activity through a lens on the past—a much more agricultural-based economy with many small craftsmen, rather than a modern industrial economy with large corporations. His model was heavily based on an agricultural economy with the landowning nobility holding ever more and more land. He incorrectly transferred his model to the rising industrial sector. He had no real understanding of productivity and how it impacted agricultural and industrial development.

Marx also focused on the role of capital in society, which is important, but again was more focused on capital as land and the rent that it produced, as opposed to a return on the investment of capital, which is so critical to modern industrial society. However, his lack of understanding of the role of capital and its return was a key factor in forcing economists to develop a viable theory of what determined the return to capital, meaning what determines the level of profits and interest rates.

So, Mr. Marx made a good effort at trying to understand the evolution of the economy and the key concepts of property rights and capital but ended up not fully understanding them due to his focus on a past economic model, which was the predominant model when he was writing. It would be clear to an astute observer, however, that the economy was rapidly moving away from this model. But, his work motivated other economists to develop an adequate theory of capital. His performance rates an A for effort and an F for results.

Breakthrough #3: Understanding Supply and Demand (Beginning of Microeconomics)

Economic thought had a third breakthrough—the development of the combined model of supply and demand. This was not as easily attributable to one person. Prior to Marx, concepts of supply and demand developed separately. Adam Smith had led the way with work on supply and supply-based pricing. Other later work developed a competing price model based solely on demand. After Marx, these concepts were combined into a unified theory of supply and demand. This combined supply and demand concept was an excellent basic theory and was a good start at understanding how markets worked. It was the beginning of modern microeconomic theory. However, it was based on an abstraction of an idealized nineteenth century grain market. For it to be used in a real economy, there had to be unrealistic constraints which severely limited its applicability to the real world.

For example, free entry into a market, as defined in the free market economic model, is critical to a true free market, but it rarely exists at the required level in most markets today. Just as the government can establish and maintain a free market, it can destroy a free market by declaring monopolies in markets to benefit friends and supporters. Adam Smith opposed this type of government destruction of free markets, and that opposition was a key motivation for developing his theory of free markets. Free markets don't benefit the individual businessmen participating in them (that's why they wanted the king to grant them monopolies), so there is a natural tendency to thwart the free market to gain extra profits. The government's role in establishing and maintaining free markets and free entry into those markets was not well understood at the time and is still not well understood. And, that's just one example of the problems underlying supply and demand models of the economy. So, theories of supply and demand are an important breakthrough but they are often highly constrained in their applicability to the real world. Overall, this breakthrough merits a C—good idea in principle, but poor in actual real-world execution.

As you can see at this point, economics was suffering in part from an overall lack of an integrated theory. Economics was a collection of theories and concepts. These concepts were usually developed by economists observing economic behavior in everyday life and abstracting that behavior into more general and theoretical concepts with broad application. That's a good way to take a first step but it isn't an overall integrated theory. And, in particular, economists were still not focusing on key issues such as property rights, technological evolution and information dynamics (the way people learn). That also means those concepts were certainly not part of an integrated theory of economics, which is critical for good economics.

Breakthrough #4: Understanding the Role of Capital and the Payment for Capital

As mentioned earlier, Karl Marx helped future economists focus on capital. This led to the fourth major breakthrough in economic thought, which was an understanding of the role of capital and the payment for capital in a modern economy. In particular, this meant understanding interest payments as compensation for the time value of money and as compensation for the riskiness of an investment. In addition, economists began to better understand an investor getting compensation for taking a business risk. They better understood the concept of return on investment, which was fundamental to the financing of the modern industrial economy.

However, theories of risk and returns need to be integrated with a better understanding of property rights to be fully applicable to the real world. Overall this breakthrough merits a B—like theories of supply and demand a good idea in principle, but poor in actual execution.

Breakthrough # 5: Macroeconomics (Monetary and Fiscal Policy)

The fifth breakthrough in economic thought is the modern concept of macroeconomics. Modern macroeconomics is in part an attempt to solve some of the earlier problems just mentioned with theories on supply and demand, which basically did not allow for the occurrence of a severe recession or depression.

Macroeconomics was developed to deal with these problems in a more sophisticated way than simple supply and demand theories, which proved totally incapable of explaining what happened. As mentioned earlier, supply and demand theories were abstractions of an idealized nineteenth century grain market. The influential British economist, John Maynard Keynes, created a more sophisticated bit of abstraction by looking at how governments had funded wars in the past through borrowing money. Monarchs had often borrowed money in the past to fund wars. Keynes broadened the concept to how governments could borrow money to stimulate the economy, or conversely to run a budget surplus to reduce economic activity. Issues surrounding governmental borrowing are called fiscal policy.

In the same light, a more modern macroeconomist, Nobel Prize winner Milton Friedman, looked at how governments printed money, which is called monetary policy. Again, printing money was something that monarchies had done to finance wars in the past so Milton Friedman abstracted this concept and applied it more broadly to the whole economy as a means of stimulating or reducing overall economic activity. This also led to a much clearer theoretical foundation for the causes of inflation.

Thus, the creation of the concepts of both fiscal and monetary policy (how governments borrow and print money and its effects on the economy) was the foundation of modern macroeconomic analysis.

However, since macroeconomics is based on abstraction, it cannot handle what will soon become one of our key tools for getting out of the mega-depression, targeted stimulation, or the even more advanced policy tools that will need to be used much later to lock the economy at full employment and zero inflation, both of which depend on a fundamental understanding of economics as a science.

The fact that economics has both a microeconomic theory and a macroeconomic theory illustrates the fundamental problem mentioned earlier—that economics does not have an integrated comprehensive theory– which suggests that neither individual theory is completely adequate. The inadequacies of these economic theories will become painfully obvious when the Aftershock hits.

Breakthrough # 6: Mathematical Models

In the post-war period, economists were able to represent the equilibriums suggested by the supply and demand model, as well as fiscal and monetary policy, by systems of equations. The system of equations could be solved, so that the model provided an equilibrium solution. Due to the many fundamental theoretical problems discussed in this chapter, these models have not been as successful as hoped in representing real world economies, but they do represent an important first step in introducing mathematics into economics. As explained in detail later in this chapter in the "Fourth Element" subsection a *static* equilibrium is not what real economies tend to reach. Real economies are more like the weather—constantly changing and reaching a *dynamic* equilibrium. As will be discussed later, for these fluctuating systems the use of numerical simulation models, which are based on a better fundamental analysis of the economy, is the preferred way to create a viable mathematical model of the economy.

Breakthrough #7: Empirically Tested Mathematical Models

Another major postwar breakthrough was the use of econometrics, which allowed a statistically based empirical validation of an economic theory or model. A model that could be empirically tested is a big step in the right direction, but the models don't work that well. Models that produce a high correlation of multiple inputs with model outputs may test well statistically, but correlation does not imply causation. So, for example, high home prices might not only be caused by high demand; there may be many other factors at work, such as property rights, and these cannot be measured or used correctly with current econometric analysis.

To some degree mathematical models can be modified to produce the results you want them to produce. Thus, they produce more what Mark Twain said about statistics—there are lies, damn lies, and statistics. So, they are often inaccurate in practical terms.

Empirically tested mathematical models are a good step in the right direction, in that they are making economics more mathematical and empirical. That is very important to economics becoming a science. However, economists are using the wrong mathematical approach and empirical approach. The econometric approach will need to be replaced by an empirical approach based on scientific experimentation.

Although there have been minor improvements to microeconomic and macroeconomic thinking and econometric modeling in the last 30 years, there have been few major breakthroughs. We are still trying to improve economic thinking with these same concepts, and it's not working very well.

Economics Needs a Breakthrough Idea, like Continental Drift

Almost 30 years ago, the evolution of economics stopped with mathematical models. Despite the massive resources spent, we have had few major breakthroughs since then. Lots of research, lots of funding awarded to think tanks, and economics research centers, lots of John Bates Clark awards for best economic scholars under 40, lots of tenured professorships given, lots of Nobel prizes awarded, lots of highly regarded articles published in the *American Economic Review* (one of the most prestigious academic economic journals), but no significant breakthroughs.

Why?

It seems as if with all these prizes and funding, the profession is having a breakthrough every day! But, it's not, and that's why economists are having such problems dealing with our current economic downturn. In fact, all the activity and prizes almost seemed designed to distract from the lack of real breakthroughs.

Like cheerleading in the financial markets, it is cheerleading in the economics profession. Using the earlier analogy of thousands of geologists studying the Appalachians with no real breakthroughs on understanding why mountains form, we could give out thousands of tenured professorships, print thousands of articles in prestigious journals, give out lots of prizes for great work on the Appalachians, but it still won't help us understand what created the Appalachian Mountains.

Unless, of course, you have someone like Alfred Wegener, who is willing to take on the status quo view of geology and come up with an idea like continental drift. Of course, when a big breakthrough like continental drift occurs, you don't need thousands of people studying the Appalachians anymore. Alfred has figured it out. The other guys were just wasting their time and need to go home despite all their prizes and funding.

Now of course, there is plenty of work to be done to develop the model of continental drift. Now that you have a powerful new understanding of geology, a huge window of new research has just been opened. But, very likely it won't be something that all the Appalachian scholars will be all that good at. It will be for a new generation to truly run with and develop the research possible now that geologists have an understanding of continental drift.

What economics needs is a breakthrough like continental drift and a person like Alfred Wegener. See the sidebar below for some

ABE Award for Intellectual Courage: Alfred Wegener

Alfred Wegener created the greatest breakthrough in modern geology, the theory of continental drift. However, he wasn't even a geologist. He received his PhD in Planetary Astronomy from Humboldt University in Berlin in 1905. He was also interested in climatology. His lectures, *The Thermodynamics of the Atmosphere*, became a standard textbook in meteorology. Obviously he had no problem getting support when he wasn't attacking the status quo.

However, with continental drift, he was attacking the status quo head on. He had reasonable but not overwhelming evidence for his continental drift idea. He had noticed the obvious fit of North America to Europe and South America to Africa. He tried to prove this theory that the continents were once connected by doing research on fossils and geology. He found identical fossils and identical rock strata on both sides of the Atlantic.

After 1912 Wegener publicly advocated the theory of continental drift arguing that all the continents had once been joined together in a single landmass and had drifted apart. In 1915, in *The Origin of Continents and Oceans*, Wegener published the theory that there had once been a giant continent, which we now call Pangea.

Reaction to Wegener's theory was almost uniformly hostile, and often exceptionally harsh and scathing; Dr. Rollin T. Chamberlin of the University of Chicago said, "Wegener's hypothesis in general is of the footloose type, in that it takes considerable liberty with our globe, and is less bound by restrictions or tied down by awkward, ugly facts than most of its rival theories."

Needless to say, no one was interested in helping him prove or disprove his theory. They simply dismissed his groundbreaking ideas out of hand without even wanting to understand them or discuss them.

In fact reaction to his ideas was so strongly negative that after the American edition of Wegener's work was published in 1925 the American Association of Petroleum Geologists organized a symposium specifically to criticize his continental drift hypothesis.

However, by the 1960s the evidence for Wegener's theories of continental drift became overwhelming. Despite all of the efforts of highly credentialed status quo defenders, Wegener's ideas succeeded because they were right. He revolutionized geologic thought and became the father of modern geology.

background on Alfred Wegener and his struggle against the status quo academic leadership to bring an enormously important breakthrough to geology, for which we award him the ABE Award for Intellectual Courage.

So Why Aren't We Getting an Alfred Wegener or a Breakthrough Idea Like Continental Drift?

It's an interesting question, and as we alluded to before, it's very much related to that huge increase in funding for economists and economic research during the bubble economy. Life has been good for economists during the bubble economy. Partly as a result of the stock and housing bubbles, universities have had no trouble raising tuition enormously—way beyond the rate of inflation. This allowed them to increase or maintain professors' salaries. It also allowed professors to spend little time teaching. Theoretically, they should have been spending more time researching, but the reality is often quite different, and what they were researching hasn't been very productive, which we will discuss in more detail later on in this chapter.

Economists Have Become Academia's Version of Financial Cheerleaders

Once professors are given tenure, it is almost impossible for them to be fired. Tenure amounts to total job security. Rewards in academia are not solely monetary. They also include quality (or ease) of life. Year-long sabbaticals are easier to get when the university has a lot of money. Well-funded retirements are also a great perk. Because of all of this, the status quo has been very good for most economists and most people naturally don't want to threaten it. People in that position don't want to see the status quo changed and have an inherent bias against ideas that would threaten the status quo. Hence, explanations of the economy tend to be biased in support of current ways of thinking and not to favor new ways of thinking that are vital for breakthroughs. The result is that economists became academic cheerleaders—the academic counterparts to financial cheerleaders. And, when you are a cheerleader, there is no hope of making a breakthrough.

In a sense, they are right to become economics cheerleaders. The alternative of having the bubbles pop is not good for them. A final popping of the bubbles would result in huge funding cuts for economists at universities and research centers, since both will be badly hit by government cutbacks in spending (due to the dollar and government debt bubble collapse) and huge drops in philanthropic giving (part of the discretionary spending bubble that will pop). In such an environment, it will be hard to protect economists from cost cutting, especially since they won't be seen as contributors to a solution due to their obvious lack of understanding of the economy that the Aftershock will show.

It's worth noting the significant cutbacks to university funding that the British government is making now, even when there is relatively little economic pressure to make cutbacks (compared to when the Aftershock hits). Economists really don't want to think we have a bubble economy for very good reasons. They are especially vulnerable to a bubble pop.

The Combination of the Demands to Get Tenure and the Rewards of the Good Life after Tenure Has Been a One-Two Punch to Creative Economic Thought

Although the life of many economists has been good, the life of someone trying to become one has not. In particular, it has become increasingly rigorous requiring increasingly high levels of mathematical skills to gain tenure at a major university. The intense rigor required is effectively freezing out people with a high degree of creativity. Sure, they can publish highly rigorous, highly mathematical articles, but they don't have the opportunity for a lot of creativity.

Not that math shouldn't be a key part of economics. Of course it should. But again, the problem is that we don't have a good model to apply the math to. Doing a lot of math when you don't have a good model for how the economy works is fairly useless. Once you have a good model, then the math can be quite useful.

However, with the intensity of focus and rigor required to gain tenure, you are effectively selecting *out* the potentially most creative economists, who might create such a new model. You get people who don't question the status quo because they can't. They aren't able to do so because they are highly focused on the enormously rigorous task of trying to get tenure, not on solving the fundamental questions of economics that would create real breakthroughs. That's just a big distraction from getting tenure.

So it is a two-pronged problem of a good life after tenure and a very difficult highly focused and rigorous path to get tenure that is making economic breakthroughs increasingly difficult.

We should add that this "breakdown in breakthroughs" is not only affecting the economics profession, but other sciences as well, such as biology and geology. The most important science—physics—which is the mother of all sciences, is facing this same issue. Without movement forward in physics, the other sciences are inherently limited as a result.

Interestingly, Lee Smolin, an American physicist now living in Toronto, recently wrote a book called *The Trouble with Physics*. It describes how physics has hit a brick wall in breakthroughs (sound familiar?). Despite massive funding, the last 30 years have

ABE Award for Intellectual Courage: Lee Smolin

Lee Smolin is one of those unusual academics and intellectuals who can spot a major problem and write very coherently about it. His book, *The Trouble with Physics,* is one of the best critiques of the current physics communities ever written. He points out, very convincingly, that the physics community, after decades of very impressive breakthroughs, has come to a virtual standstill since the early 1980s. In his many years of teaching and researching at major academic institutions, such as Princeton, Yale, and the Fermi Institute at the University of Chicago, he has seen the physics community become overly focused on string theory as the theoretical basis for breakthroughs in our understanding of physics.

More importantly, the physics community has not allowed or encouraged much discussion on other theories that might bring greater insight into the problems physicists are having such trouble solving. And, string theory hasn't gotten physicists anywhere in almost 30 years. The inability of this academic community to encourage and create alternative theories that may answer their questions is a serious problem.

What does this have to do with the bubble economy? Not much directly, but it has a lot to do with the current state of economics. In many ways economics is facing a similar problem. Although there was much progress made in the decades prior to the 1970s in a variety of areas including Milton Friedman's work on monetary policy and John Maynard Keynes' work on fiscal policy, as well as advancements in econometrics, very little has been accomplished since. The economics community has not been very encouraging or creative about major new approaches to understanding our economy. These failings are much more apparent to us than those of the physics community since they affect our pocketbook, but the failings of both communities are very similar.

Most importantly, any movement to make economics a real science, as opposed to a social science, has ground to a halt. In the end, for economics to be a real science, it has to be directly tied to the mother of all sciences, physics. If physics is having a problem, all sciences will have a problem, including economics, which needs to truly become a science. We should all share Mr. Smolin's concern about physics because it affects all the sciences and, ultimately the same problems affecting the mentality of the physics community are likely affecting other sciences as well, just as we see similar patterns in economics. Hats off to Lee Smolin for his important insights and his enormous courage.

been some of the least productive years in the last century for breakthroughs in physics (sound familiar?). And the same concerns he has about the academic community in physics are found in other academic fields. We gave Lee Smolin the ABE Award for Intellectual Courage in the first edition of *Aftershock,* and we give it to him again in this second edition (see sidebar describing Lee Smolin's work).

So, the problem is not just in economics, which makes sense because the reasons we gave for the unwillingness to question status quo thinking in economics would affect all academic departments to some degree.

Where to Now? Answer: Economics Needs to Move from Being a Set of Competing Philosophies to Being a Science

So, no breakthroughs from the economics community are likely in the near term. Still, what do we do? How do we get economics moving on the right track so that it can solve our economic problems? Where should economics go for more breakthroughs? How do we improve economics?

First we need to realize that we need a massive paradigm shift. It's not a regular paradigm shift which may be simply moving economics from being nonmathematical to being mathematical.

The paradigm shift needed is much more fundamental. Economics needs to move from a philosophical approach to a more scientific approach. There is a reason that Robert Heilbroner's great book on the history of economics and economists is called *The Worldly Philosophers*. Past economists have been philosophers first and economists second.

They look at the real world and then make an abstraction of it to try to better explain how the real world economy works. As we mentioned, an economist might develop an idealized nineteenth century grain market to better explain how a market works. It's an abstraction of the real world economy.

They also have fallen into philosophical camps—Communists, Capitalists, Socialists, and so on. Or they follow a certain philosophy of an economist or group of economists—Keynesian, Austrian, Marxist, and so on.

As mentioned earlier, two of the great breakthroughs of twentieth century economics—greater understanding of fiscal policy (government borrowing), led by John Maynard Keynes, and monetary policy (how the government creates money), led by Milton Friedman, are to some extent abstractions of how governments have financed wars for centuries—either through borrowing money or printing money. These abstractions are then taken and turned into macroeconomic theory.

So, although there have been some breakthroughs in creating a better philosophical understanding of how the economy works over the past 200 years, we have not had a breakthrough in developing a more scientific understanding of the economy.

The best analogy would be to medicine before Louis Pasteur and after Louis Pasteur. Before Pasteur, a nonscientific philosophy could be very important to medicine, such as the concept of spontaneous generation for the creation of diseases. Spontaneous generation is not scientifically based. However, using a more scientifically founded understanding of diseases, based on viruses and bacteria, created a revolution in medicine. This understanding was developed by more than just Pasteur, but the key is that medicine changed from being a philosophy of various opinions on how diseases were created to a very scientific understanding of what really caused diseases. This had a huge impact on the development of medicine and the degree to which medical science could help solve health problems in our society.

This is the paradigm shift needed in economics if it is to move from competing philosophies to a real science that can properly analyze and understand our economic problems, and thus help solve them.

So what has to happen to make economics more of a science? As we just mentioned in the analogy to continental drift and as we talked about in *America's Bubble Economy* and *Aftershock*, we need to look at economies as evolving. It is not simply cyclical; it is evolving. As we say in our many presentations to investors and businessmen, the economy of the 1850s is not like the economy of the 1950s. The economy of the 1920s is not like the economy of the 1990s. Thirty years ago China wasn't even a consideration in our economy. Now it is the world's second largest economy and very important to our economy. Our economy has evolved, not cycled.

These changes were technological, social, political, and scientific. All of these factors will continue to evolve. We won't cycle back to the technology, the social systems, the political systems, or the world economy of the 1850s. We will continue to evolve. When you look at a short period of time, such as five years, this evolution is not very obvious. But when you look at a period of 100 years or 150 years, this concept is blatantly obvious.

Four Key Elements for Making Economics More of a Science

So, to make economics more of a science, we need to take this understanding that the economy is evolving and apply it to four major elements in our economic thinking.

First Element: Information Dynamics

Information Dynamics is a theory of learning, psychology, and the costs of learning. We need to bring an understanding of learning into our understanding of both production and consumption. It also means we need to understand that learning is inherently an evolutionary process. Consumers are learning and producers are learning. This is extraordinarily important to economic growth. We need to better understand this learning process, which means we need to better understand how people learn. Specifically, we need to understand how the human brain learns.

Altogether a full understanding of how the brain learns is probably a ways off, just recognizing the importance of learning in both production and consumption and focusing on this issue is an important breakthrough toward making economics a science. The foundation of Information Dynamics in neurobiology also helps us understand the deep scientific linkages, and hence the need for a scientific and experimentally based economic analysis.

Second Element: Better Understanding of Technological Change

Technological change is inherently evolutionary, with more advanced and evolved technologies building on past technologies. For example, you need to have breakthroughs in producing electricity before you can develop integrated circuits.

At first, such an understanding of technological change would seem to be hard to develop. Focusing only on those technologies that improve productivity significantly makes it easier to develop. There are only a small number of technological changes that make major improvements in productivity, and it is important to focus on these key technological changes. Again, the close connection with engineering and science also shows how economics will eventually have a very strong scientific and experimental basis.

Third Element: A Theory of Property Rights

We define property rights as the rules society uses to allocate resources. These are both governmental rules and nongovernmental rules. Those nongovernmental rules are social and business rules. These are the rules for who gets what and how much they get.

Property rights, like Information Dynamics and technological change, are inherently evolutionary. Property rights evolve. In the United States, we moved from being a monarchy to a democracy. That was a big change and over time greatly affected our economy. But, more importantly, it was an evolution, not just a change. We're not going to cycle back to a monarchy.

The concept of property rights is very important to economics because it is an important part of production. For example, companies need capital to increase production. Governments control the banks and the capital markets, so they have a very direct impact on production.

As another example, it was no coincidence that when the United States moved from being a monarchy to a democracy, the country became a leader in the support of free markets. Monopolies had long been created by monarchs and dictators as a way to bring in revenue for themselves. This monopoly privilege of the monarchy is what Adam Smith was essentially attacking in his writings on free markets.

In the period from 1800 to 1850, court rulings by path-breaking jurists such as John Marshall and changes in laws increasingly destroyed government-granted monopolies. The United States led the world in its support of free markets. U.S. citizens saw monopolies as being beneficial to a few (which they were) and harmful to the growth of business and to individual citizens. With the vote, they had the power to change that aspect of property rights.

In a more recent example, when the U.S. Army took over Japan after World War II it established a new property rights system that dramatically changed Japanese production of goods and services. And, again, it wasn't just a change; it was part of an evolution that dramatically increased Japanese productivity and economic output. Japan is not going to cycle back to its pre-World War II property rights system.

Property rights are also forced to evolve by technology. For example, when military technology moves from swords to guns, property rights will change. The people with the guns will ultimately force their property rights system on the people with swords. Their ability to create and utilize new technologies is part of that economic evolution that extends way beyond just military technologies and affects other important technologies and social and business property rights.

Since the theory of property rights has as it basis both Information Dynamics and productivity theory, it too becomes a very scientific and experimental theory.

Understanding how property rights evolve is a key element in making economics more of a science.

Fourth Element: A New Methodology for Economic Analysis and Predictions

Currently, the mathematical models used to analyze the economy and make predictions are not adequate, which is a nice way of saying that the methods are wrong.

Without getting too detailed, current economic modeling assumes that you can reach a state of equilibrium. Economists change various inputs in an equilibrium model and see how it affects that equilibrium. But, in fact, reaching static equilibrium is never the case in the real world economy. The economy is constantly changing.

A better mathematical method to analyze the economy and make predictions would be to use numerical simulation models. These are the same models used to predict weather patterns or how our continents will move across the earth. If you used current econometric models to predict the weather, they might predict that there will be a vacuum over New York City—something that could not possibly happen in real life.

One of the key advantages of numerical simulation models is that they can be tested scientifically by seeing how well they predict what has already happened in the past. For example, a good numerical simulation model of continental drift should accurately show how North America got to where it is today. If the model keeps showing North America where South America is, you know it's wrong and have to modify it, so that it ultimately shows how every continent got to exactly where it is today. That takes a lot of work and a lot of money, but it's worth it because you are creating a model that accurately predicts continental drift in the past and hence can reasonably accurately predict where continents will drift in the future.

Increasingly, numerical simulation models are being used in all the sciences from geology, to physics, to chemistry and biology. They are also used in technological research from oil drilling and production to nuclear weapons testing. They are being used because they work. Increased use of numerical simulation models will be an important part of future breakthroughs in all the sciences.

For economics, developing numerical simulation models will be far more expensive than current econometric models. However, the advantage is that they work. It's better to put more money into something that works than less money in something that doesn't.

Being able to make models that properly predict what we know happened in the past and that can make predictions about the future that can be tested is a key test of any good scientific theory. Hence, it is a key element of making economics more of a science.

Where Do We Stand Today in Making This Transition?

So, where do we stand today in advancing our knowledge of these four key elements for making economics more of a science?

Well, fortunately a few people are concerned that current economic theory needs to change. This has been especially true after the failure of the economics community to foresee the popping of the U.S. bubble economy. Hence, some people refer to this focus on developing a new theory as the search for a postcrash model.

A physicist, Doyne Farmer, from the Santa Fe Institute, recognizes the limits of current mathematical models of economics. He believes we should be using numerical simulation models in economics. He is moving in the right direction, but his proposed model leaves out property rights, information dynamics, and technological evolution. Hence, such a model is guaranteed to be wrong, or at least quite incomplete. It is also telling that such a non–status quo idea comes from a physicist and not an economist.

A psychoanalyst, David Tuckett, from University College London, is doing work on bringing more psychology into understanding market gyrations. It's good to bring more psychology into economics, but without a full understanding of Information Dynamics, of which psychology is definitely a part, this will lead to a dead end. Again it is also telling that such a non–status quo idea comes from a noneconomist.

The Economics Profession Does Not Want to Make the Transition

That's partly because most economists don't believe there is anything all that fundamentally wrong with current economic theory.

Yes, they argue, some tweaking may be needed, but there is no need for an entirely new theory.

And some economists, like Roman Frydman from New York University, think we can never forecast the economy with any accuracy. We're tempted to respond with "What the hell are you doing in economics then?" It's like a manager who tells you that his business is unprofitable because it never could be profitable, so don't blame him.

So part of the problem in economics, as we mentioned before, is that economists are pretty happy in their current positions as professors and hence, in their current thinking that no fundamental change is necessary. Sounds a lot like the management of General Motors in the 1980s and 1990s, doesn't it?

Mark Gertler, who previously worked with Ben Bernanke, but is now with New York University, feels that the economics profession is highly competitive, and if you have a better idea in economics it is going to win out. We agree with Mr. Gertler in the long run, but it's not going to happen the way Mr. Gertler thinks.

That's because getting a job in economics requires that you think the way other economists do—from a fundamental standpoint. Not that you can't have disagreements in economics. You can have and are encouraged to have lots of little disagreements. But, in raising questions about the fundamentals of current economic thinking, you will find little support. Hence, it will be hard to get tenured as a professor.

Just as we all know that in Communist Russia even though the competition to be an economist was fierce—they were highly respected and sought after positions—the people who were hired for those positions were probably not the ones who were fundamentally critical of the Communist system. Don't expect people who are pleased with the current way of thinking to be very eager to hire someone who is not.

ABE Award for Intellectual Courage: Barry Marshall

Barry Marshall completed his medical studies at the University of Western Australia in 1974 and carried out his residency at Royal Perth

Hospital. He was interested in gastroenterology, especially stomach ulcers. He found ulcer patients had a mysterious spiral shaped bacteria in their stomachs near the site of their ulcers. Mr. Marshall thought that these bacteria might be causing the ulcers.

This was completely opposed to the status quo thinking on stomach ulcers. Generations of medical scholars had taught their doctor/students that stomach ulcers were caused by excess stomach acid brought on by stress and diet.

Marshall did a great deal of research that further convinced him of the role of these bacteria, eventually called Heilcobacter pylori, in causing ulcers. He noticed that bismuth, a component of Pepto Bismol, killed the bacteria and gave temporary relief to patients further convincing him of the bacteria's role in causing ulcers.

He presented his findings at a conference in Brussels in 1983, and the highly credentialed supporters of the status quo were *very* skeptical. Barry had limited credentials and was attacking the status quo. So, they ignored his groundbreaking research.

But he persevered and found considerable success in treating patients with a combination of bismuth and antibiotics. Lacking much support or funding for an expanded research project based on his theories, as a last resort, he finally drank a bottle of the bacteria himself! Sure enough, he began to get an ulcer. He had complete faith in his theory and so completely believed he was right that he was willing to use his own body to prove it.

In 1986 Barry was invited to the University of Virginia to further his research. After a decade of further work at the University, his theories became more widely accepted. In 1996 the FDA officially approved a course of treatment for ulcers along the lines of his ideas. He returned to Australia and was eventually awarded the Nobel Prize in 2005.

Barry had to overcome enormous opposition from highly credentialed medical scholars to do his work. Not to be overlooked, the sizable industry in performing ulcer operations would be eliminated if ulcers were easily cured by simple antibiotics. He didn't have many people supporting him. All he had going for him was the correct understanding of the problem. After much struggle, the truth won out and overcame all the highly credentialed opposition and lack of interest from leading medical research institutions, such as Harvard and Yale. It wasn't easy, but millions of ulcer sufferers around the world have Barry Marshall to thank for greatly improving their lives.

Hence, if you really want to advance economic thinking you are probably best off not depending on the economic profession for a job. You shouldn't leave the profession—quite the contrary, you should be very active in thinking about how to improve economic thought. But, what you can't do is rely on the economics profession for a job, or you will naturally be forced to think like the other economists and not focus on the need for a fundamental change in their way of thinking.

A great recent example of a scientist who faced enormous decades-long skepticism over his ground-breaking Nobel prize–winning medical research work by much more highly credentialed status quo academics was Barry Marshall. For his struggle against the status quo, we give him the ABE Award for Intellectual Courage. See the sidebar on pages 252–253 for more details on his struggle.

The Solution to the Lack of Interest in Making Such an Important Change in Economics

The solution for solving the problems of economics and making it a useful and valuable science that people in the United States and around the world can rely on and benefit from will come from addressing the four key areas described previously, and from getting other economists to focus on them as well.

Of course, we have a lot more to say about each of those four key areas and how to answer the questions that are raised in each one. We will address those issues in future books. In addition, we look forward to writing books about how to increase productivity based on these ideas. Raising productivity will be crucial to our economic recovery and future growth.

As to getting other economists to focus on those issues, well that's going to take some time. However, the Aftershock helps to speed up the timetable—a lot. That's because right now it's not that obvious that economics is totally lost. The economy is doing okay, as are economics faculty and researchers at major universities and research institutes. There has been no significant loss of funding for economists.

However, once the Aftershock hits, it will be quite obvious that economics has failed miserably. In addition, there will be a whole lot less money to go around for universities and economics research institutes. And, since economists had a lot to do with creating the Aftershock through their lack of understanding of the economy, there won't be a lot of sympathy for paying them when funding is extremely tight. Poor performers won't be rewarded in the Aftershock. There's simply no more money for it, and it will be quite obvious that they are poor performers.

Hence, a new group of economists, albeit a much smaller group and much more poorly paid, will take the place of the current group. That group will be desperately looking for solutions to the economic problems of the day and will have a huge incentive to justify their meager pay by showing some positive results from their research. It will be these people who will not only be willing to question the fundamental concepts of economics but extremely eager to do so since it is so obvious that those concepts have failed. In addition, the economists will desperately want to do something to show their work is worthwhile, and they deserve to keep their jobs.

So, in this way, what Mr. Bernanke's friend Mark Gertler said will come true. The good ideas will win in the end because economists will be highly motivated at that point to abandon current thinking and to find a different theory of economics that helps solve our economic problems. A meltdown in the economics profession may not be what Mr. Gertler had in mind, but it certainly will work by dramatically changing the incentives for supporting fundamental changes in economic thought.

A meltdown in the economy and in funding for economists may not be the only solution to our current economic problems, and it certainly isn't the best solution, but it is a solution. Most importantly it will work, and is quite feasible to implement in the real world—in fact, it is unavoidable.

■ ■ ■

To make comments on the material in this chapter or enter a discussion thread please visit our web site at www.aftershockeconomy .com/chap9comments.

Our Predictions Have Been Accurate, So Why Do Some People Still Dislike Them?

Most economists and financial analysts did not foresee the Bubblequake of 2008 and 2009, and most still do not see the coming Aftershock, nor will they agree with many of the ideas and predictions in this book. How come? Why do most people not see what seems pretty straightforward and obvious to us?

The reasons lie in the six psychological stages of dealing with the Bubblequake and Aftershock that we first told you about in Chapter 4. We were in the first stage (Denial) for a long time, and more recently we have been in the second stage (Market Cycles), in which most experts believe if we just wait long enough things will get better—in fact if you try really hard, you can believe things are already getting better right now! What is so compelling about the Market Cycles stage of thinking about this problem is that it is so *comforting*. It helps us cope with our anxieties by insisting all will be well again soon. This comforting stage is being strongly promoted and maintained by both the cheerleaders (people who say all is great right now) and the comforters—"experts" who, unlike the cheerleaders, are willing to admit we have problems, but who reassure us that the solution is at hand, or could be if we would just do A, B, or C (none of which will actually save us).

So we have both cheerleaders and comforters hard at work, keeping us from facing facts and really getting prepared for what is ahead.

Naturally, both cheerleaders and comforters do not like our books because we are saying that the economy is not in a down cycle as they say, and our economic problems will not simply cycle away as they say.

Toles Copyright © 2008 *The Washington Post*.

Understanding why some people react negatively to our book is important for understanding why the bubble economy occurred in the first place and for seeing where we are in the progression of those six psychological stages. The roots of the antagonism to our ideas are grounded in the very strong desire to hang onto the many benefits of the rising-bubble status quo and the very strong psychological need to hang onto the comforts of the known and rewarding past. The overwhelming desire for and the reassuring comfort of a rising bubble economy makes almost everyone—even the authors, at times—want to deny these problems until we have absolutely no other choice but to face them and solve them. Until then, most people want to maintain the many comforts and benefits of the status quo.

Therefore, it's important that we not only be able to analyze and predict what happens with the economy, but be able to analyze and predict the reactions people will have to our predictions, because that tells us a lot about how our country will react to and handle the coming Aftershock. It's somewhat unusual for a book to look at why people might not like its ideas, but, in this case, quite essential to a good understanding of what is happening with the economy and how it is evolving. It is also important for our readers to understand where other people are coming from so that we can better understand why so many other people might say we are wrong—and why you should resist being one of them.

Here are some of the main reasons why many people will not accept the validity of our books' predictions until after they occur.

It's Not a Cheerleading Book

Most people want a highly plausible cheerleading book that says everything is okay, or it will be soon, even if we hit some rough patches along the way. They want good news, but they also want the good news to be plausible, meaning that it has to be based on some kind of seemingly rigorous analysis. The analysis itself can be terrible, but as long as it seems rigorous (i.e., complicated), and it supports the idea that things will get better soon, that's what they want to hear.

Ideally, this good-news analysis should also square with conventional wisdom, for example, the idea of Market Cycles. But the analysis can't be too optimistic, or it will sound like fantasy. It has to be very cognizant of current problems while being fundamentally optimistic that the economy, stocks, and real estate will all inevitably go back up.

Alan Greenspan was a master at this. He was the perfect cheerleader because he was optimistic, but always sounded well reasoned and quite plausible. Greenspan never talked too much about any fundamental economic problems, except with very long-term issues, such as the long-term cost of Social Security and Medicare. However, he always brought up some negative issues that made his overall optimism seem well considered. Even when his views didn't square with reality, people still loved to hear them.

As an aside, it is quite interesting that since retiring, Greenspan has become much more outspoken about the deep problems in the economy, particularly related to the ballooning national debt, the origins of the real estate bubble, and the vulnerability of the dollar.

That, of course, does not get much media coverage. Not too many people want to hear from an old cheerleader who is no longer beating the drum for what they consider to be well reasoned optimism.

In place of the earlier cheerleader Greenspan, we now have the current Federal Reserve, which is furiously printing money by buying bonds (see Chapter 3) and temporarily boosting the stock market, which is providing short-term stimulus to the economy. As a result of this Fed-generated growth, powered by massive money printing, people are feeling more bullish on the stock market and more optimistic about the economy. That is having some short-term positive effects on consumer spending and is giving the cheerleaders some temporary ammunition to work with, as they tell us that all is well, or will be soon. In fact, the Federal Reserve is currently the biggest weapons supplier in the cheerleaders' war on rationality.

But even before the Fed began its massive money printing of the last two years, many economists insisted that all was well. For example, in May 2009, a report by the National Association for Business Economics announced that a panel of 45 economists they interviewed expected economic growth in the second half of 2009. Nearly 75 percent of those who responded to the survey said that the recession would end in 2009. Not one economist thought the recession would move beyond the first quarter of 2010.

As of this writing in spring 2011, people still love to hear that the economy will turn around in the second half of the year. Even if it takes three more quarters or even as long as another year, people still want to hear about a turnaround. Beyond the prospect of more massive money printing by the Fed, which is unsustainable over the long term, and massive borrowing by the federal government there is no good reason to believe we are in an economic recovery. It is all cheerleading and money printing.

Even when cheerleading analysts and economists are proven wrong, time and again (for example, when the housing market did not bottom out and recover in 2006, or in 2007, or in 2008, and when the economy didn't turn around in the second half of 2008, these people still retain a lot of credibility because they sound rigorous, and they are trying to be optimistic. The fact that, again and again, they have no idea of what they are talking about and are constantly proven wrong, does not matter—at least they are trying to be plausibly optimistic. The audience that wants cheerleaders still likes what cheerleaders are selling.

In this group, nobody likes a bear, least of all when that bear is right.

It's Not a Complex Book (Although It Is Based on Complex Analysis)

For some readers, a really complicated, hard-to-understand book or research paper is best. It makes the reader (and the author) feel as if they know something that very few people can understand. This makes readers feel really smart. It also obscures the upsetting truth about the economy. This group may not want a cheerleading book, but they also don't want to be too fundamentally critical of the economy or its future prospects. For example, this group might like to read about a detailed analysis of complicated credit default swaps and the intricate ways they might threaten the economy, even though the real threats to the economy are simpler and much more fundamental.

Many people in this group are very threatened by the real economy since many of them will lose their jobs in the Aftershock, including many economists and financial analysts and other professionals. But here's a question: If the people writing these complex research papers and books could not predict or even talk about something as big and important as the Bubblequake financial crisis that just hit us in 2008, exactly how good is their comlex analysis? What good does their analysis do if it could not even warn us that so many banks would fail, and the U.S. stock market would lose half its value?

If these people cannot protect us from such a huge occurrence, what exactly can they do for us? The answer is, they keep us relatively happy and in the dark. They don't draw their power from accuracy; they get it from having a certain level of credibility (at least for now), based not only on their academic, business, or government credentials, but also on group denial.

These analysts and economists don't want to see the reality of the economy because if they did, they would have to ask, "How did so many smart people make such terrible mistakes?" Maybe because they weren't so smart? But if that is the case, then what will happen to Wall Street, and what does that say about economists and politicians and their super-smart advisers? It says that they are quite likely to fail and to take the economy down along with them. That is really painful for all of us. It is much more comforting to think of these folks as credible and smart for as long as we can, than to look at this logically and say they are not so credible or so smart.

For example, the biggest mistake made in the run-up to the recent financial crisis was that people on Wall Street *and* Main Street *and* in Washington all thought that it was perfectly fine for housing prices to go up 100 percent or more, while people's incomes only went up a few percent. That was a pretty basic economic mistake to make, don't you think? The idea that the fundamental problem was caused by Wall Street gods gone bad or by risky credit default swaps is just wrong. The fundamental problem was bad investment judgment at a very basic level (because home prices cannot go and stay up 100 percent or more while incomes do not equally rise). This very bad investment judgment was made by just about everyone, from the least financially sophisticated people in America to the most financially sophisticated people in America.

Our analysis in 2006 in *America's Bubble Economy* was quite different. We looked at the fundamentals driving the housing market rather than hoping that huge price gains were well justified and would keep on coming. The analysis was spot-on and even televised nationally, when Bob Wiedemer said in February 2008 on CNBC's Squawk Box that homebuilding stocks would go down even when almost every other financial analyst felt that, for some reason, they had already gone down enough, were certainly at the bottom of the cycle, and would naturally go up.

Now we are making an even bigger mistake than before, when we were blaming Wall Street. Now we are making the catastrophic mistake of ignoring the future consequences of allowing the Federal Reserve to massively increase the money supply and creating high inflation in the long term, in exchange for the short-term benefit of boosting the stock market, temporarily stimulating the economy, and keeping lending going.

Supposedly brilliant analysts writing brilliant research papers are simply not seeing this threat, just as they did not see the problems that would eventually arise from the real estate bubble or all the rest of the bubbles. Even right up until the financial crisis of 2008 and after it, these "smart" guys were clueless and unprepared. People at the very top of the financial world were not very smart about their investments that they should have been extremely smart about. Instead, they bankrupted (or effectively bankrupted) some very impressive commercial banks and investment banks that had previously survived the greatest of our nation's financial difficulties. It's absolutely amazing that these people had such poor investment judgment that they couldn't even survive in an economy with some of the lowest unemployment levels, lowest inflation rates, and lowest interest rates in our nation's history. It was absolutely phenomenal misjudgment in the face of these easy-to-see facts. Clearly, this shows the power of not wanting to face facts and that despite being "masters of the financial universe," these people were not very smart at what they should have known best. And now they are doing it again by ignoring the future negative impacts of massive money printing by the Fed. Instead, they are thrilled by the stock market rally that the massive money printing is helping to create. As long as they are getting what they want, people can suspend logic and believe almost anything.

In the more distant past, Wall Street has shown great skill and innovation due to the fine efforts of some very impressive people, such as J.P. Morgan and Charlie Merrill. But, these great skills were not on display by the Wall Street of the past decade. That these supposedly impressive financial managers had such terrible judgment inevitably raises the question of how well the economy will do in the future. And it makes a very uncomfortable statement about the way our society is structured and about the people who are running it. It's not just bad or evil individuals that are causing us problems; it's something much more profound that is affecting our economy.

One dramatic example of how people in power can prefer complexity to cover up fundamental problems is the terrible *Challenger* space shuttle disaster. When the space shuttle *Challenger* blew up shortly after takeoff in 1986, hundreds of NASA scientists were eager to do enormous amounts of research into the problem and produced voluminous papers on the subject, and even then, they might not have figured out exactly what went wrong. Physicist Richard Feynman, on the other hand, was able to do a simple experiment of putting the rubber seals from the shuttle's booster tank into ice water to simulate conditions on the day of the launch. When Feynman pulled the seal out of the ice water, it was brittle and broke easily, thus solving the mystery of why the shuttle exploded. It was an excellent example of simple and straightforward analysis, but in some ways, it made hundreds of NASA scientists look bad and in doing so, made the whole NASA organization look bad. This made a lot of people inside and outside NASA feel pretty uncomfortable, but at least they were willing to bring Feynman in to look at the problem, which was a good step. Today's NASA might be far less willing to do so.

The ideas in our book make people uncomfortable in the same way. If it's really that simple to understand our economic problems, then a lot of people in positions of power are not doing their jobs and cannot be very smart. That's a painful fact to face.

Once the Aftershock hits, most of these folks will lose their current credibility. At that point, we won't need any more highly respected, inaccurate cheerleaders; we will need some highly accurate thinkers! Including some of the readers of this book.

It's Not a Crazy Book

Crazy books are just cheerleading books in disguise. They propose crazy economic or financial theories that aren't real. Some of these books are far more critical and radical, and more "doom and gloom" than we are. They might say much more critical things about our country. They might be far more critical of individuals such as Alan Greenspan or the Wall Street Titans. But, they are so silly that they aren't very threatening. Hence, by being so implausible, they are effectively cheerleading for the status quo. Many crazy books, therefore, become quite popular forms of entertainment.

By contrast, there have been some important examples of books that were not crazy and took on important issues, such as *Uncle Tom's Cabin* and *Silent Spring*. Both of these books were well written and were very honest about the issues they took on. They weren't crazy, but in being very realistic they were also very upsetting and many people didn't like them at all. Fortunately, many other people did like them even if they were highly critical of the status quo, as they were the right books at the right time for a nation that was already beginning to change its attitudes in the direction the books were advocating.

Timing is everything. Unless the time is right for a critical mass of society to begin to accept the new ideas in a basically accurate book, it will be rejected. Instead, many people will prefer a crazy book because it is far less threatening. Our book is not a crazy book and lays out a very reasonable and rational analysis of our current economic situation, including how it started and where it is headed. For that reason many people who would like a crazy book will not like our book.

It's Not an Academic Book

In addition to the reasons discussed in the previous chapter about why many economists don't like the ideas in this book, they also don't like the book because we are not playing by their rules. In most academic circles, an author has to be published in a refereed (peer reviewed) journal to have any credibility; otherwise academics aren't going to be very interested in the book. That actually makes a lot of sense in some ways because there are plenty of crackpots out there and this is a good way of filtering them out. However, a problem arises when the academics are fundamentally wrong in their analyses, and someone outside the inner circle has something of merit to say. Then the policy becomes a real negative because academics are not exposed to different viewpoints (in part because they don't want to be).

In addition to the problem of exclusivity, academics often have the problem of a narrow focus. A narrow focus is good—in fact, it is absolutely necessary for good analysis—but only if you have a solid understanding and a good theory of what is going on in the broader context. For example, as we discussed in Chapter 9 if you don't understand continental drift, trying to study minute changes in the Appalachian Mountains isn't going to improve your understanding of how they were formed. Without a good overall theory to provide a larger context, a narrow focus is just a way of avoiding the hard work of developing a good overall theory that explains what is really going on.

This is what many, if not most economists do. They spend decades focusing narrowly, while the larger context goes unexplored and misunderstood. Clearly, we can't all be big-picture thinkers. But equally clearly, someone has to do it, and they need to do it as accurately, rationally, and objectively as possible.

It's Not Suggesting Armageddon

One of the most common themes we see in some financial books that many people seem to like is that, rather than present an honest assessment of the problems we will face, they say that our financial problems will result in financial Armageddon. That might be combined with another Armageddon theme that says that a financial collapse will result in violent unrest across the world. Another lighter version would be the "end of capitalism" or the rise of dictatorships in the United States and/or other currently democratic countries.

As with the crazy books, some people prefer reading Armageddon books because reading them is much more comfortable than facing the reality of a fundamental change in people's economic, social, and political lives. They retreat to the fantasy of Armageddon because, even if they have some extra food stored in their basements, they know that Armageddon is not really going to happen, and reading about it is a good way to avoid dealing with changes in society or the economy that they would rather not see. *Pretend Armageddon* is simply a more comfortable alternative for some people than what our book predicts.

It's Not a Status Quo Book

All of the above reasons why people don't like our book boil down to this one common denominator: It's not a status quo book. Other books, in one way or another, more strongly support the status quo by saying so directly or by being so off base or by adding so much meaningless complexity that they offer no real threat to the status quo. This book threatens the status quo in a fundamental way because we are saying that our problems are knowable, relatively simple, caused entirely by us, and cannot be reversed.

The inevitable future consequences of the current Bubblequake and coming Aftershock will force big changes on our businesses, our government, and our society. Like the aftermath of the Revolutionary War in the United States or World War I in Europe, the aftermath of the Bubblequake will alter the status quo. Fundamental changes to our current property rights system are inevitable after the dollar bubble bursts, and that is far scarier to most people than *The Terminator* fantasies or other pretend end-of-the-world scenarios.

We are daring to say that we have made big economic mistakes in the past, that we will go through a difficult time (the Aftershock), and the final result of all the chaos created by our past mistakes will be a much, much better, and wealthier society than we have today, but one that will be fundamentally very different.

Us versus the Comforters: How *Aftershock* Stacks Up Against Other Bearish Books

On the surface, the book you are now holding in your hand may seem (to people who haven't read it) like just another "doom-and-gloom" economics book. In fact, *Aftershock* is substantially different from any other book currently available.

Some books have correctly predicted that our economy is heading for trouble. To varying degrees, each has contained some partially correct insights, forecasts, and advice. Many have offered some truly bad investment ideas. And many others have provided some very good investment advice, but for wrong or incomplete reasons.

The reason for this is that most bearish books, while recognizing that all is not well, do not fully analyze the problem but instead provide a degree of *psychological comfort* to those who benefit from the status quo (which is most of us). This allows readers who are observant enough to see we have serious problems to think about these problems while still maintaining a feeling of safety. We all like the feeling of safety, and that is the primary thing that books written by comforters give us.

Obviously, we don't have the space here to analyze the details of all the bearish economics and finance books on the market today. Instead, we'd like to take a closer look at three popular books, *Crisis Economics* (Penguin, 2011) by Nouriel Roubini, *Aftershock* (Vintage, 2011) by Robert Reich, and *Crash Proof 2.0* (John Wiley & Sons, 2009) by Peter Schiff. We chose these three, not because they are the worst or the best of the bunch, but because these well received books have attracted a lot of attention and therefore serve as good models against which we can compare our predictions and our entirely unique perspective. In their own unique ways, each has been written by what we call a comforter.

Crisis Economics *by Nouriel Roubini*

Nouriel Roubini is a popular bearish economist, sometimes referred to as "Dr. Doom," the same moniker Henry Kaufman earned when he was chief economist at Salomon Brothers. Fundamentally Mr. Roubini sees our current problems as being the result of a financial crisis (as indicated by the title of his book) that was caused by too much debt, heavy use of leverage by financial institutions, and inadequate regulation of those institutions. He believes that with better regulation of financial institutions to prevent them from making large numbers of excessively risky transactions, along with less debt, we will be able to solve the current problems and avoid future financial crises.

One might wonder why, with a name like Dr. Doom, we would call Nouriel Roubini a "comforter." To understand this requires realizing that a comforter is not a cheerleader. A cheerleader says all is well; a comforter says all could be well again, if only we would just go back to doing things as we did (or should have done) before. Dr. Doom, therefore, is a comforter. He is part of a larger group of comforter economists, such as Paul Krugman and Ben Bernanke, who strongly suggest that we look to the past, specifically the Great Depression, as a guide for how to deal with our current financial ills. Based on what worked, or would have worked, in the past, they suggest similar remedies of stronger regulation and greater fiscal stimulus. They also suggest that we should not greatly reduce the money supply as we did in the Great Depression. We completely agree. They also don't see major problems in tripling the money supply. We completely disagree.

We also differ strongly from Mr. Roubini in that we see our economic problems as being caused by a set of multiple interacting bubbles that are beginning to pop (as described in 2006 in *America's Bubble Economy*) and are now putting strong downward pressure on two much more important bubbles, the government debt and dollar bubbles (the Aftershock).

We don't see a lack of financial regulation as being the *core* problem, nor do we see printing money as the solution—in fact, printing money is pumping up both the dollar and the government debt bubble. Unlike some comforter economists, we believe we are in an entirely different situation from the Great Depression. Continuing to think that we can solve our current problems by using techniques from the Great Depression shows a fundamental lack of understanding of our current situation. It is much like the general who always wants to fight the last war, instead of taking on the current reality. The last war is the war the general knows best and is most comfortable with, not this new situation.

Unlike us, Roubini does not see any threat from future inflation. He also did not and still does not think gold is a good investment. We disagree strongly on both counts.

Unlike Roubini, we see the financial crisis as a result of the popping of the housing and consumer spending bubbles, which popped the private credit and stock market bubbles. The financial crisis was not a cause of the problems, but much more a symptom of much deeper underlying problems—the popping of our multibubble economy. Roubini and the other comforter economists still do not recognize the full magnitude of the problems caused by the two biggest bubbles, the government debt bubble and dollar bubble.

In general, the comforters tend to believe that our problems are more limited to excessive financial debt, financial risk taking, and lack of financial regulation than to a fundamental problem with a multibubble economy that is still in the process of popping—clearly a far less comfortable problem to recognize. It is far more comfortable to think that all we need is more regulation as we've done in the past and more government stimulus, which seems like something we've done in the past, even though it certainly is not at the same level that we've done in the past, given the magnitude of the increase in deficit spending and the magnitude of our accumulated debt.

The bottom line is that both the analysis of the problems and the kinds of solutions offered are much more comfortable and comforting than the actual economic situation we are in, as we have described in our books. This is a key part of why Roubini gets so much attention: he gives us a comfortable message, and he does so with greater credibility than most economists who did not foresee any problems. He did foresee some problems, so he now has some credibility, and his comforting message is relatively easy to digest.

Aftershock *by Robert Reich*

Robert Reich was Bill Clinton's Labor Secretary. He is considered a leader of liberal thought, so we thought it was important to include his book in a review of the most recent books on the economy and how we differ from them.

In the fall of 2010, Robert Reich published a book surprisingly called *Aftershock*, one year after our *Aftershock* came out. Yes, we did complain to his publisher about using our title, but they refused to change it. We're not sure why he calls his book *Aftershock* since he doesn't really describe any aftershock to the financial crisis. Maybe he just liked the eye-catching title. It is a good title—we can attest to that.

In terms of his book, Reich's primary thesis is that the rich have been getting an increasing proportion of the wealth in the nation, creating the greatest income inequality since the stock and economic boom of the 1920s. The lack of income for the middle class has forced them to take on too much debt to maintain an adequate standard of living. That came crashing down in the financial crisis of 2008, which is causing a lack of consumption now and, hence, a very sluggish economic recovery.

His basic prescription for improving the economy is more progressive taxes to reduce income inequality. In addition, he supports more unemployment compensation and other welfare-type support for members of the lower class, as well as more health and education spending to help the middle class with health expenses and to better train them for new jobs. All of this he says will stimulate the economy and encourage more spending by the middle class, which will further boost the economy.

Reich, like Roubini and others, is a comforter who looks to the Great Depression for an understanding of what is happening and what to do about it. Unlike Roubini, Reich does not focus on more regulation and instead sees the remedy as more Depression-era thinking that calls for more welfare and progressive taxes. Both are comforters because they are telling us we can solve our problems by looking to the past.

We differ with Reich in several ways. We see growing income inequality as primarily a result of, not the cause of, our economic problems. Income inequality increased as our multibubble economy rose. When those bubbles pop, the income inequality caused by the bubbles will be reduced because a lot of rich people will no longer be rich (unless they follow the advice in this book!).

We also don't feel that the middle class was forced by economic circumstances to take on too much debt. The debt related to the financial crisis for both the middle class and the upper class was much more related to the rising asset bubbles, particularly real estate, than any need for a better standard of living. Pushing up bubbles took a lot of borrowed money.

Most importantly, we see the basic problem that underlies the slow economic growth as being a *slowing of productivity growth* since the 1970s. Fundamentally, we see increasing productivity growth (not decreasing income inequality) as the key to growing the economy. Income inequality is always going to be higher during a rising asset bubble or during periods of high economic growth. Reducing income inequality is not the key factor for creating real economic growth; productivity is. Hence, our prescription for future growth is to *increase productivity*.

Unfortunately, most of the focus in the economy now is on maintaining the asset bubbles and not on increasing productivity. The popping of these asset bubbles will likely be an important part of getting the government and the public more focused on productivity growth than on maintaining the bubbles. Once all the bubbles pop, our only alternative for growing the economy will be to increase productivity. Until then, we are ignoring this.

Increasing productivity will not be easy and will take fundamental reforms to our government and the economy that will likely take time, just as real productivity growth has always taken time in the past. That is not as much fun as a rising bubble economy, but it works. Greater spending by the government to boost the economy, which is fueled by borrowing money and printing more money will not result in higher economic growth, either. All such borrowing and printing will do for us is preserve the bubbles for a little while longer and make the final popping of the bubbles that much more devastating.

Crash Proof 2.0 *by Peter Schiff*

The third book we've chosen to look at is *Crash Proof 2.0* by Peter Schiff, which we actually like more than most others. But again, just like the other authors, Schiff is a comforter. He is a "Back to Basics" thinker (one of the six psychological stages discussed in Chapter 4), who would like us to return to the gold standard for the dollar, significantly cut federal spending, and get rid of the Fed.

Schiff believes that the United States is close to being tapped out on debt, and very soon we will no longer be able to get any further loans, when in fact we will see our $15+ trillion debt expand to $20 or even $25 trillion before the U.S. government falls into default and can borrow no more.

In addition to blaming debt, Schiff also says our economic problems are due to a lack of domestic manufacturing, which we know is not the reason for our troubles—the falling bubbles are. Most industrial nations have seen the percentage of their GDP related to manufacturing decline substantially in the last 50 years. In addition, our manufacturing will increase when our currency is no longer manipulated against us. Manufacturing and productivity are not the same things. We can boost productivity without a huge increase in manufacturing.

In terms of his advice for wealth preservation, we agree that U.S. stocks are not a good place to put your money in the long term. But we also know that Schiff's recommendations to move out of U.S. stocks and into foreign stocks is the equivalent of jumping out of the proverbial frying pan into the fire. Comforters are often wrong in their investment advice, and clients can lose a lot of money as a result. We know for a fact that foreign stocks will crash for the same reasons we know U.S. stocks will crash, because we have an understanding of the larger forces that are driving this global multibubble collapse. Schiff, like many others, is missing this because he is a comforter, who doesn't see the bigger picture.

Additionally, Schiff says oil will be a good investment. We say demand for oil will fall after the Aftershock hits the world economy, making it a bad investment, except in the United States, where the price of oil will rise due to the falling dollar. He says gold is now in a bull market; we say gold hasn't even begun to hit its future bubble heights. He says to stay liquid, and keep your cash handy to pick up bargains in real estate and other distressed assets; we say it's far too soon for that. Please avoid all bargain hunting until *after* the dollar bubble pops. Again, we are basing all this, not on our intuition or lucky guesses, but on our detailed analysis of how the overall economy is evolving.

Actually, we are a lot more respectful of these successful authors than we sound here, but our point is that it is not good enough to just get some of this right, and then get a lot wrong because you are a comforter (probably unconsciously) and are looking to the past for causes and solutions. The economy is evolving, not going backward. Getting it partially right is not enough; you have to get most of it right, and you have to get it right *for the right reasons.*

ABE Award for Intellectual Courage

In the spring of 2009, we noticed an article by Simon Johnson and Peter Boone. It began by saying "Euphoria returns! Who could have guessed that Bank of America stock would rally 70 percent the week it learns that the Feds are demanding new capital equal to nearly half the bank's market capitalization." That caught our eye. It went on to question the ongoing stock rally by pointing out that 22 percent of Americans have houses worth less than their mortgages, and that there are parallel problems for commercial property. We don't agree that we are heading into a situation similar to Japan's lost decade in the 1990s as they suggested. We think the current falling bubble economy will not turn into a malaise but will continue to fall until the dollar pops, at which point, it will be a very different situation than in Japan in the 1990s. But, we were pleased that they were willing to point out that large budget deficits and trillions of dollars of new loans to the banks "are recipes for hyperinflation and, if the Fed and Treasury don't pull away from the punch bowl soon, sharply increasing inflation is very much in the cards."

Although this may not seem like a radical position, and there are certainly others who hold similar views, it is unusual that mainstream economists are beginning to speak out so boldly on these issues.

Clearly, Nouriel Roubini of New York University and Robert Shiller of Yale University have been the leading advocates of intelligent skepticism about our current economy from the mainstream economics community. They've done a good job. But hats off to Mr. Boone and Mr. Johnson, as well! Simon Johnson is a Professor at MIT's Sloan School of Management and a senior fellow at the Peterson Institute for International Economics. The Peterson Institute is one of the best of the economic think tanks and, pound for pound, does more good work than any of them. However, given their strong expertise in global economics, we would have hoped to see more sharp criticism and analysis of the current bubble economy from their staff and their director, Fred Bergsten. That Mr. Johnson is stepping out more boldly on these issues now is truly a step in the right direction.

We also want to recognize a few other people for their courage. In the field of business journalism, on the print side, *Newsweek* columnist Robert Samuelson and *Washington Post* syndicated columnist Steve Pearlstein have consistently been courageous in their willingness to give a very honest appraisal of the economy and to point out cheerleader mentality. They're the best in the print business.

On the electronic side of business journalism, few have hit the mark more accurately or more frequently than Paul Farrell, senior columnist at Dow Jones MarketWatch. Paul was simply born with intelligent skepticism in his genes.

Finally, we have to give one of our highest awards to bubble expert Eric Janszen, whose web site iTulip was one of the first to call the Internet bubble. He has also been at the forefront of poking holes in the current bubble economy in his articles and his books. We might add that in the Internet bubble days, no one had a more accurate book than Tony and Michael Perkins, whose *The Internet Bubble* was the best book written on those crazy days. Needless to say, Eric has been a long-time friend, and we owe Tony a great debt for introducing us to him.

Got Macro?

All the best investment strategies of the past fall flat without the correct macroeconomic view of what's ahead, which is why we now offer the following services:

Aftershock Advisors provides a variety of services, such as our popular Investor's Resource Package (IRP), including the monthly Aftershock newsletter, e-mail alerts, and live audio forums. You may

(continued)

sign up for a two-month free trial of the Aftershock IRP at the book website www.aftershockeconomy.com or call **(703) 787-0139**.

We also offer **Private Consulting** for individuals and businesses. Please e-mail info@aftershockeconomy.com for more information.

Through our money management firm, **Absolute Investment Management**, we provide hands-on, Aftershock-focused asset management services on an individually managed account basis. For more information please call **(703) 774-3520** or e-mail absolute@aftershock economy.com.

Epilogue

SAY GOOD-BYE TO THE AGE OF EXCESS

It's sad to see it all go. It was the Party of the Century and not just in the United States, but around the world as well. The Age of Excess was like no other time in U.S. history, and there will never be a time like it again because eventually we do learn from our mistakes, even if painfully so. And how quickly we will forget the good times and how good they were when faced with the "shock and awe" of the Aftershock that will end the Age of Excess. So, this epilogue is dedicated to reminding us how good the Age of Excess really was.

But where do we begin? There was so much excess. First, there were all the corporate executives and investment bankers, who made hundreds of millions of dollars making terrible business mistakes that destroyed the value of their companies. And better yet, the government bailed out their companies, while the executives kept all the money they made from making the decisions that destroyed their companies, and they got some nice bonuses to boot. And why not? The government could always borrow so much money, it really didn't matter. Why hold anyone accountable when we're all in this party together, right?

And let's not forget all the great Internet companies whose values kept going up, up, up, even though their revenues and profits did not. We knew they were worth a lot of money because sooner or later some other company was bound to buy them at massively overvalued prices. And why should the acquiring company worry about overvaluation? Their stock never suffered from their bad decisions; it just kept going up, up, up along with the rest of the stock market, despite terrible management.

That same party thinking worked wonders for private equity firms, the true masters of the universe. Their strategy was simple: always pay

275

a higher price to buy a company than anyone else, and then just let the ever-rising stock market make you billions when you sell it later. Some private equity firms made billions just by taking themselves public, because everyone on Wall Street knew that their strategy of buying companies at very high prices was foolproof.

Even folks on Main Street got to play at the party. Lots of credit cards and home equity lines of credit made everyday life very festive, indeed. We got to enjoy lots of big screen TVs, the latest computers, and all sorts of new gadgets and gizmos at the party. And with retirement stock market accounts rising so rapidly, why not put everything in stocks, including our future social security? Remember that one?

Even if stocks didn't go up every year, you could always count on your home as a great investment. No matter how much the price went up, we just knew it would never, ever go back down very much. Market cycles only worked in the up direction, right? Even if your income didn't rise very much, the value of your house could easily double in a few years. We didn't entirely know why, but something really good must have been happening somewhere. Whatever it was, we didn't care. It was all part of the joy of the Age of Excess. In the Age of Excess, you didn't have to think too much about why things were so good, they just were.

Even better, in the Age of Excess, good jobs never, ever disappeared. If you lost one, you could always just hop onto another— like catching the next train leaving the station. And plenty of jobs meant you didn't have to waste perfectly good money by putting it in a savings account. Let those poor Chinese peasants, who made all the stuff we bought do all the saving. Besides, saving money was downright un-American. If you saved, you were hurting the economy. And look what happened when we finally stopped buying so much and started saving a little in late 2008—the economy really started to tank. If we had just kept spending as we did before, we'd still be doing just fine.

Speaking of which, don't forget that in the Age of Excess, patriotism means doing your part to help in a war. That certainly doesn't mean tax increases—in World War II, tax rates were as high as 75 percent. No, it actually means you need your taxes decreased for all of your suffering from high taxes. It also doesn't mean a draft or volunteering for the war. In World War II, over half of Congress volunteered for the war. In World War I, Charlie Merrill, the founder of Merrill Lynch, was so interested in volunteering for the war that he drove down from New York to Fort Myers in Washington to speed up his enlistment process. In the Iraq War, there were so many titans of Wall Street volunteering that they had to set up a separate sign-up window at the Pentagon! (Not really.)

Of course, patriotism also doesn't mean cutting your consumption to help out the boys fighting the war. No, what it means to be a patriot in the Age of Excess is to put those "We Support Our Troops" stickers on your car and drive to the nearest mall. In fact, to be even more patriotic, you should buy more cars to put more stickers on, especially if those cars are one of those hot new BMWs or Mercedes. Wow, now that's real support. To show how much we supported our troops, by 2008 we had purchased 35 million more cars than we had registered drivers. That's a lot of cars to put stickers on! If only we had done that in World War II, imagine the difference it would have made. But, that wasn't war in the Age of Excess, where war has no cost.

And, finally, who could forget that in the Age of Excess, the government has no limit on how much it can borrow. If we hit a rough patch in the economy, we just convert to the bailout economy. Made a business mistake or a personal financial mistake? No problem; the government will just borrow money to bail you out. Bailouts are easy, and the government wouldn't think of raising taxes to cover bailouts when it can so easily borrow so much money at such low interest rates. That's just part of being the U.S. government in the Age of Excess. No money? No worries; the government can just borrow what it takes to tide us over. Is there any limit to what the government can borrow? Well, why worry about it? Something good must be happening to let the government borrow so much money. And that's after it has already borrowed $10 trillion and hasn't been able to pay back a penny of that debt. It's almost magical. But whatever it was, in the Age of Excess, you didn't have to think too much about why things were so good—they just were.

Too bad it had to end.

Appendix: Are the Stock and Gold Markets Manipulated?

POTENTIAL STOCK MARKET MANIPULATION BY THE FEDERAL RESERVE

This is a topic that comes up periodically from our readers, and so far we have ignored the issue in our writings. It is sometimes brought up as a reason for short-term movements in the market. There are really two parts to this issue: (1) the manipulation of bonds, foreign exchange, and banking markets; and (2) the manipulation of the stock and gold markets.

In terms of the first part, the Fed clearly and pretty openly manipulates the bond markets, the foreign exchange markets, and directly manipulates the banking markets. Open market operations, in which the Fed buys and sells Treasury bonds, clearly manipulate the bond markets. When the Fed buys Freddie Mac and Fannie Mae mortgage collateralized debt obligations (CDOs), it is clearly manipulating the mortgage market and indirectly the entire bond market.

The Fed uses foreign currency swaps, where the Fed lends money to foreign central banks, to manipulate foreign exchange markets.

The Fed directly manipulates the banking market by making it easier for banks to profit by lending to them at very low interest rates and allowing them to lend to consumers at significantly higher interest rates. The Fed essentially lowers the banks' cost of goods sold—their "goods" being money. This also manipulates the value of their stock and their ability to raise more capital by making them more profitable.

Also, by manipulating the bond, foreign exchange, and banking markets, the Fed also indirectly but powerfully manipulates the United States and world stock markets.

It also clearly manipulated the price of homes through its actions to keep interest rates low and to reduce the speed with which it forces banks to foreclose on mortgage holders. Most importantly, the government acted to manipulate housing prices by saving Fannie Mae and Freddie Mac. By saving those agencies, the government made mortgage money easier to find, and housing prices were kept much higher than they would have been otherwise.

All of this manipulation is being done to help stabilize the financial markets and thus stabilize the United States and world economy. Of course, if this manipulation also helps maintain asset price bubbles, then ultimately, it is stabilizing short-term financial markets at the expense of long-term financial market stability. That's because, ultimately, these asset bubbles cannot be maintained. It is a micro version of the much larger macro problem of the Federal Reserve printing money, and Congress borrowing massive amounts of money. It stabilizes the short-term economy at the cost of massive destabilization later.

The second part of the question, manipulation of the stock and gold markets, is a source of great interest by conspiracy theorists. However, not long after the first edition of *Aftershock* was published, it jumped to the mainstream media when Charles Biderman, the President of Trim Tabs, a well respected financial markets research firm, released a report saying that the huge increase in the stock market in 2009 was hard to explain based on the sources of funds moving into the market that normally drive up a stock market.

Trim Tabs made a common-sense analysis of the key flows of funds. An excerpt from their report, which details those flows of funds, follows:

> We cannot identify the source of the new money that pushed stock prices up so far so fast. For the most part, the money did not come from the traditional players that provided money in the past:
>
> - Companies. Corporate America has been a huge net seller. The float of shares has ballooned $133 billion since the start of April.
> - Retail investor funds. Retail investors have hardly bought any U.S. equities. Bond funds, yes. U.S equity funds, no. U.S. equity funds and ETFs have received just $17 billion

since the start of April. Over that same time frame bond mutual funds and ETFs received $351 billion.

- Retail investor direct. We doubt retail investors were big direct purchases of equities. Market volatility in this decade has been the highest since the 1930s, and we have no evidence retail investors were piling into individual stocks. Also, retail investor sentiment has been mostly neutral since the rally began.
- Foreign investors. Foreign investors have provided some buying power, purchasing $109 billion in U.S. stocks from April through October. But we suspect foreign purchases slowed in November and December because the U.S. dollar was weakening.
- Hedge funds. We have no way to track in real time what hedge funds do, and they may well have shifted some assets into U.S. equities. But we doubt their buying power was enormous because they posted an outflow of $12 billion from April through November.
- Pension funds. All the anecdotal evidence we have indicates that pension funds have not been making a huge asset allocation shift and have not moved more than about $100 billion from bonds and cash into U.S. equities since the rally began.

If the money to boost stock prices did not come from the traditional players, it had to have come from somewhere else.

Their conclusion was that it was possible that the Federal Reserve had acted to directly manipulate the stock market, and was responsible for much of the rise in 2009. They clearly indicated that they didn't have any direct evidence of this, and the evidence was only circumstantial. Hence, they lacked any real proof that would stand up in a court of law or public opinion.

Most people ignored the report as unimportant even though Trim Tabs is widely used and respected. In fact, they were respected enough that CNBC interviewed them regarding the report. Trim Tabs has a good track record in calling the 2000 bear market and in calling the 2002 bull market. But, they missed some of the 2009 bull market by having turned more bearish after the market had risen 40 percent. They said their research had shown that the normal sources of funds to buy stocks were declining and hence, the bull market was nearing an end.

They were wrong, since the market moved up another 30 percent. Hence, the few people who commented on the report released in January 2010 felt it was partly sour grapes at having missed all of the bull market.

One of the few people who bothered to respond to the report was Barry Ritholtz, certainly no cheerleader, having authored *Bailout Nation* (with Bill Fleckenstein and Aaron Task). He is also one of the more entertaining people to see on Wall Street. He was on a financial authors' panel with *Aftershock* coauthor Bob Wiedemer in New York in March 2010 and was a lot of fun to listen to.

On his website he made some key points against the Trim Tabs report. First, it would be very hard to cover up such large-scale operations over a long period of time. Second, if the Fed was trying to keep the market up over the last decade, it had sure done a bad job of it. Hence, he didn't give the report any credibility.

Barry took a lot of flak from his readers, many of whom strongly disagreed with him. It is also worth pointing out that the Fed may not be trying to boost the market long term. Instead its intention would more likely be to save the market from the big collapse of what has been a historic and, we think, very bubblish 1000 percent increase since the early 1980s.

The manipulation issue has also brought up the issue that had been raised before of whether the government has an informal plunge protection team or PPT. This would be a group of Fed, Treasury, and major bank officials who talk to each other when there is the threat of a major stock market plunge and work to prevent it or counteract a plunge once it happens.

This idea supposedly got going after the huge 20 percent stock market crash of 1987. In that case, as was well documented in a *Wall Street Journal* article written shortly after the crash, the problem the stock market faced was not Black Monday, when the market crashed 20 percent, but Terrible Tuesday, when the markets stopped functioning Tuesday morning after the crash.

The problem, specifically, was that the New York Stock Exchange's market makers had basically run out of capital and couldn't function. There was no market being made in such key stocks as IBM and GM. Market makers on the New York Stock Exchange had been somewhat thinly capitalized and were laid low by their huge losses on Monday and couldn't function on Tuesday.

A 20 percent drop in the stock market is a problem, but a dead stock market is a much bigger problem. So, the Fed and Treasury basically stepped in and told the big banks to lend money to the major market makers, and they would back up the banks if they took any losses. Well, that did the trick. The banks lent the market makers the money they needed, and the stock had one of its biggest one-day rallies in history. Terrible Tuesday became Terrific Tuesday!

After that event, the Plunge Protection Team came into being as an informal group of the same people who worked together to save the market on Terrible Tuesday to deal with any Terrible Tuesdays in the future. Clearly, such direct intervention in the stock market had worked wonders.

Could this same type of thing have happened during the May 2010 flash crash? As further investigations have shown, the flash crash was primarily due to a series of down days culminating in a big down day—the day of the flash cash. It was accentuated by high frequency traders, who do over 50 percent of the trading in the market now, exiting the market when it got too volatile. Of course, that's part of a broader problem of low volume and little long-term interest in the stock market. But, in many ways, the Flash Crash wasn't too different from Black Monday of 1987—a big bad day after a series of bad days.

The day of the Flash Crash had been going badly, but it got worse in the afternoon, partly due to a large trade by the Kansas City-based money management firm, Waddell and Reed. After that, some large high frequency traders pulled out of the market because the volatility was making it difficult for them to trade with any hope of making money. Thus, the flash crash began.

But, why did it turn around so suddenly? Did the massive increase in volatility cause the high frequency traders to come back in? That concept doesn't make sense—the higher volatility of the flash crash would seem likely to push them further away from the market. Almost like the market makers of 1987, high frequency traders exited the market because they didn't have the capital or didn't want to risk their capital in such a market. Thus, liquidity was drying up and the market was essentially dying. Seems like a perfect time for another intervention like the one in 1987. Only this time it was much quicker. They didn't act before a 20 percent decline and were able to stop the decline rather quickly and very sharply—a much better performance than 1987. But, is it true? And, wouldn't we have heard about it by now? You would think so, but it's difficult to be sure. The incredibly sharp turnaround had the telltale signs of a huge intervention.

However, all of the discussion of the Flash Crash in the media or by financial analysts was on why it went down so fast, not why it went up so fast. In fact, there was almost no discussion at all of why it went up so fast—that was considered normal and not worthy of discussion. The real question was what kind of technical trading error made it happen. Fat finger? Dumb trader? Once the investigations showed it was not a trading error, but a big market downturn accentuated by a large trade, people seemed to lose interest. And, again, no one asked why it went up so much so fast.

So, we're back to Barry Ritholtz's question. Can something like stock market manipulation remain a secret? To answer that question, let's look at other recent financial community secrets. Enron and Bernie Madoff are both obvious examples. However, both remained a secret even though there had been ample warning of problems to anyone looking at them closely. *Fortune* magazine saw something wrong in Enron, and Harry Markopolos (a Chartered Financial Analyst and Certified Fraud Examiner) actually wrote a report to the SEC detailing what he thought was going on with Bernie Madoff. So, it wasn't a secret, but no one wanted to see it.

In the end, people want to see what they want to see. Even in nonfinancial areas this is true. In the movie *All the President's Men*, someone at the *Washington Post* asked his fellow editors this question: If Watergate is true, why aren't any of the other newspapers like the *New York Times*, *Los Angeles Times*, and *Chicago Tribune* following it? Were staff members at the *Washington Post* the only ones who thought they knew the truth? It did seem hard to believe. But, often, even on big issues, people don't even ask the question.

So, is Charles Biderman of Trim Tabs correct in thinking the Fed is intervening? We don't know for sure (and neither does he), but there are clearly a lot of reasons the Fed would want to see the stock market go up. A rising stock market has probably helped out the economy more than any other single positive element in 2009 and 2010. Certainly it is the only part of our economy that has grown 80 percent. It has put more dollars into people's pockets than even all the borrowed money Congress has spent. It has certainly helped encourage the top 20 percent of our income earners who do over 40 percent of our consumer spending to get back into spending mode.

That puts a lot less pressure on the Fed to do other things like print more money via quantitative easing to boost the economy. You might say pushing up the stock market is probably one of the most cost-effective ways to spur the economy.

People who figure the Fed is manipulating the market mostly assume they are doing it by buying stock futures. That's part of the reason a lot of the upward activity in the market takes place overnight, and there are days when the market opens up with a huge increase despite a complete lack of significant good news. Of course, we really don't know how such manipulation could occur. It could also be via foreign intermediaries. But, again, we don't know the exact mechanism of how this might occur.

All of this could be explained by other factors. And clearly, the key factor has been that cheerleaders want to see the market go up. However, that cheerleader spirit is also a key reason that manipulation works. With a very skeptical market, such periodic manipulation would fail. Or, it would look more like Chinese manipulation of its currency— the currency shows a rock-solid movement up or down, based on what the government wants, with almost no volatility. It is fully manipulated all the time.

With the stock market heavily driven by cheerleaders, it doesn't take much to turn the market around from having a big fall. That's very different from manipulating the market all the time. Key manipulations done at the right time, like turning around the Flash Crash, greatly helps cheerleader psychology and would be relatively easy to perform.

And, everyone wants to see them succeed. Even noncheerleaders. What could be better than a rising stock market and an improving economy? We'd certainly be the first ones to support it if we thought it would work in the long run.

It's only an issue if it is part of maintaining asset bubbles that are unsustainable. And in that broader context, it won't work. Even with a lot of manipulation, it will fail in the end, just as blatant Chinese manipulation of their currency will fail. That's one reason most countries don't manipulate their currencies to anywhere near the extent that the Chinese do. It's not just highly risky; such manipulation never works in the long run. It is just covering up an underlying problem—in China's case it is a chronic trade surplus that China is using to boost its economy beyond what is economically sustainable. In our case it is a series of asset bubbles that are unsustainable.

Lacking a smoking gun, stock market manipulation will remain a mystery. And few people will want to investigate because almost no one wants it to be true. Plus, they also hope that it will work.

And that mentality shows up in other ways, such as the lack of interest in a Fed audit. Even though it has received bipartisan support from Congressmen as diverse as Republican Ron Paul and Democrat Alan Grayson, it didn't pass. It's almost as if people know the Fed has secrets that they don't really want people to know about. Is direct stock market manipulation one of them? If you don't ask, you'll never find out.

Well, that's probably not true. If the stock market melts down along with much of the economy, like the Enron and Bernie Madoff frauds, people will be mad, and it's likely they will ask these questions, and we will likely find out. But, of course, at that point it will be too late.

Which is why we are awarding the ABE Intellectual Courage Award to Charles Biderman, President of Trim Tabs. Not because we think he's right. We don't know. But, he did ask the question. And, at this point, that's what's important. He is a long-time well-respected financial analyst who has made good calls in the past and he backed up his question with good research and exposed himself to ridicule for asking a reasonable question nobody else wants to ask. He is also a Wiley author—a blatant plug for our excellent publisher, which, by the way is a great example of a company that can survive the ups and downs of the American economy and still thrive. They were founded in 1807. That's over 200 years of surviving and thriving—not bad at all.

Gold Manipulation

European central banks perform the most active and open buying and selling of gold by governments. European central banks have been selling gold for many years. They have agreed to sell up to about 500 tons of gold a year. This agreement is in effect today, but in 2010 very little gold was sold, whereas in past years the amount of gold sold was often close to the agreed-upon limit. This selling could be considered manipulation, but in theory it is being done so that central banks can sell gold without greatly depressing the market.

The type of manipulation that most people are concerned about would be attempts by the Federal Reserve to push the price of gold down. One potential way to manipulate the price of gold is through swaps.

Gold Swaps

Essentially, gold swaps are where two central banks literally swap hoards of gold—with the objective of doing nothing more than muddying the accounting waters.

A second type of gold swap involves only one central bank's gold reserves, which are lent for currency to another central bank. The real problem with this tactic is that the banks consider these swaps to be collateralized loans, and thus they don't appear on their balance sheets. No one knows for sure just how much gold and silver the Fed and other central banks have lent to each other in this way, but it would be worth taking a closer look if we could. A serious audit of the Federal Reserve would be a big step forward.

Clearly, gold is not as big an issue as the stock market, so we don't think the Fed is focusing on it that much, certainly not as much as many gold bugs suspect. But, gold does have an impact on the stock and bond market psychology, so we don't think they are ignoring it either. It is clearly on their minds, and it clearly is in their benefit not to see the price of gold jump too far too fast. Otherwise, it will start to undermine investor confidence in the dollar and put pressure on the Fed to do costly interventions in the form of printing money to purchase bonds to boost investor confidence in the dollar.

A final aspect of gold market manipulation would be the sale of gold by the U.S. government, ostensibly for a reason such as paying down the debt. This idea was discussed in the spring of 2011. It wasn't taken very seriously, but it can't be ruled out that the government might not sell some gold in the future if the price gets high enough. At a certain point, the money received could be substantial and valuable when the government eventually hits a severe budget crunch. Although it is not covert manipulation, selling gold would put downward pressure on the price. Even just serious talk about the government selling a significant amount of gold would put downward pressure on its price. However, once gold is moving strongly upward, it may not cause the price to fall; it may simply reduce the speed at which the price of gold rises.

Market Manipulation Summary

Bottom Line: We don't think market manipulation can be ruled out. It could be happening at times. There is certainly incentive and capability, and there is a little bit of history favoring belief in such interventions. If the Fed openly manipulates just about everything else these days, would they be that reluctant to manipulate such a key part of our economy, the stock market, that has grown so much more key over time?

An increasingly less fearful, and some would say reckless, Fed that is willing to print massive amounts of money to boost the economy and appears to be almost equally concerned about the economy and jobs as it is inflation is a Fed that would be more than willing to manipulate other markets such as stocks or gold.

Terms like "moral hazard" no longer even exist in the government's vocabulary. As we have said before, that mentality has changed so much that we predict that almost anything that gets into trouble and might threaten the stability of the economy and its asset bubbles will likely be deemed necessary for a bailout, no matter who benefits or whose responsibility it was.

If anything, manipulating the stock market would fit right in to what has become an increasing willingness on the part of the government to use its printing and borrowing powers to shore up the economy short term and a tremendous willingness to maintain asset bubbles.

Investment Impact

Long term, if manipulation exists, it will have no impact on the Aftershock scenario other than to make the meltdown that much bigger. Short term, it will certainly have an impact in forestalling the Aftershock, just as the government's other measures of borrowing and printing money will forestall the Aftershock, as we have discussed previously.

Short term, any manipulation certainly makes it harder to time the market. That's part of what manipulation is trying to do. In foreign currency manipulation that is the key impact of manipulation—the central bank manipulates the market in part to scare off manipulators from attacking a currency. A central bank does this with well-timed purchases and lots of mystery surrounding their exact purchases and the timing of those purchases. The central banks want to make the market participants sweat big time and hopefully cause them huge losses if they go against the central bank.

Of course, we don't recommend that most investors try to time the markets too closely. We strongly suggest for the reasons we mentioned in the book and the reasons we have mentioned in the past, that you make long-term deliberate decisions on where to put your investment capital. You can move short term with the bubbles, but always remember that they are bubbles and your profits depend on you not being in those markets when the bubbles pop.

■ ■ ■

To make comments on the material in this Appendix or enter a discussion thread please visit our web site at www.aftershockeconomy.com/appendixcomments.

Bibliography

Altman, Daniel. "Uncle Sam, Deadbeat Debtor?" *New York Times*, July 23, 2006.

Athanasoulis, Stefano, and Robert J. Shiller. "The Significance of the Market Portfolio." *Review of Financial Studies*, 13, no. 2 (2000): 301–29.

Athanasoulis, Stefano, and Robert J. Shiller. "World Income Components: Discovering and Implementing Risk Sharing Opportunities." *American Economic Review* 91, no. 4 (2001): 1031–54.

Baker, Dean. "The Menace of an Unchecked Housing Bubble," *Center for Economic and Policy Research*, March 16, 2006. www.cepr.net/index.php/op-eds-&-columns/op-eds-&-columns/the-menace-of-an-unchecked-housing-bubble/ (accessed October 19, 2006).

Ballinger, Kenneth. *Miami Millions: The Dance of the Dollars in the Great Florida Land Boom of 1925*. Miami, FL: Franklin Press, 1936.

Batra, Ravi, ed. *The Great Depression of 1990: Why It's Got to Happen, How to Protect Yourself*. New York: Simon & Schuster, 1987.

Berman, Dennis K. "Fistfuls of Dollars Fuel the M&A Engine." *Wall Street Journal*, January 3, 2006.

Biderman, Charles, and David Santschi. *Trim Tabs Investing: Using Liquidity Theory to Beat the Stock Market*. Hoboken, NJ: John Wiley & Sons, 2005.

Blinder, Alan S. and Janet L. Yellen, *The Fabulous Decade: Macroeconomic Lessons from the 1990s*. New York: Century Foundation Press, 2001.

Bohm-Bawerk, Eugen Von. *Capital and Interest*, 3 vols (1884 and 1889), trans. G. D. Huncke and H. E. Sennhole. South Holland, Illinois: Libertarian Press, 1959.

Bonner, Bill, and Addison Wiggin. *Empire of Debt: The Rise of an Epic Financial Crisis*. Hoboken, NJ: John Wiley & Sons, 2006.

Bruno, Michael, and William Easterly. "Inflation Crises and Long-Run Growth." *Journal of Monetary Economics*, 41(1) (1998): 2–26.

Buffett, Warren E. "Chairman's Letter to Shareholders." Berkshire Hathaway, Inc. 2005 Annual Report.

Bulgatz, Joseph. *Ponzi Schemes, Invaders from Mars, and Other Extraordinary Pop Delusions, and the Madness of Crowds*. New York: Harmony, 1992.

Case, Karl E., Jr., and Robert J. Shiller. "The Efficiency of the Market for Single Family Homes." *American Economic Review*, 79(1) (March 1989): 125–37.

Cassidy, John. *Dot.con: How America Lost Its Mind and Money in the Internet Era*. New York: Perennial Currents, 2003.

Clements, Jonathan. "The Debt Bubble Threatens to Derail Many Baby Boomers' Retirement Plans." *Wall Street Journal*, March 8, 2006.

Cooper, Jim. "A Truer Measure of America's Ballooning Deficit." *Financial Times* (London), May 1, 2006.

Coronado, Julia Lynn, and Steven A. Sharpe. "Did Pension Plan Accounting Contribute to a Stock Market Bubble?" Washington, D.C. Board of Governors of the Federal Reserve System, Finance and Economics Discussion Series No. 2003-38, 2003.

Cutler, David, James Poterba, and Lawrence Summers. "What Moves Stock Prices?" *Journal of Portfolio Management*, 15(3) (1989): 4–12.

"Danger—Explosive Loans." *BusinessWeek*, October 23, 2006.

Delasantellis, Julian. "U.S. Living on Borrowed Time—and Money." *Asia Times Online*, March 24, 2006. www.atimes.com/atimes/Global_Economy/Hc24Dj01 .html.

Dent, Harry S. *The Roaring 2000s: Building the Wealth & Lifestyle You Desire in the Greatest Boom in History*. New York: Simon & Schuster, 1998.

Duncan, Richard. *The Dollar Crisis: Causes, Consequences, Cures*. Hoboken, NJ: John Wiley & Sons, 2005.

Easterlin, Richard. "Does Economic Growth Improve the Human Lot?" *Nationals and Households in Economic Growth: Essays in Honor of Moses Abramovitz*, Ed. Paul David and Melvin Reder. New York: Academic Press, 1974.

Eichengreen, Barry. *Golden Fetters: The Gold Standard and the Great Depression: 1919–1939*. New York: Oxford University Press, 1992.

Einhorn, David. *Fooling Some of the People All of the Time: A Long Short Story*. Hoboken, NJ: John Wiley & Sons, 2008.

Evans-Pritchard, Ambrose. "SocGen Crafts Strategy for China Hard-Landing." *The Telegraph*. January 20, 2011. www.telegraph.co.uk/finance/china-business/8272388/ SocGen-crafts-strategy-for-China-hard-landing.html (accessed February 16, 2011).

Fergusson, Adam. *When Money Dies: The Nightmare of Deficit Spending, Devaluation, and Hyperinflation in Weimar Germany*. New York: Public Affairs, 2010.

Fisher, Irving. *The Nature of Capital and Income*. New York: Macmillan, 1906.

Fisher, Irving. *The Stock Market Crash— and After*. New York: Macmillan, 1930.

Fisher, Irving. *The Theory of Interest*. New York: Macmillan, 1930.

Friedman, Milton. *Money Mischief: Episodes in Monetary History*. New York: Harcourt Brace Jovanovich, 1992.

Froot, Kenneth, and Maurice Obstfeld. "Intrinsic Bubbles: The Case of Stock Prices. *American Economic Review*, 81 (1991): 1189–1214.

Galbraith, John Kenneth. "The 1929 Parallel." *Atlantic Online*, January 1987, www .theatlantic.com/doc/198701/galbraith.

Galbraith, John Kenneth. *The Affluent Society*. New York: New American Library, 1995.

Galbraith, John Kenneth. *The Great Crash: 1929*, 2nd ed. Boston: Houghton Mifflin, 1954.

Glover, John and Joe Brennan. "Greek, Irish Banks Force ECB to Print More Money: Euro Credit," *Bloomberg*. February 16, 2011. www.bloomberg.com/ news/2011-02-16/greek-irish-banks-force-ecb-to-print-more-money-euro-credit.html (accessed February 16, 2011).

Gordon, Robert J. "U.S. Productivity Growth Since 1879: One Big Wave?" *American Economic Review*, 89, no. 2 (1999): 123–28.

Gross, Daniel. *Pop! Why Bubbles Are Great for the Economy.* New York: HarperCollins, 2007.

Heilbroner, Robert J. *The Worldly Philosophers: The Lives, Times, and Ideas of the Great Economic Thinkers,* 7th ed. New York: Simon & Schuster, 1999.

Heilbroner, Robert, and William Milberg. *The Crisis of Vision in Modern Economic Thought.* New York: Cambridge University Press, 1995.

James, Harold. *The End of Globalization: Lessons from the Great Depression.* Cambridge, MA: Harvard University Press, 2001, 125 and 142.

Janszen, Eric. *The Postcatastrophe Economy: Rebuilding America and Avoiding the Next Bubble.* New York: Penguin Group, 2010.

Jung, Jeeman, and Robert J. Shiller. "Samuelson's Dictum and the Stock Market." *Economic Inquiry,* 2005.

Katona, George. *Psychological Economics.* New York: Elsevier, 1975.

Keynes, John Maynard. *A Tract on Monetary Reform.* London: Macmillan, 1923.

Keynes, John Maynard *The General Theory of Employment, Interest and Money.* New York: Harcourt Brace & World, 1961.

Kindleberger, Charles P. *Manias, Panics and Crashes: A History of Financial Crises,* 2nd ed. London: Macmillan, 1989.

Kindleberger, Charles P., and Robert Z. Aliber. *Manias, Panics and Crashes: A History of Financial Crises,* 5th ed. Hoboken, NJ: John Wiley & Sons, 2005.

Krugman, Paul. *The Great Unraveling: Losing Our Way in the New Century.* New York: W. W. Norton & Company, 2004.

Krugman, Paul. *The Return of Depression Economics and the Crisis of 2008.* New York: W. W. Norton & Company, 2009.

Krugman, Paul. "How Fast Can the U.S. Economy Grow?" *Harvard Business Review,* 75 (1977): 123–29.

Lewis, Michael. *Panic: The Story of Modern Financial Insanity.* New York: W. W. Norton & Company, 2009.

Lewis, Michael. *The Big Short: Inside the Doomsday Machine.* New York: W. W. Norton & Company, 2010.

Lindert, Peter. *Growing Public: Social Spending and Economic Growth Since the Eighteenth Century.* New York: Cambridge University Press, 2004.

Lowenstein, Roger. *Origins of the Crash: The Great Bubble and Its Undoing.* New York: Penguin Press, 2004, 2.

Lucas, Robert E. "Asset Prices in an Exchange Economy." *Econometrica,* 46 (1978): 1429–45.

Mandel, Michael. "Bubble, Bubble, Who's in Trouble?" *Business Week,* June 15, 2006.

McGrattan, Ellen R., and Edward C. Prescott. "Is the Stock Market Overvalued?" *Federal Reserve Bank of Minneapolis Quarterly Review,* 24 (2000): 20–40.

Meltzer, Allan H. "Monetary and Other Explanations of the Start of the Great Depression." *Journal of Monetary Economics,* 2 (1976): 455–71.

Nima. "Inflation & Money Supply in China," *EconomicsJunkie.* November 18, 2010. www.economicsjunkie.com/inflation-money-supply-in-china/ (accessed February 16, 2011).

Perkins, Edwin J. *Wall Street to Main Street.* Cambridge, UK: Cambridge University Press, 1999.

Posen, Adam S. "It Takes More than a Bubble to Become Japan." *Institute for International Economics Working Paper No. 03-9,* October 2003.

Prechter, Robert R. *At the Crest of the Tidal Wave: A Forecast for the Great Bear Market.* New York: John Wiley & Sons, 1995.

Prechter, Robert R. *Conquer the Crash: You Can Survive and Prosper in a Deflationary Depression.* Hoboken, NJ: John Wiley & Sons, 2003.

Pressman, Steven. *Fifty Major Economists,* 2nd ed. New York: Routledge, 2006.

Pressman, Steven. "On Financial Frauds and Their Causes: Investor Overconfidence." *American Journal of Economics and Sociology,* 57 (1998): 405–21.

Reich, Robert B. *Aftershock The Next Economy and America's Future.* New York: Alfred A. Knopf, 2010.

Reich, Robert. "The Sham Recovery," *The Huffington Post,* March 12, 2010. www .huffingtonpost.com/robert-reich/the-sham-recovery_b_497439.html (accessed February 16, 2011).

Romer, Christina. "The Great Crash and the Onset of the Great Depression." *Quarterly Journal of Economics,* 105 (1990): 597–624.

Rosenberg, Yuval. "The Boomer Bust." *Fortune,* June 19, 2006.

Roubini, Nouriel, and Stephen Mihm. *Crisis Economics.* New York: Penguin Press, 2010.

Samuelson, Robert J. "A Financial 'Time Bomb'?" *Washington Post,* March 12, 2003.

Samuelson, Robert J. *The Good Life and Its Discontents: The American Dream in the Age of Entitlement, 1945–1995.* New York: Crown, 1995.

Samuelson, Robert J. *The Great Inflation and Its Aftermath: the Past and Future of American Affluence.* New York: Random House, 2008.

Saxonhouse, Gary R., and Robert M. Stern. *Japan's Lost Decade: Origins, Consequences and Prospects for Recovery.* Massachusetts: Blackwell Publishing Ltd, 2004.

Schiff, Peter D., and Andrew J. Schiff. *How An Economy Grows and Why It Crashes.* Hoboken, NJ: John Wiley & Sons, 2010.

Shiller, Robert J. "Measuring Bubble Expectations and Investor Confidence." *Journal of Psychology and Markets,* 1, no. 1 (2000): 49–60.

Smith, Adam. *The Money Game.* New York: Vintage Books, 1976.

Soros, George. *The New Paradigm for Financial Markets: The Credit Crisis of 2008 and What It Means.* New York: Public Affairs, 2008.

Stovall, Sam. *The Seven Rules of Wall Street.* New York. McGraw-Hill: 2009.

Summers, Lawrence H., and Victoria P. Summers. "When Financial Markets Wore Well: A Cautious Case for a Securities Transactions Tax." *Journal of Financial Securities Research,* 3, no. 2–3 (1988): 163–88.

Turk, James. *The Coming Collapse of the Dollar and How to Profit from It: Make a Fortune by Investing in Gold and Other Hard Assets.* New York: Currency, 2004.

Wanniski, Jude. *The Way the World Works,* 2nd ed. New York: Simon & Schuster, 1982.

Wiedemer, James. *The Homeowner's Guide to Foreclosure: How to Protect Your Home and Your Rights,* 2nd ed. New York: Kaplan Publishing, June 3, 2008.

Wiggin, Addison. *The Demise of the Dollar . . . and Why It's Great for Your Investments.* Hoboken, NJ: John Wiley & Sons, 2005.

Will, George F. "Guaranteed Collisions." *Washington Post,* May 15, 2005.

"World Finance: The Coming Storm for Banks." *The Economist,* February 20, 2004.

Index